AN INTRODUCTION TO
NEW MEDIA AND
CYBERCULTURES

Pramod K. Nayar

AN INTRODUCTION TO
NEW MEDIA AND
CYBERCULTURES

WILEY-BLACKWELL

A John Wiley & Sons, Ltd., Publication

This edition first published 2010
© 2010 Pramod K. Nayar

Blackwell Publishing was acquired by John Wiley & Sons in February 2007. Blackwell's publishing program has been merged with Wiley's global Scientific, Technical, and Medical business to form Wiley-Blackwell.

Registered Office
John Wiley & Sons Ltd, The Atrium, Southern Gate, Chichester, West Sussex, PO19 8SQ, United Kingdom

Editorial Offices
350 Main Street, Malden, MA 02148-5020, USA
9600 Garsington Road, Oxford, OX4 2DQ, UK
The Atrium, Southern Gate, Chichester, West Sussex, PO19 8SQ, UK

For details of our global editorial offices, for customer services, and for information about how to apply for permission to reuse the copyright material in this book please see our website at www.wiley.com/wiley-blackwell.

The right of Pramod K. Nayar to be identified as the author of this work has been asserted in accordance with the Copyright, Designs, and Patents Act 1988.

Wiley also publishes its books in a variety of electronic formats. Some content that appears in print may not be available in electronic books.

Designations used by companies to distinguish their products are often claimed as trademarks. All brand names and product names used in this book are trade names, service marks, trademarks or registered trademarks of their respective owners. The publisher is not associated with any product or vendor mentioned in this book. This publication is designed to provide accurate and authoritative information in regard to the subject matter covered. It is sold on the understanding that the publisher is not engaged in rendering professional services. If professional advice or other expert assistance is required, the services of a competent professional should be sought.

Library of Congress Cataloging-in-Publication Data

Nayar, Pramod K.
   An introduction to new media and cybercultures / Pramod K. Nayar.
      p. cm.
   Includes bibliographical references and index.
   ISBN 978-1-4051-8167-9 (hardcover: alk. paper)—ISBN 978-1-4051-8166-2 (pbk.: alk. paper)
   1. Cyberspace—Social aspects. 2. Internet—Social aspects. 3. Computers and civilization. 4. Information society. I. Title.
   HM851.N385 2009
   303.48'33—dc22

                                                                    2009010790

A catalogue record for this book is available from the British Library.

Set in Minion 10.5/13.5pt by SPi Publisher Services, Pondicherry, India
Printed in Singapore by Ho Printing Singapore Pte Ltd

001   2010

CONTENTS

PREFACE AND ACKNOWLEDGMENTS

This book is an Introduction to an often bewildering variety of technologically driven and determined phenomena called cybercultures. Its focus is the wired, digital environments that inform much of our lives today – from cell phones to multiplayer games to instant messaging and emails. Communications technology has carved out realms within our material one in which bodies, conversation, identity, social relations, family structures, information gathering, and political participation have all been radically altered.

Sections of this book have appeared in earlier forms in various places, and are reprinted in revised form by kind permission of the editors.

Parts of Chapter 2 appeared as "The New Monstrous: Digital Arts, Genomic Arts and Aesthetics," in *Nebula* 4.2 (2007); www.nobleworld.biz.

Parts of Chapters 2 and 3 appeared as "Wetware Fiction: Cyberpunk and the Ideologies of Posthuman Bodies," *ICFAI Journal of English Studies* 3.2 (2008): 30–40.

Parts of Chapter 5 appeared as "The Sexual Internet" on *eSocialSciences Working Papers* (www.esocialsciences.com/Articles/displayArticles.asp?Article_ID=1391, February 21, 2008) and "Bodies and Spaces: Reading Women in/and Cyberculture," in *In-Between* 15.1 (2006): 3–21.

Chapter 6 appeared as "New Media, Digitextuality and Public Space: Reading 'Cybermohalla,'" in *Postcolonial Text* 4.1 (2008); journals.sfu.ca/pocol/index.php/pct/article/view/786/521.

Chapter 7 appeared as "Postcolonializing Cyberculture: Race, Ethnicity and Critical Internet Studies," in *LittCrit* 34.1 (2008): 3–15.

Sections were also delivered as lectures at the Mudra Institute of Communications, Ahmedabad (MICA), India, June–July 2008, and I am grateful to Rita Kothari and Atul Tandan for inviting me to MICA.

My greatest debt is to Jayne Fargnoli of Wiley-Blackwell, who responded to a short query on another series and set in motion what became a two-book project. I owe a great deal to her unstinting encouragement and infectious enthusiasm (marked by color-coded emails, variant fonts, and smileys).

Margot Morse at Wiley-Blackwell took care of the details with great cheer – and this book is better for her contribution.

For my friend Anna Kurian's attention to detail, resourceful tracking of materials, camaraderie, and boundless affection, I am immeasurably grateful.

And to Brigitte Lee Messenger for her patient and flawless copyediting – thanks very much.

A book is a history of generous acts, and this one is no exception. I am privileged to be able to thank scholars, librarians, and friends who have helped me access materials, shared their own writings, and generously contributed towards this project. They include: Padma Prakash of *eSocial Sciences*; Jeanne Paghera of the Journals Customer Service department at Wiley-Blackwell, who supplied me with some crucial journal articles; Mysore Jagadish of the American Information Resource Center, Chennai, India; Brian Yothers of the University of Texas at El Paso; Akhila Ramnarayan at the University of Dayton; Thea Pitman at Leeds University, who sent me her work on Latin American cybercultures; and Neeraja Sundaram, who found time during her own research to read selected chapters and comment upon them (and who didn't find too many horrors or "Gothics" in them).

Special thanks are due to: Colin Harrison and the School of Media, Critical, and Creative Arts, Liverpool John Moores University, UK, for inviting me as Visiting Professor in 2008, and to new friends there: Timothy Ashplant, Elspeth Graham, Joe Moran, and Belle Adams; Amy Anderson and the India Foundation (especially Harish Trivedi) for hosting me as Visiting Professor at the University of Dayton, Ohio, in September–October 2008; Akhila Ramnarayan of UD's Department of English for her friendship and support, and to the Indian Council for Cultural Relations for enabling the trip; the editorial boards of *Writing Technologies* and the *Journal for Information Technology and Politics*; and the editors and referees of numerous journals where sections of this work have appeared: *In-Between*, *ICFAI Journal of English Studies*, *Writing Technologies*, *Postcolonial Text*, and *eSocial-Sciences*.

This book has benefited substantially from some extremely fine reading (of both proposal and manuscript) by many Wiley-Blackwell reviewers, who offered generous advice, constructive suggestions, and, in quite a few cases, enthusiastic praise. My thanks go to them.

As always, I offer my gratitude to my family – my parents, Ai-Baba, Nandini, Pranav – for their patience, understanding, and enduring affection during the writing of this book (and many others). Without Nandini's care, of course, I wouldn't be writing at all.

1 "READING" CYBERCULTURES

CHAPTER PLAN

Introducing Cybercultures

The Information Society

Key Issues in Cyberculture Studies
Globalization, Technocapitalism, and Cybercultures
Materiality and Corporeality
The Digital Divide
E-Governance
Civil Society
Governing Cyberspace
Identity
Race
Class
Gender and Sexualities
Space and Geography
Risk
The Mediapolis and the Space of the Other
Aesthetics

Cyberculture Studies
Ethnographies of Cyberspace
Apparatgeist *Theory*
Cultural Studies

On January 31, 2008, a ship's anchor cut through underwater cables in the Mediterranean. Internet and communications services were massively affected across the world. India, where I was writing, experienced disruption to its business process outsourcing (BPO) operations (S. Joshi 2008). In November 2008, a report from the Indo Asian News Service, tellingly titled "Second Life Romance Costs First Life Marriage," told the story of a British couple who were getting a divorce because of an affair the husband was having in the virtual world *Second Life*: the wife refused to accept his excuse that it "was after all an affair in the unreal world" (IndiaInfo.com 2008). The two incidents capture the thesis of this book: cyberspace, cyberculture, and virtual reality remain deeply embedded in very material conditions.

This book argues throughout that cybercultures and virtual worlds have a material dimension. It pays attention to the rhetoric and discourses of and about cybercultures, while constantly drawing attention to the fact that the "hardware" of structures – bodies, cities, concrete, cables, sentiments, work spaces, and labor – that make cybercultures possible are subject to the dynamics of race, class, gender, economic inequalities, governance, and injustice.

Introducing Cybercultures

"Cybercultures" serves as a shorthand term to include the networked, electronic, and wired cultures of the last three decades of the twentieth century. Other terms used include Internet studies, new media studies, digital media studies, digital culture studies, networked culture studies, information society studies, and contemporary media studies. The number of terms available to choose from indicates the transdisciplinary nature of the field.

CYBERSPACE

Cyberspace describes the worlds and domains generated by digital information and communications technologies (ICTs). It is seen, in this book, as a set of relations and actions in electronic space.

Cyberspace is also often called "information space" or "technospace" (Munt 2001: 11). It is defined as "new social spaces fostered by computer-enabled automated information and communication technologies (AICTs)" (Hakken 2008: 216). Cyberculture, as defined by the *Encyclopedia of New Media*, refers to "cultures formed in or associated with online social spaces" (Kendall 2007).

Technically, "ICTs" include the collection, processing, storage, retrieval, and transmission of information in the form of text, video, audio, and graphics for economic, social, cultural, scientific, and political applications among individuals, groups, institutions, and nations. Information is converted into digital form and transmitted through increasingly convergent technologies where the personal computer, the phone, the Internet, and multimedia provide an integrated form of communication.

CYBERCULTURE

The electronic environment where various technologies and media forms converge: video games, the Internet and email, personal homepages, online chats, personal communications technologies (PCTs, such as the cell phone), mobile entertainment and information technologies, bioinformatics and biomedical technologies.

Cyberspace is also produced by multimedia applications such as mobile phones, electronic surveillance, and video conferencing. As more people surf the Net via iPhones and the cell phone becomes ubiquitous across the world, "cyberspace" itself has to be redefined. While virtual reality (VR) environments are fashionable for academic studies of cyberculture, they do *not*, as Lisa Nakamura (2006) rightly points out, constitute the bulk of the experience of users of digital technology. Blogs and games, the homepage and social networking, online shopping and chat are more central to the common and the everyday, and if cyberculture studies hopes to draw from the frameworks of cultural studies – which is grounded in the everyday – it must turn to the popular Internet rather than the exotic environments of VR labs. There is no *one* cyberculture: because it has been so normalized, appropriated, altered, and domesticated into our everyday lives, there are in fact many cybercultures, of which the Internet is perhaps the most common. With mobile telephony and 3G phones, we have cybercultures in the palm of our hands and access to a virtual world. This book treats cybercultures as a *formation* that is the consequence of many structures, artifacts, ideas, and ideologies coming together: the political economy, information, global finance, capitalism, the logic of the market, the structures of cables and wires, monitors, and SIM cards. Cybercultures include a multiplicity of sites and applications, from medicalization to mobilization, pornography to politics, entertainment to addictions. However – and this is the key point – the formation that is cybercultures is at various points, and in different ways, attached to, connected with, replicates, extends, and augments real-life *material* conditions.

The cyberspace environment – from the "space" of mobile communications systems to gameworlds – is throughout this book treated not simply as a parallel universe but as an *extension* and *augmentation* of the everyday one. The human as an "avatar" in cyberspace, with different and multiple identities, is not so much dispersed as *reconfigured* as an extended human. The posthuman is not a startling new form but a modified version of the human as we have known it.

Cybercultures are a "formation" which is linked to and embedded in material contexts and conditions. These conditions generate, inform, and even govern the nature of cyberspace, its production, expansion, and application. This means that we need to see cybercultures as any other cultural process/event/structure, positioning, representing, influencing, and affecting race, class, gender, sexuality, and identity in particular ways. Cyberculture studies extends the work of cultural criticism and cultural studies by locating cybercultures as affected by and affecting these actual identities of individuals.

As the Internet, digital media, and cybercultures become "normalized," domesticated, and integrated into

AVATAR

An avatar is an online identity. It is usually a graphic representation of the user in a virtual environment. It can be modified and made to look like anything the user wishes, and it can also be made to perform actions in the online environment. The term comes, incidentally, from Hindu mythology, where it signifies the reincarnations or earthly manifestations (appearances on earth) of gods. Its first use may have been in Lucasfilms' online game *Habitat*, dating back to the 1980s.

the everyday life of individuals and organizations, we need to understand how they affect that everyday life. Do all sections of society acquire the same degree (or nature) of control over virtual worlds and representations in these worlds? Are cybercultures gendered in the everyday lives of individuals? These questions are important because they reveal cybercultures to be a set of social practices. Cybercultures are, like film or television or sport, cultural formations that have their own cultural politics (of race, economy, class, or gender). This book explores cybercultures as embedded in, masking, or generating forms of power.

In order to "read" cybercultures, we need to see them as techno*culture*. This book does not treat cyberspace as an independent entity but as one that is connected to the material world with all its attendant problems and concerns. While cultures determine what forms of technologies develop, these technologies, in turn, shape cultures. Technology, in other words, is not merely an effect or cause of culture but is *both*: it determines and is determined by the culture in which it develops. There is a spirit and logic of a particular technology that feeds off and into the community and culture. In other words, one needs to locate any technology *within* its particular *material* contexts. All technology, in this reading, is context-bound. Technologies are not simply out there: they become a part of our lives, are incorporated into the everyday. They are "domesticated" (Silverstone and Haddon 1996) and, in turn, inform the way we run our everyday lives *around* them. Technologies, in addition to possessing instrumental value, also possess cultural values – of prestige, safety, and sociability – values that increasingly inform the design and development of technological devices.

The mobile phone needs to be more than a phone – it now has to serve as a personal diary, a health indicator, an entertainment device, and a status symbol. Designers therefore need to account for those values that have become important and rendered desirable within a culture, and incorporate those into the "thing." The "thing" is therefore more than that: it represents aspirations, lifestyle choices, cultural values, sentiment (empirical research has demonstrated, for example, that people are *emotionally* attached to their cell phones; see Palen and Hughes 2007; Srivastava 2006), and functionality. A cell phone must be both efficient and attractive: one is the value of *productivity* and *instrumentality*, the other is *symbolic* and *cultural*. In October 2007, Hotmail launched "Cool Hotmail" (www.coolhotmail. com). Its key "features" are all social and allow users to pick personal IDs:

> "Get cool e-mail IDs as proof of residence!"
> "Exclusive e-mail IDs created for the top icons!"
> "Find an e-mail ID that describes your personality right here!"
> "Sport, food, drink and lots of fun! IDs for all occasions. How many of these funky e-mail IDs have you got?"

And finally, as a clinching argument:

> You're in a class of your own, individuality is your key. It's all about being you, in your own space. It's about your e-mail ID!

The ideology of individualism informs the design of the desktop and email. Hence Microsoft labels its software program MS *Office*, thereby suggesting that it serves a particular class of people (who work in offices rather than, say, at masonry or gardening). These are not technical details, they are social and cultural values. The name of the software program is rooted in real material contexts where, increasingly, office work and services – or "knowledge work" (A. Liu 2004) – are given more value than other forms of labor in the informational economy.

Similarly, technologies of databasing are governed by factors that are nontechnological such as transborder access of information, security concerns, questions of privacy, human capital, or conflicts. Finance, the market, and cooperative policies between nations are also factors in the operational mechanisms of databases. Where earlier the state or the archive controlled information (tax details, criminal records, population, birth and death records), digitization opens up the possibilities of archivization to various actors. The logic of technology is thus often a sociologic.

We also need to ask whether men and women use digital technology in the same way. Does digital culture significantly alter identities in the real world where race, ethnicity, class, and gender continue to remain key markers? Such questions are not about virtual worlds or electronic communication or digital gameworlds: they are about the lived experiences of humans around the world.

Cybercultures are driven by material considerations of profit and power, and affect people in their real lives. All this goes to show how technology must always be seen as contextual, and treated as technoculture where meanings, values, and functions are integrally associated with the object. Culture and technology are therefore not distinct but linked.

Cybercultures emerge in the context of large-scale movements of people, miscegenation of cultures leading to hybridized forms, dispersed forms of production, and, most importantly, the widespread "flows" of capital. Capital's increasing moves to control the production, circulation, and consumption of commodities demands greater connectivity but also increasing controls (Stratton 1997).

Nongovernmental organizations (NGOs) research and link up with dispersed locations in their bid to effect changes in societies across the world. Migrant workers (mainly from Asia) built Silicon Valley, which eventually headquartered the research and commercial aspects of the computer revolution. The Internet emerged out of a US Department of Defense project. The entertainment industry sought to spread as widely and as deeply as it could, and the demand for greater, continuous, and more varied entertainment fueled Walkmans, mobile technologies of film, and entertainment on the move. Globalization, arguably the most decisive social/political/cultural aspect of twentieth-century culture, would not be possible without ICTs.

The focus in this book is Internet networked cultures and digital worlds, where computers, digital technologies, and communication systems play a major role. While mobile phones increasingly become terminals and nodes for Internet cultures, they figure here as extensions of such network cultures. This book examines:

- popular forms of cybercultures;
- the spaces (private, public, ageographic) generated by cybertechnologies;
- the gendered, raced, and classed nature of these new cultures.

In the rest of this chapter I outline (1) the contexts of cyberculture in terms of the information society and globalization; (2) the key issues in cyberculture studies; and (3) select approaches to cybercultures.

The Information Society

The "information society" (Webster 2003) can be defined as an order where there is

- increasing convergence of telecommunications and computing in everyday life, production, consumption, and politics;
- an increasing importance of knowledge production;
- an ever-increasing number of people involved in information work (as opposed to agricultural or industrial labor);
- networking of cities and spaces via flows of information (through telecommunications networks); and
- an increasing amount of information *exchange* in the form of text, images, and sound.

The world has moved on, according to Daniel Bell's (1973) famous thesis, to the state of a "post-industrial" society. This shift is characterized by a reduction in industrial labor and a concomitant expansion of the service industry and a "knowledge society." Instead of laborers and workers we have "professionals," a "new intelligentsia" who seek to fulfill the information needs of the post-industrial society.

The information society is intimately linked to globalization. Globalization is marked by the following features:

- The expansion of trade in terms of trading relationships and movement of capital.
- The development of transnational and global communication networks.
- The diminished role of the nation-state even within its territorial space.
- The rise of transnational cultural, economic, and political networks (such as the International Monetary Fund, Greenpeace, and Amnesty International).
- The increased presence of Western consumer products and cultural artifacts (from Levi's to Microsoft), or what is often called the "McDonaldization" of the world.

A new international division of labor facilitated by the telecommunications networks is visible in the age of globalization. Global and offshore finance, outsourced work, multiple and fractured sites of production and consumption, and cultural flows are all enabled by the new ICTs.

The increasing dependence on information collection, processing, and distribution in a globally connected world has led to what Manuel Castells characterizes as an "informational order" where the "flows" of information are of paramount importance. Cash flows are in fact information flows (Castells 1996).

Key Issues in Cyberculture Studies

This section summarizes the key concerns in cyberculture studies. Many of these issues are examined in greater detail in subsequent chapters, and are included here mainly to indicate the possibilities within cyberculture studies.

Globalization, Technocapitalism, and Cybercultures

Globalization has been enabled by the advent of high-speed communications. Capitalism is increasingly becoming *technocapitalism* because the distributed nature of production, marketing, and consumption demands technological linkages and synchronous, 24/7 communications. Manuel Castells's work, as noted above, has demonstrated how the flows of information assume prime importance in this context. It is the management of information and financial flows that becomes the key focus in globalized technocapitalism.

As an example of such flows in the age of informationalism, consider Amazon.com. Amazon.com is arguably the most successful .com company today. Having survived the .com bubble burst in 2000–2001, it has expanded astronomically since its founding to become the foremost example of the linkage between globalization, technology, and commerce.

Amazon.com is a unique company because of the way it localizes itself. While its name and web address are now a brand, the company uses a flexible screen geography – as Martin Dodge (2004) points out, the screen is a micro-geography – so that local cultural and even personal elements can be incorporated. This makes it a local "firm" for users, something like the old grocer down the street, because the Amazon.com website is designed for and by the individual user, to the extent that the entire website is in the local language. Amazon.com is a Seattle-based company, but it is a transnational one whose flows and networks of finance and product distribution are global. Finally, even if Amazon.com does not own a physical store, it possesses a massive material infrastructure "substrate" to its website.

In addition to the theme of commerce and globalizing ICTs, other features draw our attention here. Increasingly, people, classes, and territories that are not significant for the informational society are excluded from the wired world. The old, African nations, the mentally ill, and inner-city ghettoes are all peripheral to the globalizing ICT movement. Just as capitalism was driven by the logic of capital accumulation and production, the high-tech age is driven by the need to possess ever greater amounts of information, and those who lack this (the "information poor") are left out of the race. Human labor power is, however, central to this new condition as well. Automation, information gathering, and labor are, argues Douglas Kellner (1999), analogous to mechanization in the earlier age of capitalism. In such a new capitalist order, the information poor fall through the gap.

Globalization has very clear material consequences – from profits to poverty – and these are the conditions in which cybercultural forms, the informational economy, and ICTs exist and function. This book believes, therefore, that cyberculture studies constitutes a vital aspect of globalization studies itself.

Materiality and Corporeality

Studies of cybercultures such as that by Howard Rheingold (1994) celebrate virtual worlds for enabling the user to transcend geography and the body. Disembodiment, it is argued, is the overcoming of the body's limitations in favor of pure rationality and thinking. When Hans Moravec (1988) describes the body as "mere jelly" (p. 116), the key assumption is that information, thinking, and the mind are more significant than the body (even though cyberpunk is often critical of such views of technologized bodies, which often represent cultural anxieties about "informatization"). The theme of disembodiment and bodily transcendence also forms the basis of the work of cyber- and digital artists like Stelarc. The body's limitations – disease, degeneration, aging – can be overcome through technological prosthesis. What we have is an *augmented* body: the posthuman.

Subjectivity and identity are no longer rooted in the body. Subjectivity in the posthuman condition is "dispersed throughout the cybernetic circuit" (Hayles 1999: 27). The incorporation of data from the outside into the body and the extension of consciousness into other spaces through VR or cybernetic circuits suggests that consciousness need not be confined to the body. However, while the transcendence of the body's limits is attractive – since in some respects it does away with degeneration and aging – it poses its own problems. Since suffering, politics, and emancipation continue to be *embodied*, the transcendence of the body does not help. Besides, for women, minorities, and the socially marginalized, claims for justice must remain rooted in the *body* rather than in pure, disembodied, and abstract "consciousness."

It is also significant that any technology of corporeal transcendence can only be built through rigorous labor by very material bodies, often working in sweatshops and for low wages. On the more positive side, new developments in computer-driven prostheses and medicine can significantly improve the functions and therefore material life of differently abled, aging, and diseased bodies.

Cyberculture studies explores the impact, consequence, context, and manifestations of computer technology and ICTs on the social, cultural, economic, and material (i.e., fleshly) conditions of real bodies, and examines the shifts in the nature of living for material bodies via ICTs and new media. In the chapter on cyberbodies (Chapter 3), we return to these and other corporeal themes.

The Digital Divide

It is a truism that resources and power are not evenly distributed among the people and nations of the world. The rise and rapid expansion of ICTs are subject to a similar condition of unequal access between, for example, Africa and Europe, leading to a "digital divide." Focusing primarily on Internet access as the focal point of networked culture, Pippa Norris suggests a three-layered digital divide: the *global divide*, referring to the divergence in Internet access between developed and developing nations; the *social divide*, referring to the divergence between Internet access and use between classes and sections within a particular society (termed "information rich" and "information poor"); and the *democratic divide*, referring to the difference in the nature/quality of use of the Internet and digital resources between users (Norris 2001: 4). An example of this digital divide, identified in September 2007 (Internet World Stats 2007), would be the rate of Internet use and population penetration:

- Africa has 14.7 percent of the world's population and constitutes 3.5 percent of the world's total Internet use (though it shows the largest expansion of Internet use – 874.6 percent between 2000 and 2007).
- Europe has 12.3 percent of the world's population and constitutes 27.2 percent of world Internet use.
- North America has 69 percent Internet penetration, even though it has only 5.1 percent of the world's population.
- Within Asia, Afghanistan constitutes 0.1 percent of total users in Asia, and has 2.0 percent of its population wired. India constitutes 13.1 percent of total Internet users in Asia, and has 5.3 percent of its population wired. Hong Kong has 68.2 percent of its population wired, and Japan 68 percent.

The difference between users and Internet penetration is obvious from the statistics. However, the significance of this difference is not so obvious at first, and it is the nature of the digital divide that concerns us here in terms of agency, ability, and questions of power and identity.

DIGITAL DIVIDE

This term is used to describe the uneven nature of access to and quality of Internet access, electronic communication, and cyber-cultures in general. It gestures primarily at the difference in digital cultures – including production, dissemination, and use – between First World and Third World nations, though the "divide" within the former is also increasingly described under the same rubric.

The First World is increasingly "informatized," networked, and linked. The digital age in such cases might mean, for particular segments of society, *increased access* to health services (networks of healthcare workers, data, and expertise), education (distance learning, access to information), financial transactions (e-commerce), and civic engagement (online voting, public debates via the Internet). The personal computer and faster and cheaper connectivity alter the individual's or community's role in the public sphere, enabling individuals and communities to access information and therefore improve their lifestyles or conditions.

Within First World nations, however, racial and class inequalities exist in access to and use of digital resources: there is differential access for blacks and Chicano/a populations, and there is a rural–urban divide. The digital divide therefore needs to be studied at the level of the nation, the institution, and the individual (Norris 2001: 14–15). White students without a PC at home might access the Internet in other places more than non-white students. Studies have shown that Caucasian children surf for humor and entertainment sites while African American children of the same age group often look up information, education, and race support activities, though the popular Internet seems not to show a racial divide among children (Jackson et al. 2007).

However, the digital divide is not merely a question of access to a PC or the Internet. Other cultural factors such as language (the lack of English, for instance, among immigrants in the USA, who may need to find information about social welfare or laws) can determine the number of users. This brings us back to the question of *power* in debates about the digital era. The Internet arose as an elite, selective formation and expanded into a full-fledged techno-elitism determined by capital. Differential access, infrastructure, and costs determine the power of individuals to spend time on the Internet or to form online communities. Questions of authority, including peer review, control of resources, respectability, and policy-making capability – their *genealogy*, to be accurate – continue to inform cybercultures. These are ultimately questions of power and are precisely the areas where subcultures like hackers make their *agency* known.

AGENCY

Agency is the capacity of individuals to make choices to alter the course of their lives, and to implement those choices. Agency in social theory is the cornerstone of identity and rights, where the demand for rights is the demand for individuals to be able to pursue their goals, ambitions, and aims without hindrance.

Cyberculture studies' emphasis on the political economy of ICTs pays attention to issues of power and justice, the social agenda, and the political consequences of ICTs. Cyberculture studies calls attention to the raced, gendered, and classed nature of the "information revolution," the effects of this revolution on different sectors of society, and the question of power that determines the course of the revolution.

E-Governance

A key element in the digital divide debate is that of e-governance. Enthusiasts of digital democracy argue that the expansion of the Internet and digital resources will enhance civic participation, communications between citizens and the state, and the state's responses to society. E-governance includes increased public services ranging from community health care to civil servants' responses to requests for local consultations. Where face-to-face meetings are difficult and expensive to arrange, networked cultures can fruitfully enable such interactions in cyberspace. Government and public service websites offer information about official processes, often for free. Research organizations have collated data from various countries and found that the UK and USA possess the highest number of government webbed operations (Cyberspace Policy Research Group 2001).

The two key aims and principles in cases of e-governance are "informational transparency" and "communication interactivity" (Norris 2001: 119–120). The first describes the amount of information offered by the government, while the second describes interactions between state agencies and citizens. Online publication and availability of official reports, administrative decisions, and policy-making processes could help citizens in voting, making representations to the state, understanding policies and regulations, and perhaps even making their own interventions. It could be argued that the process of e-governance seeks to increase transparency and enhance state–citizen communication. However, the mere availability of information does *not* ensure the quality or reliability of the information supplied.

Cyberculture studies is concerned with the role of ICTs in the formation of legislation and the impact of new technologies in the realm of political participation. Proceeding from its concern with the political economy of ICTs, cyberculture studies addresses issues of empowerment, control, political uses (and abuses) of new technologies, national identities, and new ways of citizenship participation in politics and governance.

Civil Society

With their potential for greater connectivity both within the community and between the community and the state, digital technologies have been commonly understood to enhance civil society. NGOs, activists, experts, and the general public now have greater access to information and greater chances of linking together to lobby. In 1999 during the World Trade Organization (WTO) meeting in Seattle, environmentalists, activists, anti-globalization protesters, and labor unions came together to demonstrate. The International Civil Society website provided an hourly report on the demonstrations – reports that were distributed/telecast to hundreds of NGOs worldwide. Such examples are taken to indicate a strengthening of grassroots activism.

Social movements increasingly use the Internet as a medium of communication, propaganda, and political mobilization. Citizens' forums, state feedback mechanisms, and NGOs use the Internet and digital resources to strengthen their infrastructure, responses, and public interface.

Social movements with various focal points – the environment, anti-racism, gay and lesbian rights, anti-globalization, women's empowerment – have turned to the Internet as a space where solidarities might be forged and reinforced. Listservs, online petitions, and emails have solicited funding and political support. People who might otherwise have refrained from street protests or similar expressions of political opinions swell the ranks of online petitioners. Political protests have gone online in other, more "damaging" ways – blocking and defacing government websites, for instance – in order to attract attention (an example of this is pro-Palestine hackers defacing American pro-Israel websites in 2000). More importantly, there is the possibility of globalizing the movement itself because transnational linkages between organizations and groups are helped in their processes and public outreach programs by the medium. Protest and social movements are able to transmit their ideologies, beliefs, and values to a greater number of people and over larger territories than ever before. Manuel Castells suggests that the slow erosion of traditional political formations such as the political party and the trade union has enabled loose coalitions, ad hoc assemblages, and spontaneous mobilizations to "substitute" for permanent and more organized structures (Castells 2001: 140–141).

Citizen networks in towns and cities are now able to offer greater opportunities for the community and individuals to participate in debates about issues concerning them. University networks, local community networks for senior citizens, and help groups reach out to greater numbers through the medium of their websites, helplines, feedback mechanisms, and online discussion forums. Democratic processes of feedback, opinions, and debate are facilitated by the new ICTs, marking a whole new era for civil society and enhancing political, social, and cultural agency – from opinion dissemination to political action.

However, it should also be kept in mind that such online political action might not have a *material* effect (the protests against the WTO or the Myanmar regime, for example, did not alter the course of events). There is a risk that cybercultural resistance or activism remains at the level of the virtual, with little or no impact upon the real world. A false sense of social commitment and empowerment emerges in online political activism – putting one's digital signature to an online petition is not the same as barricading a civil servant or blockading the road to obstruct traffic in order to articulate demands. We would also do well to recognize the irony that online petitioning could lead to a *withdrawal* from the material political demonstration that attracts attention and action.

With its interest in the political economy and material bases of information technology and digital cultures, cyberculture studies explores the ways in which organizations, individuals, campaigns, and civil society in general have appropriated or resisted ICTs.

Governing Cyberspace

While the digital era may herald improved citizen–state interaction through a democratizing technology, at least in post-industrial societies, cyberculture and networks are themselves subject to governance and regulation. The "freedom" of cyberspace demands careful examination in the face of the hagiographers of "Internet culture."

Governance concerns not simply the hardware of wires, drives, terminals, and routers but also the consequence of modes of data transfer through codes, or protocols. Protocols (Transmission Control Protocol/Internet Protocol, TCP/IP, and the Domain Name System, DNS) are the material substrate of the Internet's distribution system and can be regulated. A protocol is defined as "a language that regulates flow, directs netspace, codes relationships, and connects life-forms" (Galloway 2004: 74).

Protocols – software rules – are about power.

With the Reston, Virginia, conference and the International Forum on the White Paper (IFWP) in 1998, mechanisms began to be put in place to regulate the "root." The Internet Corporation for Assigned Names and Numbers (ICANN) sought what it called "technical management," but it was in fact an organizational system that initiated "Internet governance." ICANN, Milton Mueller emphasizes, is a new international regime formed around the Internet's use, where technical coordination is tied to the regulation of the industry (Mueller 2002: 217–218).

PROTOCOL

The set of rules that determine the allocation of Internet addresses, domain names, and servers.

Allocation of domain names and categories (.xxx such as .kids) also involves issues of authority of the root administrator, as Mueller (2002: 9) points out. Who decides whether the sites under the label .kids really are appropriate for children? Address space allocation is influenced by *technical*, *economic*, and *policy* matters such as the uniqueness of identifiers, efficiency of consumption of the resources, and disputes among assignments of names (Mueller 2002: 29).

Finally, the commercial interests of AOL or Microsoft drive and constitute the *institutional* governance of the Internet. Copyright laws, domain names, and national security concerns can result in regulation, via protocols, of the inherently uncontrollable, distributed Internet. Even search engines have their own politics and serve the interests of corporations like Microsoft or Yahoo! when they become transformed into advertising domains rather than "neutral" search mechanisms (Introna and Nissenbaum 2000; Spink and Zimmer 2008).

Identity

Contemporary social and critical theory rejects the notion of a stable, unified, and coherent identity, instead seeing identity as the cumulative effect of a series of negotiations, differences, and discourses (Butler 1990; Hall 2000). In cyberspace identities are malleable as never before. Avatars (online identities), homepages, email IDs, and bodies are all inherently unstable. The disconnect between representation and the body (still a primary source of identity in the "real" world) is, by definition, infinite in cyberspace. Cyberspace allows one to pick an identity, to masquerade, mimic, and transcend bodily identities and interact with the world as somebody else. In a world where race, class, gender, and sexuality can become obstacles in interactions with the world, cyberspace allows one to *choose* an identity that may have nothing to do with one's "real-life" gender or race. Critics see this as an enabling condition (Turkle 1995). It allows the closet gay to assert his identity, just as a woman can be involved in the "unfeminine" space of political discussion by masquerading as a man in relative safety. The ugly body can be (re)presented as beautiful and attractive in cyberspace because software allows individuals to choose the color of their skin, hair, and eyes as well as change their shape. They can play any role they choose because it is difficult to authenticate the identity presented in cyberspace.[1] The individual's subjectivity exists in a dispersed state, where the boundaries of the self are no longer the body or skin (Hayles 1999: 72).

Identity in cyberspace can be *augmented* by making additions from a variety of choices. This shifting, malleable, and unstable identity in cyberspace is therefore often treated as "fluid." Once again, cyberculture studies' interest lies in the consequences and appropriation of new technologies.

Questions of identity must be further pared down to specific kinds of identity: racial, class, and gender. The latter forms the subject of Chapter 5 and includes sexual identities.

Race

In February 2004, *Wired* magazine's cover showed a South Indian woman with her hand partly obscuring her face, dressed in what appeared to be bridal finery. The palm of her hand was inscribed with *mehndi*, a traditional form of bridal decoration in many parts of India. The *mehndi* were actually the text of computer code and instructions. The cover story by Daniel Pink, "The New Face of the Silicon Age," that complemented this visual image dealt with outsourcing and how high-tech jobs were being lost to India.

The visual was accurate insofar as the demographics go: South Indians constitute a sizeable chunk of programmers in the computer industry. The racial and gendered interpretation of the employment and technological scene by *Wired* is, of course, problematic. It not only racializes and genders the technological contexts of business process outsourcing (which is based primarily on lower wages in India: Pink writes that the Indian female programmer "could do your $70,000-a-year job for the wages of a Taco Bell counter jockey"), but also exoticizes the "worker." The bridal finery suggests an identity that is full of promise and potential, even as the write-up expresses a definite antagonism and anxiety (Indian programmers are described by Pink as "the cause of fear and loathing," not only because Americans lose their jobs to them, but also, he adds, because they are forced to train these Indian software workers). This anxiety has visible cultural, social, and political consequences: organizations seeking to protect American jobs from the menace of outsourcing have sprung up (e.g., the Coalition for the Future American Worker, www.american worker.org/), and people stand for Congress on the anti-outsourcing ticket (John Kerry, the presidential hopeful in 2004, and Mike Emmons from Florida were two such candidates).

The Internet may facilitate the construction of pseudonymous and anonymous identities. However, this kind of "transcendence" of identity has two aspects that are more problematic than a simple question of "alternate" identities.

1. *Agency*: Do minorities, the disempowered, and the marginalized wish to transcend the crucial matrix of race, community, and gender, and if they do, or are they capable of doing so?
2. *Representation*: How is race represented on the World Wide Web? This again links to issues both of power and agency. What ideologies inform the "coding" of race on the Internet? Since the Internet is a social process, cultural factors such as race are surely integral to the function, shape, and use of the technology.

There exists a fundamental paradox at the heart of cybercultures, one that fits right into the cultural studies paradigm where corporeality and materiality are central constituents of identity and power.

First, cyberspace is a "raced" medium where disembodiment, transcendence, and fluid identities are the privilege of the white race (Nakamura 2002). When the entire cyberspace universe is made up of reconstituted, simulated, immaterial copies of the "real," where all identities are suspect, and where the difference between "original" and "copy" is blurred, there is a concomitant cultural anxiety about authenticity. That is, in times of uncertain identities, stereotypes of "authentic," unchanging, stable "natives" or the racial Other proliferate. It is in the context of the modified, unstable posthuman that there is a simultaneous search for the recognizable Other. This recognizable Other is often the woman or the black person. People who adopt different identities in cyberspace often have recourse to established stereotypes of gender and race (Nakamura 2002: 14), and thus essentialize and commodify the native, the woman, or the black person because they constitute the unchanging Other against which whites can conduct their posthuman alterations of identity. To adapt Donna Haraway's (1991b) formulation, the cyborged human functions as the inappropriate/d posthuman only because there are suitably appropriate(d) stereotypes – or what Nakamura (2002) terms *cybertypes*.

Second, and more worryingly in discourses of fluid identities, avatars, and disembodiment in hagiographies of the digital age (Turkle 1995), is the denial of embodiment. Real-life practices and experiences, issues of citizenship, the law, and medical science rooted in the body (the citizen is an individual *body*, the law categorizes/incarcerates individual *bodies* based on their actions, medicine treats diseased *bodies*) are very corporeal and material. Transcendence of the body is not an option for those who desperately need the body – raced, classed, gendered, sexualized: a solid, recognizable, identified body – for the sake of identity. Disembodiment becomes one more technocapitalist mode of *denying agency*. The discourses of multiple, shifting, fluid identities make absolutely no sense to people like minorities, women, or the differently abled because it is their embodiment that needs to be recognized and empowered. Online avatars, however glamorous or perfect they may be, do not erase or alleviate the problems of the offline body in an unequal society.

Finally, the matter of race does not end with the body but has a larger *material* context. It must be remembered that, genealogically speaking, the new ICTs grew out of the labor generated mostly by non-white workers in Silicon Valley. BPO works that enable global networking depend almost entirely on Asian labor (India, where I write, is a center for the BPO industry). Bill Gates is reported to have stated that Microsoft's Beijing research center is one of his company's most productive, before adding that when he met his company's ten best-performing employees, "nine of them had names I couldn't pronounce" (Weber 2006). At this point it is important to see how power operates within technological development and innovation:[2]

- How does Microsoft control the research and harness the efforts of Asians in Silicon Valley and its offices worldwide?
- How much of black or brown agency is "free" and how much of it is "owned" by Microsoft?

These questions are of *raced* power equations.

Companies regulate employees' lives, the acquisition of materials, the route taken by research and development, and the marketing of products. Their advertising arm also informs and influences consumer actions. Power here includes financial, social, and political power where the agency of the employee and the consumer is, at least invisibly, directed and controlled by the corporation or the state. In terms of race, the question of power is about the differentials that exist between cybertechnologies of categories such as white/non-white or First World/Third World.

Differential wages and work benefits, profit sharing, and institutional structures are *raced* structures. These are matters of power, identity, and "materials." Software programs written by Asians in Silicon Valley (by 1996 nearly half of the US government's temporary visas for high-tech workers were issued to Indians), BPO units in Indian cities, and the financial centers in First World nations, where decisions about software, copyrights, and company acquisitions are taken, constitute the *raced* social, cultural, and material contexts of cyberspace.[3]

If the *augmentation* of the body is the *apparatgeist* – the spirit of the apparatus (see below) – of ICTs and the digital age, this augmentation is rooted in raced and classed structures that govern the design, research, circulation, and marketing of ICTs. Cyberculture studies is alert to this raced and classed nature of the informational economy.

Class

Questions of access, class, and techno-elitism shift the focus on to more material matters such as cyberpower. Cyberpower includes discussions about the freedom to access information (and therefore the politics of access), control over the Internet and the digital domain (hence the question of governance, domain name control, and the infrastructure that produces cyberspace), rights to privacy, and elitism.

New York City has the largest concentration of fiber-optic wired buildings in the world, of which Harlem has one; South Central Los Angeles (the site of the 1990s race riots) has none (Sassen 1999: 60). The difference in digital resources and connectivity in Sub-Saharan Africa and Singapore or Finland is very real and very worrying, especially since crucial areas such as health care and finance are increasingly worked through enhanced connectivity and rapid transmission of data and resources.

Even though these differences in infrastructure are being eroded, there is a considerable demographic, class, racial, and national distinction between the wired and unwired. The distribution, working, and structure of the Internet, mobile phone, router, and .com website that the ordinary person uses is controlled by a technoclass. The high-tech domain remains firmly in the hands of the techno-elite, who are predominantly white and male. In terms of social capital, the world's consumer societies privilege gadgets, connectivity, and speed, thus bestowing higher status upon those who possess all three. Status is also, in a sense, augmented through techno-elitism (Dear and Flusty 1999; Gray 2001; Rutsky 1999).

Gender and Sexualities

If identities can be reinvented in cyberspace, what consequences does this facility have for gender? How do women use ICTs for their own empowerment? And how do the new environments of information technology portray women? How do women use mobile phones? Do they use them more to stay in touch with their family and homes than for pleasure and work? Do women surf for entertainment and pleasure rather than for information alone? Do women maintain separate, disguised identities in cyberspace that allow them to escape the constraints of their bodies and gender in the real world?

To begin with, there is the key problem of *access*. How many women have access to the wired world? This question needs to be further qualified and fine-tuned by paying attention to the class and racial profiles of women who do or do not have access.

A second problem is the *role of women* in the making of technology and as instruments of technical innovation and change. Feminist critics of technology (e.g., Wajcman 1993) have pointed out that not only do women *not* have equal rights of access to high tech, they are also rarely involved with the design and research that create the technology. Social constructionists (e.g., Bijker 1995) argue that women may serve the purpose of (cheap) labor in the factory or laboratory, but they have little say in how the design is finalized and how the technology is adopted.

The third key problem is that of *representation*. Since cybercultural terms such as "matrix" (derived from the Latin *mater*, meaning "mother"), motherboards, and "jacking in" are clearly coded in gender terms, it becomes important to ask how cyberspace becomes gendered. Representations of women as "techno-tards," sexualized beings, and passive users reinforce the gendered power equations from the real world. Feminist readings have found that stereotypes from the real world pervade even passing, camp, and drag on the Internet, thus suggesting that even cyberspace is as gendered as the real world.

Cyberfeminists therefore seek to feminize cyberspace by ensuring that the technology is appropriated for their use. Cyberfeminists seek to disturb power hierarchies by representing themselves in cyberspace, by seeking to control their online identities, and by being upfront with their sexualities. Their popular terminology – contamination, virus, contagion – suggests a disturbance within the cybercultural domain (Flanagan 2002; Gajjala 2003; Haraway 1991a/1985; Plant 1995; Sofia 1999).

As the chapters on cybersexualities and the cyber-public sphere demonstrate, cyberspace is gendered not only in terms of access but also in the ways in which women appropriate cyberspaces.

Space and Geography

Twentieth-century critical theory has been obsessed with space. Cybercultures that create alternate spaces and virtual universes, and alter our experience of spatiality and location, have, unsurprisingly, provided fertile ground for geographers and students of space. Numerous spatial metaphors have entered the discourse of cyberspace: information *highway*, electronic *neighborhood*, virtual *travelers*, *surfing* the World Wide Web, and web*sites*.

Cyberspace's apparent lack of political boundaries lends it a certain glamor and exoticism. As such, our ideas of the nation-state, which are firmly tied to matters of territoriality, have altered. Transnational activities such as global markets, television, knowledge networks, and finance (and including, unfortunately, terrorism) have made it imperative that we modify what we understand as space.

Electronic space or cyberspace is different from the lived environment in significant ways. Where the lived environment, or social space, involves structures and artifacts such as schools, homes, factories, and hospitals that provide the location for social relations, electronic space consists of pictorial, aural, and textual artifacts that enable and mediate social relations. Cyberspace is a network of myriad electronic connections, linkages, interactions, and knowledge sharing. This is the *logic* of cyberspace – a system of random or calculated linkages, which themselves are the result of social and cultural values, beliefs, and needs. It is also a space with its own contradictions. ICTs enable us to transcend borders and spaces – we can be here and there at the same time – while *simultaneously* providing us with precise information (via GPS) about our exact location. It is, clearly, difficult to privilege virtual spaces and virtual life when the real, material, and corporeal remains the center of surveillance and possible threat. Cyberspace is a site of social relations, a process rather than a thing.

These networks could be of the market (Sassen 2005), of sociability, or of knowledge sharing (Bach and Stark 2005), but they are basically *spaces of interaction*. Hence the term "digital formation" (Latham and Sassen 2005), which gestures at this socioculturally informed/influenced dimension of interaction as the feature that generates spaces, seems appropriate to describe cyberspace. This means that cyberspace can be subject to the same stresses, strains, and manipulation as "real" social space, since it is embedded in the social.

It is possible, as Douglas Cowan (2005) has eloquently argued, that the experience of cyberspace as another place is basically the effect of its visual representation: we believe and imagine we are in the virtual shopping mall because it *looks* like a shopping mall. Indexicality – by which we distinguish between places – is based primarily on visual cues on webpages and images. Places are organized online for us around the experiences and expectations of/in that place, where the place is the site of possible action. This possible action could also be the platform for the formation of a community.

The Internet itself possesses a geography: its *technical geography* (the telecommunications infrastructure, routers, fibre optic cable networks, transmission hardware), its *user geography* (as manifest in the distribution of users in national/regional statistics), and finally the *economic geography* of Internet production (Castells 2001: 208–224). If the first is governed by corporate houses and business ventures, mergers, and acquisitions, the second is informed by the distribution of users and the third by the profits generated, e-commerce, and technocapitalism. AOL, Microsoft, Ericsson, Nokia, and IBM, with their control over the hardware, software, routers, and, more than anything else, the labor force, concentrate the ICTs in the hands (and coffers) of conglomerates and corporations. The economic geography of the Internet is precisely this selective, metropolitan, First World corporate control over large distances, manufacturing units, peoples, and media services through regulated and carefully plotted flows of capital (Castells and Hall 1994; Wheeler et al. 2000).

We will return to the theme of the geography of cyberspace in Chapter 6.

Risk

A small icon in the corner of my Windows menu announces that my computer is now protected against 914,000 viruses. Why is it important for me to know this piece of information about my everyday workstation? It worries me that, but for this wonderful firewall/anti-spyware/anti-virus, 914,000 possible infections, invasions, and disasters could strike my PC. On an everyday basis, I live with the risk that my hardware, software, and, consequently, wetware (me) could be invaded. Websites assure me that they are "secure" and that I can carry out financial transactions without worry.

New and faster technologies seem to augment risk. Cybercultures generate their own forms of risk: computer crashes, cybersex addictions, privacy invasion, financial fraud, and stalking, among others. Building on Ulrich Beck's (1992) influential formulation of a "risk society," Joost Van Loon (2002) suggests that we live in a state of anticipating risk. Risk is always *potential*, always waiting-to-happen or "becoming-real" (2002: 130), and technoscience is called upon to both conceal and reveal the risks involved (2002: 156).

In the digital age, the environment of "cybernetic space" is constituted and constructed through a process of flows and transcoding between commerce, law, media, and the military. The virtual becomes "real" only when all these elements add up. The system (hardware-software-wetware) and the environment (cybernetic space) constitute each other, where the boundaries between the two are increasingly difficult to find. This is the dialectic of the virtual and the real.

In the case of cybercultures, the risk-aversion ethos is more complicated than a mere outlining of the risk. The appearance of a computer virus poses a risk to systems. An indirect risk proceeds from this recognition: programmers, webmasters, and users send dozens of emails warning people of this potential risk, thereby adding to the load on the system. Thus, not only does the risk element – the virus – proliferate self-replicatingly through the medium, so does the process of risk warning and risk management.

Donald MacKenzie (1998), exploring computer-related accidental deaths, has found that most of the catastrophic accidents may have involved faulty human–computer interaction rather than being "pure" computer failures. MacKenzie suggests that the risks involved cannot be based on past evidence (with computers or other forms of technology) because the incidence and complexity of computerization are increasing. What is needed to assess risk, he suggests, is addressing not only the computer's technical aspects but also the cognitive and organizational aspects of their "real-world" operation (1998: 210–212). Developments in medical informatics and medical cybercultures have given rise to their own "brands" of risk. The debate over nanotechnological particles in the USA and UK is an example of what is termed "stigmatization," where popular science writing and fiction (the novels of Michael Crichton, especially his *Prey*, 2002, are a case in point) highlight the risks of nanotechnology. Nanotechnology represents both a highly advanced medical and engineering technology and an invisible risk because of the scale of the objects. Newspaper coverage in the UK, for instance, offered a mixture of hope at the new technology's potential and anxiety over its side effects (Wilkinson et al. 2007). Wilkinson and colleagues prove how debates about risk are primarily about public policy and media coverage of the technology. This is the key moment in risk culture where the social implications of any technology occupy the foreground along with the scientific component.

The Mediapolis and the Space of the Other

The Internet is a medium through which we access distant parts of the world, strangers, and our immediate circle of friends and relatives. It serves an important social and political purpose. As Roger Silverstone envisages it, the mass media is a "space of appearance" (2007: 25–55). The Other appears to us, is made known to us, only on our screens. It enables us to see difference. "Mediapolis" is the "mediated space of appearance in which the world appears and in which the world is constituted in its appearance, and through which we learn about those who are and who are not like us" (2007: 31). The screen and the media construct the world for us, even as the medium is itself constructed *by* the world.

This means that we need to ask what "versions" of the Other or the world appear on our screens. How does the Internet orient the world to us and inform our orientation to the world? This set of questions takes us, Silverstone demonstrates, into the realm of ethics; it is

> because the media provide … the frameworks … for the appearance of the other that they, de facto, define the moral space within which the other appears to us, and at the same time invite (claim, constrain) an equivalent moral response from us, the audience, as a potential or actual citizen. (2007: 7)

This "moral response" turns the issue of representation into one of possible global citizenship where one is called upon to respond in certain ways to images of suffering, exploitation, and injustice.

Minority and alternative voices that manage to find expression help constitute, in Silverstone's argument, a framework for the culture of globalization, even when the media are governed by global capital. It might enable people to be cosmopolitan – a "citizen of the world" – with the increasing shareability and accessibility of the world. The stranger, the neighbor, and the Other all appear before us.

The mediated space of appearance provides the setting where decisions and judgments are made. This marks the potential for a new civil society – or a virtual one, to turn to its synonym – where the Other is somebody we can recognize and hope to understand.

Within cyberculture studies, the question of ethics, representations, and consumption of the Other on our screens and through information is a key one.

Aesthetics

Apple's Cube was the first computer in history to be displayed in the New York Museum of Modern Art's "Design" section. This transformed it from a machine into an art object with aesthetic appeal and values. Sean Cubitt (1998), David Jay Bolter and Richard Grusin (1999), and Bolter and Diane Gromala (2003) have focused on the design of the computer and specific art forms that have appropriated new media technologies.

In 2006, an anthology of essays exploring the possibilities of *aesthetic computing* appeared (Fishwick 2006), marking the beginnings perhaps of a new "project" in the interface of computer technology, aesthetics, and art. Aesthetic computing is the "application of the theory and practice of art to the field of computing" (Fishwick 2006: 6). It includes looking at the internal, mathematical structures of computing, the use of software to create art (often called "software art"), or the art of the interface. Aesthetic computing focuses on specific areas such as human–computer interaction (HCI), visualization, or discrete structures. It also includes looking at the semiotics of the computer – such as the location and design of the desktop or the arrangement of the hardware.

In terms of aesthetics and computers, computer art presents a different order of art. Computer-assisted art generates larger philosophical questions about the very *nature* of art. Since most computer artists use commercially developed software, what is the role of the individual "creator"? The computer is not simply an artist's tool because it performs a variety of functions and expands the artist's corporeal and mental abilities. It should therefore be treated as a creative partner of the artist (Humphries 2003: 22–24).

While computer art seems to involve a more or less direct incorporation of computers and computing into the production of art forms, a less commonly noticed dimension is the art of the computer itself. The interface – the most visible and immediate dimension of computing for the ordinary user – can be regarded as a set of *signs*. Signs, as we know, are *cultural*. The interface consists of visible graphics that are the consequence of invisible software. This interface is also, as Nake and Grabowski (2006: 62–63) emphasize, tied to our embodied existence. We perceive these objects that appear on our screen or emerge from our speakers. The interface often changes with a change in the way we operate, through our bodies, the mouse, or the pointer. That is, there is on the one hand the design and art of the "basic" interface that appears on the screen and, on the other, the changing "landscape" of the interface as we negotiate it via the cursor and clicks.

There is also the visualization – from cell biology to outer space – we see in news reports and on our screens. Visualization techniques involve a lot of computing and constitute what Stephen Wilson (2002) has termed the "information arts."

Finally, aesthetic computing includes looking at interaction digital design. Jonas Löwgren (2006) suggests that digital materials have to be shaped in such a way that users find them "good." Interaction design is the "shaping [of] the digital materials to create conditions for good use" (Löwgren 2006: 384). Löwgren identifies 19 use qualities of digital designs, including playability, seductivity, usefulness, surprise, fluency control/autonomy, elegance, and relevance. These are features to be accounted for and incorporated at the moment of design in order to enable and engage the user to use the interface and the program.

Cyberculture Studies

Clearly, cybercultures are a congeries of the economic, the technical, and the socio-cultural. Cybercultures involve questions of labor and finance, of political control and power, of the individual and community. Any study of cybercultures must address all aspects of the information society. In order to do so, the approach must be eclectic and multi-sited, dealing with multiple aspects of cybercultures without sacrificing any. Most studies, including introductions such as this one, are a brico-lage of approaches.

Thus, while it is tempting to reduce cybercultures to Internet cultures or digital cultures, the increasing convergence of technological forms invites a more broad-based perspective. Several innovative readings of and models for approaching cyber-cultures have been proposed, engaging the attention of scholars in media and communication studies, cultural studies, sociology, and the humanities.

Ethnographies of Cyberspace

If the Internet is a social formation or a social process, then it follows that, like social and cultural artifacts, it can be examined ethnographically. Following Christine Hine (2000), three key areas for studying the Internet can be isolated ethnographi-cally: travel and face-to-face interaction; text, technology, and reflexivity; and the making of ethnographic objects. The first calls for a redefining of what face-to-face interaction means. The Internet is a collection of texts, and the task of the ethnogra-pher is to understand the meanings generated by these textual practices. Finally, the Internet must be treated as a cultural artifact that is linked to offline relationships and contexts, to situate it within larger contexts and see how the two complement each other.

Ethnographies of cyberculture, suggests Arturo Escobar (1996), need to look at the ways in which software and applications are designed as well as used, the crea-tion of online communities and networks, the popular cultural forms of such tech-nologies (from cyberpunk to computer games), the cultural identities that emerge in the new technospaces, and the political economy of cyberculture (especially the relationship between capitalism, global economy, and power). An instance of such an ethnography would be the London School of Economics Young People New Media project studying the use of media by young people, the "individualization" that results from this, and new forms of leisure, literacy, and sociability (see Livingstone 2003).

This book covers something of all these domains, moving across political econ-omy, questions of the public sphere, gender and other identities, and popular cyber-cultural forms. In each case, it seeks to foreground questions of power, agency, and identity, both of the users and "creators" of cyberculture.

Apparatgeist Theory

James Katz and Mark Aakhus (2002) have developed a theory of *apparatgeist* to convey the logic and spirit of the new communications technology. "*Apparatgeist*," a neologism from "apparatus" (meaning "materials needed for a purpose" and "equipment") and the German *Geist* (meaning "spirit" or "mind"), gestures at the sense of movement, direction, and motive in any technology. It captures the individual and collective aspects of societal behavior, even as it proposes the imbrication of the cultural situation with the extant technology. The *apparatgeist* of communication technology (Katz and Aakhus are working with mobile phones and personal communications technologies (PCTs), it must be noted) is that of "perpetual contact." Perpetual contact is its logic and its spirit, and governs the premises of design, development, and use of PCTs. It describes the logic of the very language of, say, MS Word. For instance, if one were to run a right-clicked synonym search for "contact" on MS Word, this is what turns up:

> Get in touch with
> Make contact with
> Call
> Phone
> Speak to
> Write to
> Drop a line to

These synonyms cover the range of possible modes of communication, as MS Word and its preloaded Thesaurus perceive communication.

Katz and Aakhus suggest that there is a sociologic of perpetual contact. People have explicit reasons (form, function, costs) and implicit ones (how others perceive them, beliefs about usefulness, appropriateness) for choosing particular models and designs (2002: 309–310).

The *apparatgeist* of perpetual contact can be used productively to formulate an approach to cybercultures because it

- locates technology within the realm of social interaction;
- locates individual and cultural factors within technology;
- gestures at emotional/subjective and social/impersonal aspects of technologies of communication by foregrounding personal values, folk theories of contact, and even physical pleasure;
- emphasizes the symbolic aspects of technology by paying attention to issues of class, and social roles and structures such as the family;
- links the individual, the material, and the social realms with the hardware–software elements of technology.

This last point takes us back to the social basis for technology by suggesting that the logic of perpetual contact is a sociologic that is rooted in social formations, structures, and therefore ideologies and politics. However, it must be noted that Katz and Aakhus (2002) suggest *one* "spirit" or logic here. As we know, "cybercultures" are a composite of many things. They are a world medium of communication (Rasmussen 2002) and a storage and memory device. They mark the beginning, for some critics (Silverstone 2007), of a global "mediapolis." Their key features include participation, collectivity, and connectivity (Thacker 2004b). The Internet, perhaps the most significant component of popular cybercultures, is ageographical and supposedly democratic. It can also serve as a useful instrument of technocapitalism through surveillance and databanks.

The inherent complexity and myriad forms of cybercultures means that there cannot be any one spirit that informs and influences the domain. Thus, I propose, in addition to the *apparatgeist* of perpetual contact, a second one: that of *augmentation*.

Cybercultures constitute a significant condition of augmentation. This "spirit" applies to the design of cybercultural devices – from iPhones that seek to *improve* reception to search engines that pursue *faster* and *more efficient* searches to *faster* computers. *Greater* storage, *enhanced* security, *more efficacious* medical technologies are the keywords in the *culture of augmentation* facilitated by the new technologies. *Greater* participation and connectivity among a *larger* number of people – more and more of the Other appears on screens today than ever before – drive the Internet as a medium of communication, even as the state and the technocapitalist corporate body seek greater control over the medium (and this is the contradictory movement within the culture of augmentation: on the one hand the drive toward wider dissemination and greater freedom; on the other, the move for greater control and regulation). Wired and altered body states seek to *augment* the human in the move towards a posthuman condition.

"Perpetual contact" and "augmentation" capture the spirit and logic of contemporary cybercultures.

Cultural Studies

Cyberculture is perhaps best "read" through the lens of cultural studies. The definition of cultural studies given by Cary Nelson and colleagues serves as a starting point here: cultural studies is "committed to the study of the entire range of a society's arts, beliefs, institutions, and communicative practices" (1992: 4). A society's culture is taken to mean both a way of life and the set of practices, institutions, and structures of power that constantly negotiate meanings, where, through processes of inclusion and exclusion, some meanings, groups, and "texts" are valorized at the expense of others. Cultural studies involves a *political* reading of structures of power that influence, and often determine, meaning production in a culture, that harness the agency of others (including machines) for their ends, focusing on groups that are disempowered in cultural practices. Cultural studies, therefore, is interested in meanings (of poems, architecture, politics) and the structures in which meanings emerge (government, "literature," academia, industry). More importantly, it focuses on the way meanings are generated in everyday life through mass cultural forms (films, blogs, cookery shows) and social interaction rather than within high culture.

Cultural studies foregrounds four basic themes: agency, genealogy, identity and power, and social space and corporeality (Slack and Wise 2006: 143).

Agency involves questions of the capability of individuals, communities, or objects to assert their will and effect changes.

Genealogy is the location of a particular technology or cultural artifact within specific histories, discourses, and power struggles. It involves questions of need, sentiment, power structures such as the law or medicine, financial profits, and symbolic power. As we have seen above, the new media and cybercultures have emerged within multiple contexts that provide their genealogy rather than a simple linearity of "progress." The Internet began life as a defense strategy planned and constructed by the US government in the eventuality of a nuclear war. Questions of control, therefore, continue to remain central to the so-called democratizing technology of cybercultures, where protocols of data transfer, censorship, and surveillance seek to deploy the Internet as systems of control rather than freedom.

Identity is seen less as an essential or core "self" than as the product of social relations situated at the intersection of multiple discourses. Identities are seen as *constructs* rather than as immanent. They are negotiated rather than self-evident. In this view, technology is never neutral because it involves political questions about identity. Thus, questions about technoculture from a cultural studies perspective would be: How does the mobile phone or the Internet help construct an identity? Does technology influence communities' visibility and therefore validate identity?

Finally, a cultural studies approach to technology treats it as a contingent *social agent* that influences the use of space. This involves addressing three kinds of space: public "built" space, social space, and the body's space. The increasing surveillance of public space alters the experience of that space, and involves issues of rights of access and security. Social space includes the realm of politics; in cybercultures, this must be taken to include issues of electronic voting, opinion expression, and state feedback mechanisms, all of which contribute to the social and the political. NGOs and activists use ICTs to promote specific causes, often subversive to mainstream state politics, thus transforming cyberspace into a tool of political counterculture. The use of Internet technologies and digital devices radically alters the way humans use their bodies, augment them, and in specific ways transcend the body's problems and deficiencies. Devices that augment and enhance abilities enable users to exercise greater agency via the body. Penetrative scans, neurological implants, and surgical interventions that rely on transmission of data from and into the body, from the level of the skin to the DNA, are also factors that inform agency. Thus corporeal space is a crucial dimension in analyzing the cultures of technology in the digital age.

For cultural studies, "cybercultures" is thus an articulation between three crucial elements or actors: hardware (machines, computers, cable networks), software (programs), and wetware (humans). Extending this proposition via the cultural studies approach, "cybercultures" throughout this book is also the articulation between these three elements and others such as gender, race, symbolic and cultural forms, economy, politics, and identity: in other words, the "ecology" of digital culture. To separate the digital from the nondigital (say, the material) is to miss the crucial fact that digitization is inextricably linked to the social, cultural, and material. Hence Robert Latham and Saskia Sassen's term "sociodigitization" for the process of digitization, where activities and their histories in a *social* domain are transformed into codes and databases (Latham and Sassen 2005: 3, 16–18). Sociodigitization extends the interaction at the level of the household or the workplace into the digital realm. Thus, the logic of social formations – which, for cultural studies, will involve questions of class, race, gender, power relations and practices – informs the nature and shape of any "digital formation" too.

There are "real," physical elements or actors in the cybercultural network, but there are also more fluid, unquantifiable elements such as sentiment (online romances), economics (unequal access even in wired societies), and politics (control over domains or software via stringent copyright laws). Cyberculture is the articulation between hardware, software, and wetware, all three of which are *deeply embedded in the social and historical contexts of the technology*.

Cybercultures – which, it is worth emphasizing, include mobile phone culture, Internet culture, biomedical cultures, digital networks of corporate bodies, the state and NGOs, financial flows, military appropriations and entertainment – inform the identity of individuals or communities, determine profits and political responses from the state, and alter the body for a different or better lifestyle.

Thus cybercultures here are a *rhizome*, an *assemblage* of flows where multiple elements are connected, in contingent and dispersed ways, and all of which are embedded in the social and historical contexts of the technology. Cultural and material contexts influence telecommunications networks and cyberspace, and vice versa, in a kind of "recursive interaction" (Graham 1998: 174). That is, one cannot treat cybercultures of the new ICTs as flows without locating these flows in actual material, cultural, and social conditions. In other words, digital formations are mixes of computer-centered network technologies and social contexts. We will come back to this nature of digital formation in our discussion of cybernetic space below.

It is not the technology or a particular element that focuses our attention, but the *connections* of that technology or element with (and within) others. In short, it is not possible to see cybercultures as simply ICTs without reference to questions of:

- power (financial, political, cultural, agential);
- identity (gender, racial, individual/community, sexual);
- ideology (the politics of technocapitalism);
- culture (art, sport/games).

Cyberculture studies takes into account these questions as it explores everyday digital cultures. However, this book does *not* restrict itself to popular Internet studies but also looks at macro-issues such as the governance of cyberspace and the political economy of digital formations. While recognizing that these questions may not be resolved, it argues that such issues should be examined. It is also possible that, like the rhizome it explores, the trajectories of this book are also contingent, shifting, aporetic, and multiple.

The emphasis on social agency and the politics of representation and meaning in a cultural studies approach to cybercultures means that we do not treat the virtual world as a separate entity, or the digital network as a separate space. Cyberspace and cyberculture are always rooted in the material, the fleshly, and the concrete. Cyberculture's technologies are social, and cyberspace, like material space, is made up of a series of social processes and interactions.

Cybercultures, this book argues, are recursively linked to, perpetually rooted in, return to, repeat, and reflect the material. Problems of agency, identity, and power from the domains of everyday material life are also reflected in, extended into, and inform cyberspace and cybercultures. Hence, throughout this book, these concerns will keep appearing – not unlike those pop-ups!

Thus we need to see computer games, online communities, electronic voting, or information databases of the body as always looping back into or connecting with the bodies that make and experience these "virtual," "immaterial" spaces. Dissociation of the virtual from the material runs the risk of depoliticizing both its creation and its consequences. This means being alert not only to the cultural politics of the production, design, and dissemination of new media forms, but also to the ways in which people have used and subverted these forms. That is, while there is a politics (and profit) involved in the production of cybercultures, there is also a politics in their consumption. Protest movements that use ICTs, tactical media, feminist cyberpunk, and hacking patches in computer games are often unintentional appropriations of digital cultures. If power relations govern the production of cybercultures (in terms of design, funding for research, production, copyright, and monopolistic control), then power is also something the users possess and deploy in their appropriations of cybercultures. As we shall see in later chapters, power and ideology remain the cornerstone of analysis in cyberculture studies because cybercultures affect the lives of people, and affect is often a question of power (cultural, economic, political, and social).

In keeping with the breathtaking diversity of cybercultures, this book's theoretical approaches are manifold. They include feminist and poststructuralist theories of bodies and discourses, popular culture studies, political economy studies, and communication theory, among others.[4]

This book treats cybercultures as a "formation" and the Internet – the keystone of the cybercultural arch – as a cultural artifact that informs and is informed by multiple contexts such as political economy, popular art, discourses of emancipation, and bioethics, even as it extends earlier forms of communication, sociability, surveillance, and archiving. It looks at Internet cultures at a *multiplicity of sites* – all of which use PCs, software, connections, and the Internet to varying degrees and in differing ways – including, among others, homepages, blogs, fictional accounts of cyberspace, media reports, design (such as the desktop), and art forms that work with computers.

This chapter has outlined the key contexts, terms, and approaches in/to cyberculture studies. It has suggested that cyberculture is not one but many. There are many sites, designs, and applications of cyberculture, which is therefore not a coherent entity but a series of processes, uses, applications, negotiations, and structures. What we have argued, therefore, is that there is not a cyberculture but cyber*cultures*.

This chapter has proposed the book's thesis that cybercultures cannot be treated as simply virtual worlds created by computers but as a formation linked to, rooted in, affected by, and impacting upon the material and the real. This formation is the consequence of many structures, artifacts, systems (economic, legal, political, social, and cultural), ideas, and ideologies coming together: political economy, information, global finance, capitalism, the logic of the market, the structures of cables and wires, monitors, and SIM cards. It has argued that cybercultures must be treated as embedded in and connected to the real and the material world, where questions of economy, race/class/gender identities, politics, and power are crucial.

It has situated cybercultures within the contexts of the information society and globalization. It has provided a brief sketch of the key issues in cyberculture studies: globalization and technocapitalism, materiality and corporeality, the digital divide, e-governance, civil society, governing cyberspace, identity, race, class, gender and sexuality, space and geography, risk, the mediapolis and the space of the Other, and aesthetics. Finally, it has outlined the key approaches to cybercultures: ethnographies of cyberspace, *apparatgeist* theory, and cultural studies.

NOTES

1 A different situation arises when online relationships and identities shift to real time. People playing roles in cyberspace reveal themselves to be somebody else. This feature of cyberspace has come in for criticism and is a source of anxiety, especially with pedophiliacs and rapists masquerading as different people and meeting potential victims offline.
2 Following Anthony Giddens (1979) I treat power here as relational, as the transformative ability of an individual/group/institution to utilize the agency of others – human, animal, and machine – to further one's ends.
3 Incidentally, Asian Americans cannot be treated as disadvantaged. Rather, they are deemed to be privileged users of the Net and are targeted as markets for web-based commerce. Yet even here a differential exists – they are treated as targets for *commerce* rather than as empowered communities (Nakamura 2005).
4 David Bell, in his introduction to the second edition of *The Cybercultures Reader* (2007: 3–4), lists 19 parameters within which we can read cybercultures!

2 POPULAR CYBERCULTURES

CHAPTER PLAN

Science fiction (SF) suggests that there could be aliens in outer space. The artist Stelarc wired his body into the Internet for others to have easy "access." Harry Potter fans use software to showcase their admiration and affection for their celebrity icon by creating fansites. These are *popular* cybercultures. Sophisticated technology invariably circulates in the public domain through such popular forms of recreation or entertainment. Cybercultural technologies are no exception to this appropriation.

Cybercultures enjoy an astonishing variety and popularity in ways that belie the sophistication of the technologies behind the mobile gaming device or the iPod. Such "domestication" of technology within popular forms of cyberculture is the subject of this chapter.

Cyberculture, as noted earlier, includes diverse new (and popular) technologies and forms. New media cultures, a term encountered often in the late 1990s, extend cybercultural forms like the Internet and incorporate others like mobile phone technologies. The earlier text-based webpages are giving way to audio and moving video, even as communication technologies like the mobile phone become modes of entertainment with movie-music downloads and games. Print, visual, and audio are all merged in popular cultural forms on the desktop or the mobile phone screen.

This chapter examines, first, the key features of the popular expressions of ICTs. From this it moves on to discuss specific forms or genres within popular cybercultures – popular literature, fan works, games, social networking, and new forms of cyber-art. In particular, it is interested in questions about alterations in everyday life through the incorporation of these technologies.

- How does popular culture appropriate and represent sophisticated technologies?
- Are technologies such as search engines neutral or do they also have political consequences through, say, the use of commercial advertisements?
- Are virtual worlds delinked from material ones?
- Does cyberpunk's glorification of cyborg, posthuman bodies lead to a new norm of modified bodies?
- Is the hype around interactivity (of gameworlds) justified, and do users really "possess" this kind of interactivity?
- Does the emergence of game and fan cultures cause a new form of individualism, or does it reconfigure sociability?
- What forms of art emerge in the age of genetic engineering, bioinformatics, and ICTs, and what are their visions of the human future?
- How do avowedly social technologies such as social networking sites affect privacy, individuality, identity, and community?

Key Features of Popular Cybercultures

Cybercultures are a "formation" that emerges in the intersection of technical, social, economic, and social contexts. This "formation" draws on such contexts for its production and consumption, even as it affects them. These contexts, especially in the case of cybercultures of the everyday – the popular Internet, personal communications technologies (PCTs), workplace digital cultures, and the information-entertainment cultures of the new media – are characterized by four key features.

Convergence

Convergence, a term popularized by Henry Jenkins (2006b), is the coming together of various media forms on a common platform or interface. The TV serves as an Internet interface. Personal digital assistants (PDAs) and mobile phones help surf the Net, make movies, and broadcast (podcasts).

Remediation

Bolter and Grusin (1999) demonstrate how new media forms extend and expand the potential and structure of earlier media. Thus the Internet expands the working of movies and television.

Remediation is driven by a double logic. On the one hand it seeks *immediacy* or liveness, where the technology tries to make the audience feel as though it is right there without any intervening, mediating medium/technology. That is, it seeks to erase the *process* and technology of mediation itself. On the other hand, all forms of media also draw attention to the *hypermediated* context: the audience picks which camera angle to follow, or which link to click for a particular character in the "live" show (say, in *Big Brother*). Thus split screens, graphics, voiceovers, video feeds, sound effects, and news text all underscore the fact that our experience of the real or the live is heavily mediated. This contradictory logic of immediacy and hypermediacy is the oscillation, argue Bolter and Grusin, between transparency and opacity (1999: 19).

Consumption

Consumption refers to the consumer culture engendered by the new media technologies. Electronic gadgets constitute one of the largest components of the global consumer market. Cyberculture is inextricably linked to consumer culture. Movies drive computer games, and computer games generate fansites, movie plots, and toys. Every medium now is a *cross-over medium*, adapting, borrowing from, or echoing another format. I see every media form as being *augmented* in consumer culture where the phone serves as an email device, a film camera, a conferencing facility, a gaming platform, a personal diary, a community-forming device, and a compass or geographic mapping device.

Consumer culture's emphasis on the individual means that products are designed to ensure that all technology is *personal*. Thus mobile phones and other PCTs can be linked to the Walkman, iPod, or the personal diary. Consumer culture seeks to ensure that you are constantly connected to your personal data, your loved ones, and your workplace. "Personalizing" is a key word in consumer culture, where everything from avatars and webpages to mobile phone rings and caller IDs are supposed to reflect your identity.

In the age of mass-produced software and products, consumer culture plays on the need to be individualist. Cyberculture, like all consumer cultures, works with the paradox of consumption: on the one hand there is increasing standardization, and on the other there is the drive to personalize, to distinguish oneself from the crowd. Consumer culture thrives on key themes such as family, individualism, connectivity, and security in order to sell cybercultural products like the mobile phone, software, or PCs. Whether it is Hewlett Packard with its "the computer is personal again" or the glossy *Wired*, the "product space" (a term used by Silverstone and Haddon to describe the cultural and other spaces in which a product is sold; 1996: 53) builds on specific ideologies of home, privacy, safety, ease of access, and security. Thus mobile phones have engendered emotional and very personal responses (Srivastava 2006). In other cases, digital technology, Photoshop, or satellite communications enable the religious to "connect" to their deities and gods. In each of these examples we see another kind of convergence – that of *social and cultural contexts* and *technoculture*, a convergence best exploited by cyberculture.

Consumer culture also merchandizes various products – computer games, video recorders, software, mobile phones, stereo sets – together. Cyberpunk fiction often focuses on the commercialization of information technology, from the latest model of the PC to advanced conversion software, in addition to the booming black market in pirated software and film/music DVDs and CDs.

Sony, Macintosh, and Microsoft control the consumer cybercultural domains. Capitalism finds cyberspace a new market to exploit where youth, for instance, represent a rapidly expanding market for gadgets, games, and software. This class represents the target for the large, capitalist corporations (what Aurigi and Graham 1998 term "digital shoppers," as opposed to the "digital elite" who control the economy).

A related dimension of consumer Internet culture is the growing surveillance of online consumers and searches. Search engines like Google, Microsoft, and Yahoo! all acquired online advertising companies in 2007 (Google bought DoubleClick, Microsoft bought aQuantive, Yahoo! bought Right Media). Eric Schmidt, CEO of Google, even declared that Google might henceforth function "first as an advertising system" (Vogelstein 2007). This marks an interesting shift for the Internet as a whole, and for marketing consumer culture in particular.

Yet technology also fuels its opposite. If media conglomerates make use of technology for advertisements, tactical media (see Chapter 4 on cyber-subcultures) and

SUBVERTISEMENTS

These are spoofs or humorous reworkings of advertisements, often carrying political messages about corporate strategies, profiteering, or government oppression.

radical groups generate "subvertisements" – a subversion of advertising often called "culture jamming" (Tim Jordan 2002 terms it "semiotic terrorism"). When Greenpeace created its anti-ExxonMobil logo declaring "Exxtreme Drought: Global Warming Powered by ExxonMobil," it ran a subvertisement that carried a political-economic message about Exxon's business and anti-environment techniques. AdBusters (www.adbusters.org) has been a pioneer in such radical reworkings of media signs.

Personalized search engines – an advance over the "routine" ones of the early browsers – often leave a trail of the user's queries that generates a fair amount of data about the user's personalized preferences. When a sufficient amount of such trails from large numbers of users are compiled, then the marketing sections have profiles of entire collectives. Thus, it is not the individual user but a collective or demographic group that is profiled and used to predict user behavior and demand. This combination of surveillance, personal search, and marketing is, in Theo Röhle's (2007) analysis, the merger of "online search and online marketing into a singular technical and economical system." This means, simply, that the so-called choice of the consumer and the power of selection (whether browsing or seeking specifics) is intimately linked to (1) questions of privacy (marketing agencies following your surfing/purchases to tabulate your taste/preferences), (2) the unobtrusive selling of products via pop-ups, organization of URLs on the search engine, and (3) stealing of data in the form of credit card thefts. Personalized search engines can also function as personal surveillance mechanisms.

Online games also work to situate virtual worlds within the real one, especially in consumer-economic terms. As one commentator put it, "the gaming is virtual, the profit is real" (Wallace 2005). In 2003, *Second Life* granted Intellectual Property Rights (IPRs) to products created in the virtual domain and in the real one. Kline and colleagues (cited in Herman et al. 2006) have demonstrated how, in addition to the *cultural* (the players and their "roles" and agency) and *technological* (the interaction between software, players, and computers), games embody a third process – that of *marketing*. A player's use of the software and game situation generates satisfaction and pleasure, which in turn ensures continued gaming, consumption, and product development in a recursive relationship. When Linden Labs (which runs *Second Life*) transformed game into work – where the players work at producing or "authoring" virtual artifacts, and the artifacts are their intellectual "property" – they were exploiting this recursive relationship. *Second Life* makes it clear that marketing and commerce are as central to the virtual as they are to the real:

> The Marketplace currently supports millions of US dollars in monthly transactions. This commerce is handled with the in-world unit-of-trade, the Linden dollar, which can be converted to US dollars at several thriving online Linden Dollar exchanges. (*Second Life* 2007)

This means that a virtual world like *Second Life* effects very concrete changes in the material one. Once again this takes us back to the basic premise of the book: that the virtual is never simply virtual alone, but has serious and material effects in the real world.

Interactivity

Interactivity refers to the changing role of audiences, listeners, and viewers. Audiences are no longer passive consumers but are often involved closely with the structure, format, and story of the cultural artifact. Audiences appear increasingly to play the role of "producers" of TV programs that solicit their opinions, ideas, poll participation, and even scripts. Television merges with the World Wide Web, and webTV and TV audiences are now invited to participate as players, commentators, and voters.

Television merges with the World Wide Web in myriad ways. This could be through reviews of TV programs reprinted from newspapers, TV listings, and official websites of TV programs (the latter are also linked to consumer culture in a literal sense because many official sites also sell merchandise about/from the program). Large numbers of unofficial websites of these programs and fansites also exist. These might develop their own versions of the soap opera, and fanzines soliciting stories and dramatizations of cult texts such as *Star Wars* or *Buffy the Vampire Slayer* are now an integral part of cyberculture – an instance of "fan production" (Fiske 1992). Successful TV shows such as *Big Brother* also reached larger audiences by their narrowcast 24/7 dispersion online. Such online presence and activity could signify either a "depth" or an "extension" relationship (Deery 2003: 166–167). Interactivity itself might be "deep" when the audience determines the shape of the show – for instance, through voting.

Interactive storytelling – which, according to leading hypertext theorist Marie-Laure Ryan (2005), includes things and genres as diverse as computer games, interactive TV, interactive movies, smart toys, augmented reality gaming, interactive cartoons, hypertext fiction, and interactive fiction – is another vision of software professionals for the consumer's pleasure. The "author" of the story in *Choose Your Own Adventures* is the user-reader, who uses the help of the preloaded software and "clues" or themes to develop his or her story.

Marie-Laure Ryan proposes that the degree and level of interactivity differ from layer to layer in the story. At the first layer, interactivity is about the presentation of the story where the story exists before the running of the software. At the middle layers, interactivity concerns the user's personal involvement in the story, but the plot is still predetermined. Finally, at the inner layers, the story is created dynamically through the interaction between the user and the system. *Façade*, an interactive drama created by Michael Mateas and Andrew Stern (www.interactivestory. net/), asks the "viewer" to help develop the plot. The marriage of a couple in their mid-thirties breaks down during the course of an evening's conversation. The user writes lines of dialogue to which the couple respond, with progressively more abuse, slander, and accusations. Eventually the database runs out of possible dialogue combinations and the "visitor" has to leave, thus indicating the limited level of interactivity possible, given the database.

It remains indisputable, however, that such "interactivity" is limited to the narrative of the gameworld because the overall control of the form of the game, and its marketing and profits, rests with the company or corporation.

These four features, convergence, remediation, consumption, and interactivity, figure in varying ways in the several "genres" or forms of popular digital cultures. The rest of this chapter explores these various forms.

Cyberpunk

Technology, along with other social, cultural, political, and economic factors, influences – mediates – the way (most) people live in metropolises across the world. In Nigel Thrift's formulation, "software has come to intervene in nearly all aspects of everyday life and has begun to sink into its taken-for-granted background" (2005: 153). Cyberpunk is the literary genre that looks at such science-fictionalized lives where many people spend large portions of their life wired into another world.

> **CYBERPUNK**
>
> Cyberpunk is a science fiction genre that emerged in the 1980s which works mainly with cybertechnology, including virtual reality, often positing subcultures in a world of technocorporate capitalism.

Bruce Bethke coined the term with his 1983 short story "Cyberpunk," published in *Amazing Science Fiction Stories* (57/4, available at project. cyberpunk.ru/lib/cyberpunk/). Bethke's term attained a major generic status in popular writing after William Gibson's *Neuromancer*, published a year later. Cyberpunk had its heyday in the 1990s with the work of Bruce Sterling, William Gibson, Pat Cadigan, Melissa Scott, Neal Stephenson, and others. Bruce Sterling, editor of the first cyberpunk anthology *Mirrorshades* (1986), isolated the following as the key themes in cyberpunk:

- body invasion through prostheses (technology is "visceral": Sterling 1988a: xiii);
- genetic alteration and/or mutation;
- implanted circuitry; and
- cosmetic surgery.

Sterling argued that cyberpunk extended the concerns of SF, while adding countercultural elements such as rock video and hacking as themes to the mix (Sterling 1988a: xiii, xv). Cyberpunk is the literary expression of both, a technologically minded (and propelled) counterculture and an ethos (or, if you prefer, philosophy) of posthumanism.

Cyberpunk treats technology as incorporated into everyday life. In effect, it rejects *techno-elitism* and thus becomes a countercultural movement.[1] The key theme is the popularization and mass consumption of high-tech where hackers and vendors possess, use, and distribute sophisticated software that was once the monopoly of giant corporations.

Cyberpunk mixes genres – classic SF and the detective story, fantasy and the romance, thereby blurring the boundaries between high and mass culture.

Cyberpunk is posthumanism's literary expression because it champions the view that the limits of the body can be transcended. Like the work of Stelarc and cryogenic engineering, cyberpunk sees facets of human life such as aging, decay, and disability as disappearing through technological means. The obsolescence of the body seems imminent in all cyberpunk.[2]

POSTHUMANISM

Posthumanism is a point of view, ideology, and belief that the limitations of the human body – age, disease, appearance, disability – can be overcome and its capabilities – looks, intelligence, strength, disease resistance – can be augmented through technological intervention.

Blurring Boundaries

Cyberpunk works to convey a new taxonomy of the human, proposing a human that is perpetually a *cyborg*.

Cyberpunk proposes a new sub-species of the human, where human/machine/animal boundaries break down and where the body is transcended (at least while in cyberspace). Cyberpunk heroes, of which the prototype is Case in Gibson's *Neuromancer*, are often leather-wearing techno-savvy punks, seamlessly merged with cybernetic circuits, jacked in, and often running on drugs.

The cyborg demands a redefinition of concepts like "nature" and artifice. The non-natural – the realm of machines and technology – is now incorporated into the human frame, even as cloning and transplantation

CYBORG

A portmanteau term coined by Manfred Clynes and Nathan Kline in 1960, cyborg means a **cyb**ernetic **org**anism. It refers to a man–machine system where the human body, and sometimes the mind, is interfaced with technological (including computer) systems.

ensure the breakdown of the distinction between "original" and "copy" and between the "natural" and the non-natural/synthetic. In cyberpunk, all humans are prosthetic in one way or another. Cyborgized bodies thus have real, material import for disabled, diseased bodies, high-risk jobs (including soldiery), and surgical procedures.

Other ethical issues follow from the emergence of the posthuman and the cyborg. For instance, what happens to human rights in the case of posthumans? Are they entitled to the same rights as non-modified humans? Chris Hables Gray's "Cyborg Bill of Rights" (2001) proposes a series of amendments to accommodate the altered characteristics of posthuman bodies. Paul Lauritzen, writing on stem cell research and human rights, believes that the "new biology threatens our existing ethical commitments" (2005: 28). Andy Miah and Emma Rich point out that Gray's manifesto appeals to the concept of the cyborg in order to "address the interests of marginal groups whose humanness is not given full moral or legal recognition" (2008: 113). These are all questions of justice, political responsibility, and human rights in the age of posthumanity. If human rights depend upon a narrative tradition where the human is defined, then, I propose, such a tradition is already in place where cyborgs and posthumans make claims for rights: cyberpunk, texts like Mary Shelley's *Frankenstein* (1818), and cyborg films (Nayar 2008e).

The Body

In William Gibson's *Count Zero*, a human body is reworked in this way:

> They cloned a square of skin for him, grew it on slabs of collagen and shark cartilage polysaccharides. They bought eyes and genitals on the open market. (1994/1986: 9)

The body is often deemed to be a prison in cyberpunk. The emphasis on the mind and consciousness that can be expanded into other worlds and time zones is linked with the theme of the "limited body." The body has to be upgraded in order to allow full play for the mind. Hence the body becomes less and less biological or organic and more and more synthetic, plastic, and electronic.

Reproduction

A new taxonomy of humanity with new and emergent sub-species also of course suggests the possibility of a whole new way of life. SF has always been fascinated by the theme of reproduction, both human and alien, and the threat to humanity is frequently from breeding aliens (inaugurated by Mary Shelley's *Frankenstein*). Bruce Sterling's continuing fictional concerns about aging and continuity (*Holy Fire*, 1997, for instance) are an extension of the theme of mortality, itself linked to the question of reproduction.

Alien reproduction in Octavia Butler's Xenogenesis trilogy (*Dawn*, 1987; *Adulthood Rites*, 1988; *Imago*, 1989), Margaret Atwood's *Oryx and Crake* (2003), and cyberpunk's own theme of cloning deal with possibilities of overcoming mortality through machine-aided reproduction.

Cyberpunk exhibits a clear cultural anxiety, not only about the new forms of human emerging through technological actions but also about the possible extinction of the human species as we know it. Will this breed of monsters reproduce and replace humanity, transforming humanity into slaves or worse?

Time and Space

Cyberpunk dissolves traditional notions of time and space. Real time slips under cyber-time, with lags, speeded-up movements, and the surreal nature of interaction with pre-recorded, delayed transmission of messages/pictures/conversations. Gibson's Case is often disoriented after a sojourn in cyberspace: while his "meat-body" is in the here and the now, his consciousness has been traversing an else-where. The theme of surreal time and space ensures that the distinction between real and unreal worlds breaks down. Cyberpunk shares this feature with the post-modern fiction of William Burroughs and Thomas Pynchon, in which reality as defined and regulated by clock time and space merges messily with another "order" of reality.

Environment

An air of surreality is responsible, in cyberpunk and in films like *Blade Runner* or *The Matrix*, for an entirely new atmosphere: a post-apocalyptic world of lawless-ness, powerful corporate interests, software domination, and some resistance. The erosion of boundaries between real and cyberworlds means that the question of inside/outside also breaks down. The human is embedded in an environment, even as the environment enters the human through electronic networks. The body occupies a "metaverse" (Neal Stephenson's term from *Snow Crash*, 1993), an elec-tronic universe that is surreal, hallucinatory. This universe multiplies and expo-nentially expands in many directions, thus exhibiting the features of a live organism. Cyberpunk merges electronic data, computer-generated maps, and human spatiality as characters occupy worlds that are neither here nor there, both here and there.

Information

Central to all cyberpunk is the theme of information: its collection, control, and dis-semination. This theme seems natural in an informational age where the right kind of data is truly priceless or dangerous. Personal information such as credit card details or physical location is increasingly subject to violation and theft. Industrial and military secrets are on a par with financial ones, and everything is of course open to possible hacking since all information, at some point in its collation and transmission, is subject to computerization. It is this link between information stor-age and abuse that interests cyberpunk.

Computers are therefore the keystone of the cyberpunk arch. Control over com-puters and their databanks is the key theme in much cyberpunk because informa-tion can be manipulated and experienced in real time as *effect*. The possibility of changing IDs in cyberspace means that the human body in the real world can expe-rience a different reality – once its online or databank identity has been altered or stolen, its real life identity is also altered. Computerization, suggests cyberpunk, runs the risk of transforming reality by transforming data.

Cyborg

Between the human and the machine, cyberpunk discovers a third category that seems to share the characteristics of both and is able to cross over: the cyborg.

The cyborg in cyberpunk fiction, computer games, and film is the site of both fascination and anxiety. (In fact, if a cyborg is the interface between man and machine, even computer game players are cyborgs, since they are linked through a cybernetic loop to the machine and the game environment.) Fascination because the cyborg body has transcended the human one's limitations – whether the iron-muscled Schwarzenegger in *Terminator* or the highly sexualized body of Lara Croft in the eponymous computer game. It instills anxiety because human control over the chip or the network remains open to doubt. As cyborged bodies become increasingly common, cyberpunk worries about the impossibility of distinguishing between humans and machines.

This anxiety is underscored in the depiction of the cyborg as a relentless, remorseless machine lacking "human" qualities such as emotion. It works on the anxiety that the cyborg is limited by its programming – it cannot, for example, destroy its creator even if it wishes to do so. Cyborgs are driven by their circuitry and chips to perform their agenda. While they can possibly mimic human emotional expressions and articulate (recorded) messages that are sentimental, these are empty enunciations. Cyberpunk suggests that it is their lack of emotions that makes them inhuman. With this, of course, cyberpunk attempts to define the human as a being that is emotional (it is worth recalling the increasing humanization of the cyborg in *Terminator 2/3*). In effect, cyberpunk is concerned with contemporary technology in terms of the philosophical question it begs: what makes us human – thought? emotions? Cyborgs seem to be all body with little mind (except for the preprogrammed chip) and no "soul." Ironically, this subverts the theme of bodily transcendence (Holland 1998).

It is a sign of the cultural anxiety of the times that most cyborg films end with *human* victory. The machine or the inhuman must be made to obey or must be "retired" (the term used in *Blade Runner*). It is thus interesting to note the change from *Terminator 1* to *Terminator 2*. In the second, T2 is ordered by Commander Connor (in 2029) to return to 1991 so that he (Connor) can be protected from termination: the cyborg is entrusted with the duty to protect the human, once again marking the cyborg or machine as a servitor to the human race.

Cyberpunk Politics and the Feminist Response

Most cyberpunk texts suggest an insidious and evil link between the state, technology, and capitalism. Information itself is linked to the capitalist economy of the new age in cyberpunk. Hacking, which disrupts the nexus between information, computer technology, and capitalism, is therefore central to the theme of power in cyberpunk. Hacking, which can also be linked to the open source movement that resists the control of knowledge and software, is thus a major political theme in cyberpunk.

However, other dimensions of cyberpunk suggest a more conservative politics. The emphasis on brands and consumer products – from keyboards to appearances – suggests an ideology of (capitalist) consumption. Finally, it is in the realm of gender that the most conservative thinking in cyberpunk becomes visible.

Cyberpunk constructs a macho-cyborg. Feminist critics (e.g., Cynthia Fuchs 2003) argue that cyberpunk embodies a certain "male hysteria" about the question of human reproduction and male identity. Colored people, minorities, and women often constitute the underclass in cyberpunk, who are denied access to technology. It is to be noted that Japan and its techno-exoticism figures prominently in cyberpunk, often as a villainous counterpart to the Euro-American hero. Technology becomes a marker of social and even racial difference, and feminist cyberpunk posits a situation where women seek control over technology in order to survive. The feminist critique of cyberpunk reveals the genre to be a literary expression of real social conditions of sexism, patriarchy, exploitation, and injustice. Cyberpunk, feminist writers (Cadora 1995; Flanagan 2002; Haraway 1985; Harper 1995) believe, packages existing sociocultural prejudices and ideologies as new techno-fads.

Feminist cyberpunk proposes that women have historically experienced technology, capitalism, and war very differently from men, and this experience has not found expression in mainstream (male) cyberpunk. This demands a new genre that emphasizes women's experience of high tech. Feminist cyberpunk begins with the assumption that cyberpunk reinforces existing gender inequalities. The genre foregrounds technology in the material conditions of the real world, where control over technology is concentrated in male, capitalist hands and serves the purpose of racialized and gendered exploitation. The woman cyberpunk, when not a part of the underclass, becomes a code for the alien Other (I shall return to this theme later), where she always remains outside as a source of threat. Feminist cyberpunk reverses this binary, suggesting that the Othering of the woman is in fact a version of male hysteria where the racial Other is feared. Feminist cyberpunk posits the female robot or cyborg as a category that lies outside such binaries as native/foreign, white/non-white, and male/female.

Interestingly, Pat Cadigan, Mary Rosenblum, and Melissa Scott reverse the traditional cyberpunk theme of disembodiment and dispersed subjectivity (see Chapter 3 on the body). Proceeding from the assumption that fragmentation and disembodiment deny the woman her body except as marginal, colored, and subordinate, feminist cyberpunk reasserts the body. Male cyberpunk rarely identifies the "console cowboy" as "white male" because it is assumed that white male bodies are the norm. Feminist cyberpunk centers the woman's body in order to explore the woman's experience of technology.

The dispersal of the subject as proposed and fantasized by canonical cyberpunk denies the woman her *agency* as subject. One cannot transcend skin color or the physical body because in the real world these continue to remain sites of exploitation and discrimination. What is needed is a reiteration of the black or female body, but one that seeks an embodied subjectivity and agency. It demands a different relationship with technology, where the woman appropriates technology for her own purposes.

Games

From *Spacewar* (1962) to Massive Multiplayer Online Role-Playing Games today, the computer game is easily the most popular application of digital technology. Gaming is now bigger than even the $20 billion home video industry. When *Halo 2* released in November 2004, it took in $100 million on its first day alone (*Spider-Man 2* took in $40 million) (Nichols et al. 2006: 5). The industry and popular use of games is now big enough to warrant an annual World Cyber Games where participants from over 100 nations take part.

The following are the accepted "genres" in gaming:

- Strategy (*Rome: Total War*; *Battle for Middle Earth*; *RollerCoaster Tycoon*).
- First-person shooters (*Halo 2*; *Return to Castle Wolfenstein*).
- Platform games (*Mario, Rayman*).
- Sports (*FIFA*).
- Simulators (*FS Flight Ventures*).
- Driving (*Grand Theft Auto*).
- Action/Adventure (*Lara Croft: Tomb Raider*).
- Role-playing games (*World of Warcraft*).
- Management (*The Sims 2*).
- Beat 'em ups (*Mortal Combat*).

Video games established themselves as *arcade* and *parlor* games (there were dedicated areas in public spaces where consoles were installed and players "gamed"). Sega and Nintendo, dedicated game consoles, changed game culture radically in the 1990s when gaming moved from public space into the home. Whether it is the now-standard battle games or PBS Kids' assorted games from children's books and TV series (Tom and Jerry games), gaming is an integral part of digital culture today. Indeed, it could be treated as a subgenre of *simulation* – that integral part of cyberculture – itself.

Battle simulations, soccer, assorted chases and obstacle courses, puzzles, even game versions of novels have proved enduring. In addition to video games (console games played on TV screens) and computer games (CD-ROMs or downloaded from the World Wide Web) we also have arcade games (installed in entertainment sections in malls, multiplexes, and other public spaces) and the handheld game. Young men in particular have been the pioneers in making gaming an important facet of cybercultures (Nichols et al. 2006).

The gaming phenomenon is now so well established as a central component of mass culture that media scholars have turned to game studies, with specialized journals like *Game Studies* emerging to bestow on it the status of a discipline. The fact is that games are extraordinarily profitable commercial-consumer products (for statistics see Jansz and Martens 2005; Nichols et al. 2006).

Such a game culture has transformed the desktop, the television set, and the mobile phone. Games are now available at each of these "terminals" for the user. Thus the *cultural form of television* has undergone a significant change when it doubles up as a game interface.

Games are social. One cannot relegate games to a realm separate from that of everyday life: games are central to the everyday because they have serious *material*, *social*, and *cultural* consequences (Malaby 2007). In addition, they possess value and hold the player's interest because they are simulacra of more or less familiar realities.

Cyberculture's popularity is due to the highly interactive nature of the games. The game situation demands an active role from the player. Even though this interactivity is tightly structured and segmented (Newman 2002), and the rules and codes are built into the game structure itself – in *Counter-Strike*, one could either be a terrorist or a member of the elite corps – the freedom such games ensure mark them out as an advance over passive audience roles in other cases.

We cannot treat games and game culture only in terms of the interface or visual representation. Games are, Espen Aarseth (2004) points out, about other kinds of experience – kinesthetic, functional, and cognitive. With EyeToy the player's real-time physical movements in response to the gameworld can be detected. Players thus copy on-screen movements (avoiding enemies, saving, swerving). With the dance mat – made up of nine pressure-sensitive squares linked to a gaming device that displays moves on the screen – the dancer follows the patterns with his or her feet and so learns the dance steps. In each case we see new forms of cognitive and kinesthetic actions as responses to a simulated environment. Thus, for instance, our "game gaze," as Barry Atkins (2006) terms it, is different from the cinematic gaze because what we are fixed on is something *not yet here*, which will become visible only if we interact "properly" with the interface. Our visual desire drives our gaze, but always seeking something that is next in line to come to the screen, an *impossible* gaze.

Responses to games have ranged from anxiety about children withdrawing into the indoors (from, say, sports outside the house or in the park) for individual gaming, or their abandoning of reading in favor of "mindless" gaming, to more academic studies that argue that gaming is quite often a substitute for doing nothing (Fromme 2003). The European Union, alarmed at the amount of violence in games for children, adopted a classification system from 2003 (though a voluntary age rating already existed for video games), overseen by the Interactive Software Federation of Europe.[3] Games such as *Columbine Massacre RPG!* represent a screen culture of violence and have given cause for anxiety (Guertin 2007). Once again, this foregrounds the linkage between online worlds and the material one where violent *screens* become violent *events*.

Of the three perspectives to games outlined by Aarseth (2006) – gameplay, game-structure, and gameworld – the last one seems more suited to a cultural studies approach. The gameworld methodology includes looking at the aesthetics, art forms (graphics), history, and media use of games.

The New Sociability

Multiplayer games like *Quake Arena* or *Everquest* constitute a *social* space, not unlike the theater or the sports stadium. Unlike other forms, members of the mass audience in open source games (available on the Net) are also *communicating* participants.

Massive Multiplayer Online Role-Playing Games (MMORPGs) and Live Action Role-Playing Games (LARPs) involve avatar-based physical action, large numbers of players, looser narrative control, and intense player–player interactions (Tychsen et al. 2006). This makes gaming a significant mode of social interaction, and therefore of community, culture, and identity, or what Mortensen (2006) terms "social gaming." Real-time interaction is possible across time zones and generates a new sociability, though some commentators (e.g., Juul 2001) looking at narrative and time in gaming have argued that one cannot have both interactivity (which involves synchronous time) and narrative (which involves the time of the plot and the time of narration).

Within families, the younger generation brought up on computers and games are highly skilled players. This form of the "digital divide," research has shown, encourages sociability within a family when teens demonstrate to and teach their parents and grandparents the basics of gaming (Aarsand 2007), thus creating a new sociability and linkages within families.

It is therefore necessary to treat computer games as marking the emergence of a new form of community and communication. Gaming, especially of the LARP kind, marks the emergence of both: a new form of sociability and public culture. This calls for a radical redefinition of *public culture*, where the "public" could very well be people sitting in the privacy of their homes but engaged with a community of players from around the world in a gameworld.

It is here that the full scope of the common term "interactive" becomes visible. Interactive originally meant "influencing each other" and implied a group activity, a collective *interaction*. But interactivity is also the engagement with contexts – the ecology of the situation or event or artwork. Game culture works with both these ideas of interactivity: (1) a collective play, work, or communication and (2) an engagement with the contexts of the medium/art. Commentators believe that "affinity communities" based on common interests such as cars or sport within virtual environments will emerge, even if participants lead very different "real" lives outside the gameworld (Nichols et al. 2006: 48).

Skills, Responsibility, and Games

In "construction" games like *Civilization*, players build an entire empire or culture. In fact, one mode of dealing with video and computer game culture is to see how these games are, at their core, older paradigms of play like role-play, construction, "playing house," chase, and so on (Lauwaert 2007).

Proponents of popular culture (e.g., Johnson 2006) have pointed out that while reading might instill concentration and the ability to read a narrative sequence, even non-literary popular culture (like gaming) hones different mental skills including visual memory and manual dexterity. Henry Jenkins, noted media theorist and principal investigator for the New Media Literacies Project, argues that gaming helps children through the development of four key areas: play (through exploration and experimentation), performance (of various identities), expression (the creation of new content where children even "translate" school curricula into game content), and collaboration (within the game community). Jenkins (2006a) calls for an increased use of such devices in pedagogy, arguing that by asking children to look at and *judge* how games depict the world, we can instill in them an ethics about making choices as game players and therefore as citizens. Another commentator suggests that games educate children on larger issues such as death and mortality: the end of the game reminds one that that particular "life" is "over" (Leland 2006: 103).

Arguably, such an aim (of provoking questions about ethics, responsibility, and choices) for gaming is visible in virtual pet games. Virtual pets – heralded by the Japanese Tamagotchi in 1997 – enable children to be both spectators, watching their cyber-pets play, perform, and live (for a few days), and active players when they perform the functions of parents such as caregiving. As Mara Pets, an online games site, puts it:

> You will need to regularly feed your pet when it is hungry, put it to sleep when it is tired and play with it when it is bored. Virtual pets can catch diseases and illnesses and need to be cured. If a pet is neglected and left sick or starving it will die. (www.marapets. com/pets.php)

Such games require the development of a sense of responsibility with their "nurturing theme" (Bloch and Lemish 1999). They foster a sense of intimacy (with the virtual pet) that is unusual in other kinds of games.

Narrative

Computer games cannot be treated as a *narrative* like a novel or the cinema (Juul 2001). Time is experienced differently in games, and the relation of viewer/ reader to the object is radically different in the case of games where the audience and the player merge.

However, many games offer a basic sequential plot structure. The task of the player is part of the narrative, and this is where the game differs from the movie: it is the task of the player (who takes on the role of a character in this "story") to take on the aliens and return the planet to safety and equanimity. If, in the case of cinema or the stadium, the audience is merely "spectatorial," the player in the video game is a character in the game that is being played, where the "character" is a set of characteristics or equipment that is utilized by the controlling, real/embodied player. This also means the choices the "real" player makes for his or her character limit or determine what the character-player can do *in the game*. This "embeddedness" of the audience *as* player leads Ted Friedman, following Electronic Arts executive Trip Hawkins, to describe computer games as the "New Hollywood" (Friedman 1995: 77). Computer games constitute, for Friedman, "interactive cinema" where the player takes on the role of the protagonist.[4]

The player controls the *time* of the interactive game's events and situations. Future events are determined not by a narrative logic (except if the player has been unable to execute a maneuver) but by the player's moves. There is, according to Markku Eskelinen (2001), only one movement possible in the computer game: from the beginning to winning, though it is entirely up to the player to choose the many combinations. Interactivity here is governed by the codes that run the game. Thus, if a battle game requires that the enemy be shot dead, then only shooting dead the enemy constitutes victory. The gamer succeeds when he or she learns how the dynamics of the game work. In short, the "winning" is a *demystification* (T. Friedman 1999) of the processes of the software that built the game. Gamers learn the consequences of every move and learn to anticipate the computer's response, and then respond accordingly (Garrelts 2005a: 10–11). In fact it could be argued that the thrill of the game continues as long as one does not quite know *how* it works.

In games with dynamic environments such as *Civilization* (1991), players can expand the structure/space of the gameworld itself, thereby altering the relations between players. *Civilization*, for example, demands a certain amount of decision-making prior to alterations in the gameworld on the part of the player. These could be negotiations with opponents, the choice of city location (that the player then builds), agriculture or building, and so on. Games like *Second Life* enable players to be "constructive," to give their avatars a teleology and path or craft objects.

There are two main forms of electronic games: game-focused stories and story-focused games (Unsworth 2006). In the former the game activities constitute the stories. BBC's *Spywatch* (now available for educational purposes) is the story of a group of children who help investigate and track down a spy in their town. In Warner Bros' *Arcane* (www2.warnerbros.com/web/arcane/home.jsp), players have to find clues and solve the puzzle of the "stone circle." In *Clues* (www.boardgamecentral. com/games/clue.html), players have to navigate links to find the clues that will help them move on and solve the mystery. The main focus here is the game activities that *generate* the story's narrative.

In another type of electronic game, the story-focused game, a story exists elsewhere, and the game is based on this story. Thus *Harry Potter* (from the Electronic Arts group, harrypotter.ea.com) or *The Lord of the Rings* (Electronic Arts) are games whose adventures and narratives follow the plot of the story published in the real world. They are virtual worlds based on fictional worlds played by real players.

Role-Playing

The "work" of such games is often ignored in favor of dealing with these as simply "play." Role-playing games often allow us to choose a role, which we have to then *work* at. In *Star Wars Galaxies* (starwarsgalaxies.station.sony.com/) there are, for example, a wide variety of careers to choose from – from fashion design to biotechnology and pharmaceutical marketing. In *Second Life* you can "play" a landowner or business person, or acquire and sell land or properties (in July 2006 alone, 380,000 objects changed hands in *Second Life*; Mayer-Schönberger and Crowley 2006: 1787). These games teach competitiveness, planning, management, and basic economics. In other single-player games such as *Alice Greenfingers* (www.alicegreenfingers.com/) for children, the player learns to farm, make profits, and plan various agricultural activities from planting to harvest and sale of produce.[5] These games are worlds where we play roles that take off from and extend our material ones; they require *work* and therefore are demanding, even resulting in burnouts in some cases (Yee 2006). *Second Life* encourages players to buy and sell, build and operate. By 2001 people were selling their virtual weapons and virtual currency on eBay and Yahoo! for real money. Avatars for *EverQuest* were auctioned for rates varying between $500 and $1,000 (Castronova 2001). This reinforces my thesis that the virtual world remains recursively connected to the real. Each realm, I suggest, is *expanded* and *augmented* by the other.

The character in the game is thus configured at the interface of the "real" human player and the computer-generated figure on the screen and is not completely autonomous.

Gameworlds and their Politics

Games are framed in particular ways, in terms of both their production and consumption (the latter in the daily lives of people). "History" in these games, as Kevin Schut (2007) has argued in the case of *Rome: Total War*, is often based on stereotypes of gender, race, and nationality. As an example, let us take *Civilization IV: Beyond the Sword* (2005). Its "India" civilization is "marked" for the user/player's benefit by a few items that are recognizably "Indian": one is Mahatma Gandhi, widely known across the world as the apostle of peace and non-violence, the other is Emperor Asoka, who, after a particularly bloody battle, renounced violence and took to Buddhism. The "framing" narrative of the game is India's non-violence – this is what is up for attention and consumption rather than Indian technological development or nuclearization. Gaming is here clearly a *cultural* practice, based on a set of beliefs and circulating and therefore recognizable myths about particular "civilizations." The hooded "terrorists" in *Counter-Strike* subscribe to now well-known "images" of terror. In a sense, the popular game frames a civilization for people to continue with these same myths (*Civilization IV* offers two routes into India: spiritualism and mining!). *Alice Greenfingers* teaches profit-making strategies via increased *production*. It does not mention saving. Instead it entices the "player" to purchase – i.e., spend – commodities at the store. It forms a direct line from productive labor to profits to consumerism.

In the case of other gameworlds, consumer culture figures prominently in the form of advertisements, endorsements, and hidden forms of promotional rhetoric. When Lara Croft became associated with Lucozade in 1999 (even though the gameworld itself never showed Lara Croft guzzling the fizzy drink), the game character appeared in advertisements for the product (which even got christened Larazade for a time), bringing consumer culture and cyberculture closer and boosting sales for Lucozade (see Nichols et al. 2006: 28–31). Once again we see a cybercultural phenomenon affecting the material world – in this case, profits – even as research into the size of banner ads and the semiotics of online adverts proceeds apace (see Moorey-Denham and Green 2007; Robinson et al. 2007).

"Advergaming" is a new strategy that locates cyberculture acts such as games within promotional culture. The online game *Jeep 4x4: Trail of Life* was used by Chrysler to promote its Rubicon jeep, and 500 of the first 1,500 people who purchased the Jeep Rubicon had piloted a virtual jeep prior to purchase (Nichols et al. 2006: 32). In-game advertising becomes more and more prominent. *Sims Online* clearly showed McDonald's, for example. The space of the gameworld therefore functions as any other space for promotion. This is what David Nichols and colleagues (2006) see as the future of gaming: brands in gameworlds.

SIMCITY teaches players that power comes with expansion of cities – so if you want to be mayor, you have to ensure that the city grows. What is interesting is that the city in SIMCITY is modeled after *American* cities (T. Friedman 1999; Lauwaert 2007: 198).

Civilization's basic program gives players the chance to "grow" Egyptian or Indian cities, based on preconceived notions about these cultures. It does not allow skyscrapers of the American variety in the Egyptian or Indian city. Thus, what we see here is a *cultural* context to simulated cities and role-play.

In terms of gameworlds analysis, such popular cultural forms of cyberculture also possess significant pedagogic value. A game like *Civilization*, or the less successful *Colonization*, can be used to explain (and experience) not only historical eras but also particular situations of diplomacy, warfare, trade, navigation, or architecture (Squire 2002). In *The Wishing Cupboard* game (www.libbyhathorn. com/lh/Wishing/Default.htm), Tan, a Vietnamese boy, waits for his mother to return from Vietnam. His grandmother, in order to keep him entertained, opens the Wishing Cupboard. The task of the game player is: to open the cupboard doors one after another. Each cupboard has one ethnic, Vietnamese object. The grandmother then appears and explains the significance of the object. Thus, one cupboard reveals a "cool green" Buddha. Then, when the player continues, we get Tan's query: "What religion are we, Gran?" Gran then proceeds to educate Tan (and the players) on Buddhism. Accompanying this is a detailed, but very lucid, description of Vietnamese pagodas, Buddhist fables, and themes. In these games there is a certain pedagogic intent, where different cultures are made visible, accessible, and understandable for the player. Many such story-driven games help the child player to think and to coordinate activities. For example, in *Alice's Adventures in Wonderland* (Joriko Interactive, 2000), Alice has to be led through a succession of tricky situations to safety and success.

Indeed, the role of computer simulation in military technoscience – which brought the digital computer into existence (Crogan 2006: 76) – is something to be kept in mind when looking at the production of military and war games on the PC.

The game creators' ideologies and cultural biases have been subject to critical scrutiny in the late 1990s. Feminist critics like Helen Kennedy (2002) have pointed out that a game like *Lara Croft: Tomb Raider* might mark a departure from traditional battle games – a male-centered genre – in casting the woman as the central character, but what cannot be denied is that the game combines physical prowess with a high degree of *sexuality* (here the comparison is with other such "heroines," Buffy the Vampire Slayer being an example). It is possible that the game builds on both the masculine desire to control the female body (here Croft) and a "double consciousness" of the gender of the cyber-body and the player's own (Flanagan 2002). The near-perfect body of Lara Croft ensures that the player realizes her femininity at all times and the woman's cyber-body is the means, vehicle, and *sexualized* object of manipulation.[6]

Studies of the use of games on women and girls and their effect on them have yielded interesting results. The shift from arcade games to consoles that could be installed in the home had a gendered effect on the consumption of games, since arcades were essentially *boys'* game zones, and the console enabled more girls to play games within the safety and comfort of their own homes/rooms (Guins 2004). Whether this marks a shift from a relatively public form of recreation (sharing the arcade space with several screaming, sweating teens playing away) to a more individualist mode (within the comforts of home) is an arguable point, since LAN and LARP games do embody a collective and social gaming experience.

Video games themselves, empirical studies show, have replaced other forms of media entertainment for men (Slocombe 2005). Such research has focused on the *representations* of women in these games (as seen above) or on women *players*. For adult women, gaming has presented different kinds of opportunities. Women have integrated games into their everyday lives, utilizing them as modes of defining their selves. Risks taken, competition thwarted, and victories gained have contributed in a major way to their sense of self. Thus "power gamers" – a class of women who are regular and skilled players – enjoy the added skills, competition, and "encroachment" into masculine (game) territories. Clearly, as Royse and colleagues (2007) demonstrate, games are "technologies of the gendered self" where their involvement with game culture also affects their "real" lives in significant ways. Victories within the game arena and adventure alter the woman player's sense of self and self-worth, and this makes a difference in her identity in and negotiations with the real world. A racial politics pervades gaming – in terms of both users and the virtual world of the games. Contemporary market studies – such as Nielsen Entertainment's 2005 survey of active gamers – have shown that black and Latino players are now seen as an emerging market for games (PRNewswire 2005). When a training camp for video gamers (the "Urban Video Game Academy") was held at a school in Washington, DC, the statistics were interesting: most were African Americans, the rest Latinos, and nearly a third were girls (Vargas 2005).

For a long time there were few black characters in games. When they did begin to appear, they were very often the "bad guys" who had to be arrested and put away for the safety of the social order. Studies have revealed that the nature of black characters in games for children was skewed: African American females were more prone to violence and black characters were rarely given to groaning in pain, thus suggesting a high degree of tolerance to violence (Children Now 2001; Kilman 2005). Even the rhetoric of criticism about video games speaks of "final frontiers," new conquests, and borders in the discourse of (what was surely raced) colonialism (see, for instance, Jenkins 1998).

Black characters were absent even in popular extreme sports games like *Dave Mira* or *Amped*. In other games such as *SSX* and *BMX XXX*, the colored characters are stereotyped: the hip-hop black man, the exotic Asian woman, and the Latina woman wearing war paint. Games like *Shadow Warrior* (1997) have, for similar reasons, attracted criticism for their "digital terrorization of the Asian body" (Ow 2000: 54). The hypermasculinity of the male characters, their defiance of social rules, and their swagger in such games conform to the stereotype (Leonard 2005). Further, even the spaces of black people – the ghettoes – are fetishized in many of these games (Leonard 2005: 118).

New Media Art

Movies on mobile phones, visuals on desktops, music on the web, web telephony, literary texts in SMS format: new forms of visuality, aurality, textuality, and tactility constitute the cybercultural turn. These are also forms that are often *user-generated*. "Convergence culture," as Henry Jenkins (2006b) calls it, within cybercultures gives an enormous amount of power to the user to design interfaces, aesthetics, and modifications within the computer world.

New media art has been a significant manifestation of such user-generated, technologically informed artifacts.

New media art alters the very nature of the audience and the "text." In hypertexts we can now experience total language – VR performances with visual spectacle, music, song, text, and dance. Visual poetry such as that by John Cayley exploits the spatial and geometrical arrangement of words on the screen, and thus affects our experience of "reading." Art software such as The Impermanence Agent – which monitored users' web browsing to create customized artworks – gives a whole new dimension to the notion of text and authorship. The ephemerality, reader freedom, decentered text, sense of play and randomness, and reading as fluid, discontinuous movement of a hypertext (Ryan 1999: 101–102) question the basic conceptualization of literature as an author-driven work.

As Lev Manovich's (2001) groundbreaking work has demonstrated, the language of new media is built on databases rather than narrative (which suggests a cause–effect ordering), and the user transcodes from one format to another.

Digitextuality

Digitextuality refers to the collage of forms, registers, and signifying systems that are visible in the new media. New media technologies build a new text not only through the "absorption and transformation of other texts, but also by embedding the entirety of other texts (analog and digital) seamlessly within the new" (Everett 2003: 7). Digitextuality treats every text as an interface of many *forms* of texts – visual, aural, moving. The Graphical User Interface (GUI) was a move towards a kind of visual interface where the computer screen becomes split along several windows, each a possible source of independent interaction. Now, with audio input and streaming video also available on the desktop, again in the form of windows, the GUI is more than just "graphic."

Digital or new media art can take several forms, where each "art object" itself combines several forms and media.

Digitextuality is an example of convergence. Convergence, as we have seen, is when many kinds of media meet on a common platform. However, as Bolter and Gromala (2003: 100) point out, what we have is not a single convergence but a series of convergences, where technologies combine provisionally (the laptop that plays DVDs, palmtops that have notebooks, calendars, and clocks, iPods that function as radios, mobile phones that work as movie devices). What we see in convergence is miniaturization, where many forms of technology become smaller so that the interface/PC can accommodate more and more functions.

> **DIGITEXTUALITY**
>
> Digitextuality refers to the convergence of multiple forms of media in the digital age where print, audio, video, and graphics can be simultaneously accessed and processed through one common software application.

A point that Bolter and Gromala miss in their otherwise prescient discussion is that convergence also includes the convergence of technology *into the human body*. The body of the visitor/viewer is the site of the technology's effect. Viewers construct art through their interface with the technology. The boundaries of the art object extend outward and move into the body of the viewer. The line separating the object from the viewer breaks down when the viewer's actions and behavior determine the very nature of the object.

Active Audience Art

In contemporary art forms, computers, sensors, and digital technology ensure a participatory relation between the art object and the viewer. Such art forms offer a different order of community and social interaction in increasingly fragmented worlds. In the age of individualism and solitary works, such art forms provide an interesting social interaction with art and the artist.

In Jeffrey Shaw's *The Legible City* (1988–1991), 3D letters formed words and sentences as the user navigated a virtual city on a stationary bicycle. In Rafael Lozano-Hemmer's "relational architecture," physical architecture is augmented by a virtual one. His *Displaced Emperors* (1997), designed to transform Linz Castle, superimposed the Aztec empire (whose Quetzal-feather crown was housed in the Ethnological Museum in Vienna) on the Mexican one. The visitors' movements, tracked by motion sensors, seemed to penetrate the interiors, which were then projected on the castle building. The audience could also summon up the feather headdress through buttons placed on the building's various stations. *Adrift* (1997–2001) by Jesse Gilbert, Helen Thorington, Marek Walczak, and others also mixed real and virtual spaces. Such art forms reanimate the audience, and hence could be described as *active audience art*.

In certain kinds of installation art, computers generate responses from inanimate objects, responses that are governed by the audience's presence or movements. In Kenneth Rinaldo's *Autopoeisis* (2000), 15 robotic sculptures with arm-like structures were suspended from the ceiling. Sensors inside the arms monitored the movement of visitors, and responded accordingly. The structures also communicated with each other through a centralized computer so that the entire structure worked as a living organism, responding to the environment.

TEXT RAIN (2000) built on the interaction between the viewer's body and the exhibit. The visitor stops in front of the screen, even as her face and silhouette are captured by video cameras and projected on the black and white screen. This is accompanied by a shower of colored letters, falling like rain from the top of the screen. Whenever the letters come in contact with the viewer's image they stop falling, and they only move when the viewer moves. The exhibit invites the viewer to form patterns of letters by moving.

The audience or viewer is no longer passive: he or she is a *user* who creates the artwork through use. David Marshall (2004) suggests that we need an "active audience" approach to unravel the productive qualities of media consumption. As we have already noted, the interactive approach in contemporary new media art means that the form and content of the art object are determined by the user, who is therefore more active producer than passive consumer. All new media is interactive in the sense that the art object is sensitive to the audience's presence (an engagement with the context), even as the audience constructs a certain form of the art object.

All new media art is therefore, I suggest, *personal*: within the boundaries of the software code, every user is at least partly the producer-artist. This is where the distinction between personal mobile phones or ring tones and any art object "out there" breaks down: all are equally *personalizable*.

Remediation

Contemporary artworks such as TEXT RAIN are good examples of remediation (Bolter and Gromala 2003), where, as we have seen, new media forms emerge out of old ones. TEXT RAIN mixes the virtual and the physical. In the installation art discussed above, we see video combining with recorded images and sound, all of which are activated and modified through the movements of the audience. The click of a mouse or the movement of the visitor's hand alters not simply the content but the very *form* of the object. This fluidity of form in contemporary art is remediation too, but an *audience*-driven one because it revives older forms of audience–performer interaction (the singer reaching out to the crowd, or museums with DIY objects, especially for pedagogic purposes and in children's museums).

Liveness

The nature of "live" performance is itself called into question with artworks like Wolfgang Staehl's *Empire 24/7* (2001). This is a constantly evolving photographic image of the Empire State building, capturing changes of light and shade during the course of a day. As Christiane Paul points out, on the one hand it is "live" and, on the other, it is mediated (by the cameras). Processing, aestheticization, and mediation are central to what we see of the building. And yet it is live because we can never see it again except as a recording (Paul 2003: 102–104).

Liveness is also performance with a certain amount of unpredictability written into the script – as in hybrid adventure-drama reality TV such as *Survivor*. When audiences vote off a player in *Big Brother*, they participate in the living nature of the program. In the case of TEXT RAIN, the audience animates the artifact, just as the artifact animates the audience. It is "live" art facilitated by technology.

Web browsers are themselves becoming more aesthetic, altering the way the interface works. This is also "live" in the sense that it appropriates users' moves and preferences in order to evolve. Browser art, using Webstalker, for example, allows the user to build a collage from various sources or sites on the Internet. Netomat ignores the page and format of the traditional browser and even the data source. In response to a query, the browser looks for the content in the World Wide Web. It then delivers the text, images, and audio simultaneously on to the user's screen without regard for the data source's format.

New media art foregrounds the *recursivity* of the artifact: that it is intimately connected to the real world via the audience's bodies, perceptions, senses, and actions. Contemporary new media art refuses to separate the artifact from the audience viewing it. In fact, what new media art does is to shift the artifact from being simply a spectacle or a view to being an *environment*.

The artifact is the environment through which the audience moves, and the artifact-environment is shaped by this movement of the audience. "Interactivity" is this mutual linkage: the rootedness of the artifact in the audience and the audience-experience being shaped by the artifact. Art forms that depend on cybercultures once again highlight the fact that cyberculture cannot be studied independently of the real and the material.

PCTs, iPods, and Podcasting

The personalization and individualization of media were heralded in a radical new way by the Sony Walkman (see du Gay et al. 1997). In terms of popular culture, portable, individualized music has proved to be the most enduring of consumer products. Reproducibility, transferability, and individualization mark the iPod and the portable music system.

Podcasting is a related phenomenon. Podcasting allows an individual to distribute music or any other entertainment/information files. It is now used extensively by educational and public institutions, and even by churches and places of worship to distribute prayers and services. Podcasts can be customized to suit an individual's or institution's tastes or needs.

The key features of iPods and podcasting are *customization* and *augmented distribution*. Unlike the Walkman or Discman, which treated the listener as simply a passive consumer, podcasting transforms the consumer into a producer. The technology allows any individual or institution with the right software to distribute media files, thus making them part of the production side rather than merely consumers. Its biggest role has been in education. Students initially used podcasts only to record lectures and instructional materials (Lee et al. 2007). However, they soon began to develop their own materials for peer-to-peer distribution. What this suggests is that podcasting becomes a way of creating an *alternate mode of knowledge creation and transmission*, one that is not dependent upon institutions.

Podcasting moves from the acquisition model of learning to the participation model where users generate their own materials (Lee et al. 2007: 9–10), critically examine instructional texts, and provide their own clues and "help" for peers. Greater student control over the technology, being experimented with in various institutions, means that they will have a greater role in knowledge production.

Healthcare and medical professionals have their own podcasts to listen to journal articles and research data while on the move. Highly respected journals like the *New England Journal of Medicine* (content.nejm.org/misc/podcast.shtml) and groups like www.medicine.net use the technology extensively for transmitting health news, research, and trends in medicine.

Genomic Arts and Biomedia

Art forms of the 1990s appropriated and aestheticized contemporary developments in technoculture, especially in biology, medicine, and genetics. The integration of biology with computers and electronics – even before genetic arts entered the scene – is best exemplified by the work of Stelarc. These art forms, I propose, exhibit *both* a fear of *and* a fascination with

- the possibilities of genetic engineering;
- the cyborgization of bodies;
- the "monstrous" mix of animal, human, and machine.

Stelarc (Stelios Arcadiou) interfaces his body with machines and the Internet (see Chapter 3 for a discussion). Marcel.lí Antúnez Roca's interactive experiment *Epizoo* (1994) also allowed audiences to manipulate the artist's body. "The body is obsolete," announces Stelarc on his website (www.stelarc.va.com.au/).

Posthuman art combines computer technology with the body and appropriates genetic engineering and its concepts to art. Genetics is *mediated* for popular consumption, at least in the West, by advanced visualizing techniques and through a process of aestheticization. The Wellcome Trust – a science funding organization – has organized a "sci-art" program to encourage collaborative work between artists and scientists. Future-directed genomic art projects have been established such as SymbioticA and Tissue Culture and Art at the University of Western Australia's School of Anatomy and Human Biology by cell biologist Miranda Grounds, neuroscientist Stuart Bunt, and artist Oron Catts (www. symbiotica.uwa.edu.au).

Artists like Karl Sims (*Genetic Images*, 1991), Christa Sommerer and Laurent Mignonneau (*A-Volve*, 1994; see Mignonneau and Sommerer 2001), and Steve Grand (*Creatures*, 1996) have used artificial or virtual life forms in their installation arts. In 1997 Sony Communication Network Corporation released the PostPet artificial-life email software, which allowed users to have digital pets that delivered their emails. Sommerer and Mignonneau also created *Life Spacies* in 1997, a program that allowed visitors to their installation exhibit to type in a few lines of text. This text then generated a *life form* in the virtual world, and the visitor could take care of the "pet" (from feeding to mating). Here, the typed text is the genetic code for the creature/artificial life form.

In 2000 the Exit Art Gallery in New York focused on the artistic possibilities of biocybernetics (the combination of computer technology and biological science). Alexis Rockman's *The Farm* (2000) depicted a soybean field that showed recognizable plants and animals, and speculated on how they might look in future. These are *transgenic* art forms, blurring the boundaries between human, animal, and vegetable, transcoding these bodies into something else altogether. They are chimeras – organisms made from cells and tissues from two or more species (the term was first used to describe species crossover under laboratory conditions in 1968). It is important to note that chimeras have traditionally been regarded as monstrous because they blur species boundaries and categories. Bryan Crockett's *Oncomouse* symbolizes the first genetically patented transgenic laboratory mouse. In 1986 geneticist David Ow combined tobacco and firefly genes to produce plants that glowed in the dark. In 2000 the Oregon Regional Primate Center created a rhesus monkey that carried GFP (green fluoroscent protein), and was thus a bioluminescent monkey. Eduardo Kac's installation *Genesis 1999* is described as "transgenic art linked to the Internet," highlighting genetic transfer from one organism to another so that unique living beings result. Kac's rabbit "Alba" is fluorescent. Laura Stein's *Smiley Tomato* suggests that we should be able to produce fruits and vegetables with smiley faces. Ronald Jones's life-size sculpture of the genetic structure of cancer is about modeling and simulation in medicine. The organization Art to the Nth Power (at www.artn.com) describes various such art forms. Larry Miller of genomic licensing fame installed the portraits of 11 living artists in linear arrangement, alongside their DNA samples.

Exhibition

The medical image of a body (sliced less than a millimeter thick, photographed, digitized) is an exhibition of the internal body. It turns the body inside out – literally, in Gunther von Hagens's exhibition "Body Worlds" (www.bodyworlds.com). When it comes to genes and chromosomes, the smallest component of the human is inflated into a visual treat. In the case of genomic art, modified animals and plants are exhibitions and renderings of the "natural" processes of evolution, growth, and decay. The only comparable image-making is of images of space published in newspapers. These images of planets or astronomical phenomena often have the caption "artist's impression" beneath them, where the artist has used the digital data that are transmitted to provide an image.

Genomic art is about the aesthetization of ultimately secret processes of the human body. Deformity or perfect forms represented in genomic art are attempts to show possibilities. It is cybercultural art that takes the human form and future in the context of heavily technologized environments very seriously. In order to emphasize the possible transformation of the real/bodily through technologies, it has recourse to particular aesthetic forms.

The Monstrous and the Grotesque

One way of describing the aesthetics of such genomic art and bio-art would be to treat them as the "new monstrous" (Nayar 2007a). They are "monstrous" in the sense that they occupy the space between categories (subject/object, art/biology, organic/computer-generated) that might just be about the future.

"Monster" is etymologically linked to the Latin terms *monstrum*, meaning omen, portent, or sign, and *monere*, which means "to warn." However, it also indicates the malformed and the grotesque (the birth of deformed animals or human babies was seen as a portent in early modern Europe, when the term was first used). There is, therefore, a certain *revelatory* and *futuristic* imperative in the term itself.

What the images, performances, and installations in Rockman or Stelarc tell us – especially after the doctor has explained it to us – is the course our *future* life could take. The Pig Wings project calls attention to this aspect:

> Rhetoric surrounding the development of new biological technologies makes us wonder if pigs could fly one day. If pigs could fly, what shape will their wings take? The Pig Wings project presents the first use of living pig tissue to construct and grow winged shaped semi-living objects. (www.tca.uwa.edu.au/pig/pig_main.html)

The modified animals in Bryan Crockett, Eduardo Kac, and Alexis Rockman are monstrous in the sense that they are *potential* forms (virtual actually means potential, awaiting actualization: so virtual life is life awaiting corpo-*realization*). They are future-directed in that they reveal what is possible through cloning and genetic manipulation.

The "monstrous" in medical imaging and genomic art is an icon that directs our attention toward the future. It reveals to the eye the inner workings that *can* lead to these forms. This is not necessarily dystopian, though it combines death and life in an ambiguous way, leading Catherine Waldby (1997) to term it a "digital uncanny." There is a sense of the ghostly in the artifacts we see, something that we can recognize and other elements that we cannot. This means the monstrous in contemporary art is an attempt to create a new rationality that reflects the breaking of the older one, where questions of borders and identities are irrelevant. They also represent – in the true tradition of the monstrous – a cultural anxiety about what the "human" is. The monstrous is the aesthetic of expansion-extension, the exhibition of something that is a warning, a portent of the shape of things to come, as a 1993 cover of *Time* magazine showing the "new face of America" – a computer-generated picture culled from many racial types – suggests. It is the vivid imagining of a world through the ever-improved copying of life forms.

With genetics it is possible to collapse categories. It must be remembered that classificatory regimes and categories are integral to aesthetics (the grotesque, for instance, thrives on "species confusion" and breakdown of categories, as Geoffrey Galt Harpham 1982 has demonstrated). The dissolution of bodies/borders in *Oncomouse*, *The Farm*, or *Cremaster 4* (Matthew Barney) marks "it" (the body) differently. In genomic art, animal-plant-human borders become permeable: each can take on the form, function, or feature of even the utterly alien *other*. The monstrous in genomic art, like cyborgs, redefines boundaries and categories, creating visions of new biomorphic forms and possibilities. Yet it also suggests a cultural anxiety about the "purity" of the human race, and about laboratory and genetic experimentation (Anker and Nelkin 2004: 109).

Informational Bodies

Eduardo Kac has suggested that genomic art represents a cultural shift – the transformation of biology into an information science (Kac 2005a: 218). Kac's installation

Teleporting an Unknown State (1994–1996) consisted of a single seed on a pedestal with earth in a very dark room. Through a video projector suspended above and facing the seed, individuals could send light through the Internet to enable the seed to photosynthesize and grow.

Eugene Thacker describes the new forms of the body in biology and information sciences as "biomedia" – a term that seems to best describe Kac's own "bodies" (Thacker 2004a: 13). In biomedia, the body is a medium and the media themselves are indistinguishable from the biological body. The term also captures the kind of art that we have seen in Sommerer and Mignonneau's *Life Spacies* – the body of the virtual creature is code *embodied*. The transcoded body here needs to be understood in two ways – as a biological, molecular, species body *and* as a body that is compiled through modes of visualization, modeling, and datasets. Kac's harnessing of information technology, biological processes, and mechanical devices to generate art is an aestheticization of both biology and cyberculture, collapsing the boundary between art and nature, while probing the consequences of reducing the body to a database devoid of the contexts in which DNA produces particular forms of behavior of the body. As Steve Tomasula (2002) argues, genomic art addresses questions of change in society – while debating its ethical dimensions by revealing the possibilities within artificial (rather than "natural") change.

Control

Cybernetic art probes the limits of the human form and consciousness. It pushes the frontiers, albeit with some anxiety, of the technology–human interface. It proposes new forms and species, while revealing how science depends on cultural contexts for its work and its dissemination. It teaches responsibility by asking uncomfortable questions about appropriation of information (in the Human Genome Project, for example) and genetic engineering (such as the creation of new species in the laboratory). Art here serves the dual purpose of popularizing cutting-edge technology and interrogating it by revealing its less likeable side effects.

The artists discussed here also point toward another desire in contemporary technoscience: the desire to control the future. Rather than leave evolution and adaptation to "natural" processes, science seeks to take charge of them, even as artists envision this future (see Nayar 2007a).

The posthuman as it appears in art forms today is the culmination of the human tendency to take charge of destiny itself.

The final words on the possibilities of posthumanism and its art forms belong to the artists Stelarc and Eduardo Kac:

> The body's form is enhanced and its functions extended … electronic space restructures the body's architecture and multiplies its operational possibilities. (Stelarc 1991)

> Transgenic art [Kac is referring to GFP Bunny] acknowledges the human role in rabbit evolution as a natural element, as a chapter in the natural history of both humans and

rabbits, for domestication is always a bi-directional experience … [It] can help science to recognize the role of relational and communicational issues in the development of organisms. It can help culture by unmasking the popular belief that DNA is the "master molecule" through an emphasis on the whole organism and the environment (the context). And finally, transgenic art can contribute to the field of aesthetics by opening up the new symbolic and pragmatic dimension of art as the literal creation of and responsibility for life. (Kac 2005b: 272, 276)

Social Networking

Instant messaging, SMS, email, the mobile, and now social networking are modes of relationship making and relationship building. This is so particularly for youth, who have figured prominently in studies of new media (Kim et al. 2007; Livingstone 2003). Social networking sites (SNSs) like MySpace, Bebo, Facebook, Orkut, and CyWorld, are the new social spaces to hang out in.

An early example of the SNS is SixDegrees.com, launched in 1997, but it is from around 2003 that SNSs really took off. SNSs are defined as "web-based services that allow individuals to (1) construct a public or semi-public profile within a bounded system, (2) articulate a list of other users with whom they share a connection, and (3) view and traverse their list of connections and those made by others within the system" (boyd and Ellison 2007). SNSs are most often characterized by easy-to-use technology, profile building by members, and regular interaction through "scraps" and responses.[7] SNSs offer photo or video sharing and mobile connectivity, and are spaces of communication and exchange. Blogging services with SNS features in Xanga, LiveJournal, and Vox also widened their user base.

SOCIAL NETWORKING SITES

Web-based services where people can host profiles, chat, and communicate, social network sites are a kind of virtual social-public space.

However, boyd and Ellison distinguish between social networking and social network sites. "Networking," for boyd and Ellison, suggests relationship initiation between strangers. In the case of SNSs, while networking is possible, it is *not* the primary practice on many of them (Beer 2008 prefers the term social "networking," even though he offers Web 2.0 as a larger term to describe these new forms of online cultures).

A significant feature of SNSs has been their *user-generated* content. Websites were quick to cash in on this and became social media. Examples of this are Flickr (photo sharing), YouTube (video sharing), and Last.FM (music sharing). MySpace was able to tap into the relationship between bands and fans by creating a space for them to meet, advertise forthcoming albums, or show and reinforce their admiration.

Social networking sites blur the distinction between the public and the private because one spills over into the other. An existing social relationship is affected, altered, and reinforced by online "friending." The converse – where online interaction leads to offline meetings and relationships, as dating services discovered – is just as true. SNSs therefore consitute a "third space" between public and private where online and offline identities and relations are merged. Sharing a home video on YouTube and describing a personal favorite movie or book is the building of a profile for public consumption that could lead to a social relation.

Questions of Privacy and Profiles

The popularity of SNSs among youth and even children has had other consequences. MySpace's role in sexual harassment, stalking, and other predatory behavior prompted legal action and generated a moral panic (Consumer Affairs 2006). Once again we see cybercultural forms affecting the *material* world.[8]

Whether individuals on Friends in SNSs share the same sense of privacy is a crucial factor in social networking. Personal information included on scraps and profiles can be "leaked" or viewed by strangers. Questions of privacy, especially concerning physical addresses, finances, and even physical appearance, are actually questions of safety. What we see here is a close link between online details and networking and very real offline safety issues.

Identity thefts online are a constant threat when users reveal their identities or create profiles. In a recent case, noted author Philip Pullman had to send out a warning email to a listserv after he discovered that somebody had created a Facebook profile for him. Pullman wrote: "I would like to personally go and strangle the wretch" (quoted on BridgeToTheStars.Net 2008, the fansite for Pullman's *His Dark Materials* trilogy).[9] Phishing and identity thefts are matters of both offline and online lives. Indeed, as Vogt and Knapman (2008) point out, it is the very open nature of such personal web spaces that has led to such complications.

Exclusivity and privacy return as key features of SNSs, and sites such as Microsoft's LiveSpaces and aSmallWorld now offer private networking, open only by invitation and patronized, according to one report (Vogt and Knapman 2008), by prosperous people in the USA and UK. Ironically, the openness of the web replicates ghetto conditions of exclusivity, privacy, and patrolling in real life.

Augmenting Relations

SNSs could be an extension – *augmentation* – of existing social relationships when friends hang out in virtual space, or they could facilitate the creation of new relations when strangers come together due to shared interests. The "advertisement" of an individual's "Friends" on his or her profile enables viewers to explore the network of that particular individual.

"Friending" online is the coming together of online and offline relationships. Or, to put it differently, friendships are increasingly *mediated* and *technologized* through online interactions (I agree with David Beer – and against boyd and Ellison – that one cannot imagine a social structure or situation that is *not* mediated; Beer 2008: 521). There is a *recursive* relation between offline and online relations. Offline relationships inform online ones, and vice versa, because technology makes the difference between "being with someone somewhere" to "not being with someone" when one is (electronically) still linked.

In effect, therefore, SNSs reinforce my thesis: they are grounded in the *material* world because they help people who already know each other in the real world to communicate and exchange almost continually. Along with the "perpetual contact" that informs the everyday life of relationships now, *augmentation* is the logic of the SNS where we continue to "be" with someone even if physically separated.

The extent of communication online is dependent upon and informed by the relationship offline. If MySpace allows "perpetual contact," it is also driven by the accompanying spirit or logic of cybercultures that I proposed in the opening chapter: *augmentation*. In the case of the fan–band relation in MySpace noted above, we see this logic of augmentation at work. Local music stores advertise passes and shows on MySpace for fans to acquire them. Fans, in turn, popularize their affiliations. In effect, what is augmented in cyberspace SNSs is the cementing of a very strong *real* relationship between the fan and the music group. MySpace does not always generate fans, but it *helps already existing fans to network better.*

In this sense, SNSs contribute to an individual's *social capital.* Research has shown that networked individuals are more likely to receive help from one of their online "circle" (Boase et al. 2006). Other studies show how, even after people have moved away from a geographic location where they had strong ties (i.e., social capital), SNSs have enabled them to get assistance from their *previous* community. That is, people were able to remain in touch with an earlier community even after being physically disconnected from it (Ellison et al. 2007). What neither of these studies notices is that this SNS-driven social capital is an *augmentation* of preexisting social capital. More importantly, such social capital has very *material* consequences for the individuals.

This "augmentation" of social and cultural capital could relate to particular ethnic and cultural ties. Former community sites such as AsianAvenue, MiGente, and BlackPlanet upgraded themselves into SNSs between 2005 and 2006, thus increasing their functionality and usability by their respective communities.[10] Here SNSs *replicate* conditions of social interaction found in the real world: community bonding remains a cornerstone of virtual interactions too. Campaigns using Facebook and MySpace have been run at specific universities (one study reports that campaigns to reduce drinking age and in favor of legislation allowing same-sex marriage were the most popular among Facebook users; Charnigo and Barnett-Ellis 2007). Such SNSs create a sense of community *without* a place (a psychological sense of community), even though spatial metaphors and lingo can be used to "meet" in cyberspace (on the sense of community in SNSs, see Goodings et al. 2007). There is good reason, therefore, for Sean Rapacki to describe MySpace and other SNSs as "virtual commons" (2007: 29). They become a means, as Charnigo and Barnett-Ellis (2007) argue, to engage students in library events and services because they enable librarians to communicate better with several segments of the youth population in their area (for a different view on such "community" formations, see Byrne 2007).

Youth Culture and SNSs

SNSs have appealed most to youth and are now an integral component of youth cultures across the world, although this trend is now shifting in the UK, according to an OfCom survey of social networking in April 2008 (40 percent of adults in the UK regularly use SNSs, a higher total than in the USA or Japan, and 62 percent are on Facebook) (Whiteside 2008). Teens flocked to MySpace from around 2004; later, the SNS changed its policy to allow minors to join too. In 2005 Facebook started allowing high school students to enroll. According to boyd and Ellison (2007), MySpace (arguably the most popular of the SNSs) has three distinct "populations": musicians/artists, teenagers, and the post-college urban social crowd.

For youth (as for other) users, social networking becomes a mode of self-representation and display. It expands the community of "viewers" of their profile and can be seen as an important mode of social interaction and, as Sonia Livingstone (2008: 400) has argued recently, their "identity needs." Social interaction and behavior are based on self-representation, self-management, and self-promotion. The profile on an SNS becomes a means of doing this. With instant updates on Twitter, the self is always publicized and always connected, even if the connection (as Vincent Miller 2008 has recently argued) is merely phatic – signifying empty and often pointless communication without any real exchange of information – and not substantive.

Profile management and self-representation on SNSs are components of a social identity, even if that identity is only online. Such representations have been termed "online textual performance of self" (H. Liu 2007). Profiles become indices of taste when individuals detail their preferences in music, clothes, games, and books. These are "cultural signs" and "taste statements" (Liu 2007). Such taste statements inform the individual's social life online. Therefore, it becomes imperative for individuals to develop and maintain the kind of profile online that they do in real life in order to ensure both authenticity and sustained popularity. As scholars have demonstrated (e.g., Dwyer et al. 2007), the issue of trust is paramount in social interactions online.

Taste statements can become the means of acquiring social capital when one's online network is widened. What is important is that an online life dependent upon taste statements and profile management spills over into the real, just as real-life behavior and tastes inform online searches for like-minded people (via interest tokens on SNSs), friendships, and relationships. Thus the choice of video-sharing practices on YouTube, one study has revealed, reflects existing social relationships (Lange 2007). It could thus be argued that online profile management is now an integral component of real-life identities as well because, increasingly, people meet both online and offline and media practices reflect and affect existing social behavior, interaction, and relations.

User profiles on Facebook and other SNS spaces become commercially usable data. SNSs fit right into the "knowing capitalism" (Thrift 2005) of the twenty-first century. "Knowing capitalism" uses information (Thrift takes the example of small talk and gossip) otherwise unavailable to – or seen as unimportant by – the business sector in order to further its agenda. David Beer, building on Thrift's work, raises a crucial point about SNSs when he suggests that the small talk and vast amounts of seemingly innocuous information could actually become valuable sources for businesses (Beer 2008: 522–523). With SNSs, what is available is a whole archive of consumer preferences that they can tap into. "Knowing capitalism," tying in with the new forms of knowledge gathering – among which I include SNSs, scraps, and profiles – can build on what people say about brands, styles, and preferences to advertise, promote, and target customers on SNSs.

SNSs clearly have enormous commercial value, if one accepts Beer's arguments (as I do). The wealth of information about consumer tastes available on MySpace or Facebook surely serves the purpose of selling as much as it serves as advice to future buyers.

Companies have now turned to SNSs to generate publicity and develop linkages with consumers (Neuborne 2007). Blogging, SNSs, and presence in *Second Life* are modes of widening the consumer base. Online communities are the new terrain for market research and advertising.

Clearly, forms of popular cyberculture and new media cultures are multiplying and reaching wider population segments. They carry their own ideological and political baggage, as this chapter has demonstrated. In every case these cybercultural formations remain connected, however tangentially, to real-life social, economic, political, and cultural contexts. What is evident is not just the embeddedness of cybercultural forms in the everyday and the material, but the increasing mediatization of the everyday through and with these technologies.

NOTES

1 Counterculture – a term coined in the 1960s to describe the hippie movement – questions the values and norms of dominant cultures. Thus the opera or the politics of war and military business becomes the subject of punk, which uses anti-war themes, the street, and casual styles.

2 This is not entirely fantasy, if we look at the nature and degree of surgical interventions, genetic alterations, and computerization of the human body to rectify painful and debilitating illnesses. We see the everyday lives of senior citizens, the differently abled, and the diseased being altered through technological interventions ranging from prosthesis to computer chip implants.

3 Gambling has also been a significant form of online gaming. PartyGaming (behind the UK's Party Poker website) entered the London Stock Exchange in mid-2005, with a mind-boggling initial value of £5 billion – more than British Airways and EMI combined!

4 Empirical studies in Europe and the USA have demonstrated the gendered nature of game playing (Jansz and Martens 2005). The top three genres of men's games were

sports, action/adventure, and simulation. Women chose puzzle-solving, platform, and sports genres (Consalvo and Treat 2002, cited in Royse et al 2007: 557).

5 I am grateful to Anna Kurian for drawing my attention to this game, and sharing with me her son's experiences with it.

6 However, it also allows young male players to experiment with a female "form" in cyberspace, thus complicating the gendered nature of the game (see Schleiner 2001).

7 Profiles on SNSs have different degrees of visibility depending on the SNS. Profiles on Friendster and Tribe.net are visible to anyone via search engines, LinkedIn controls what viewers may see based on whether they have a paid account, MySpace allows users to choose whether they want their profile to be public or "Friends only," and in Facebook, users who are part of the same "network" can view each other's profiles, unless the profile owner has decided to deny permission to those in their network.

8 Employers and governments have had a role in trying to regulate the booming business of SNSs. Thus, the US military banned soldiers from accessing MySpace (Frosch 2007) and the Canadian government prohibited employees from using Facebook (Benzie 2007). Employers have scrutinized student profiles on SNSs before offering them jobs, and job offers have been rescinded based on the content of messages on Facebook (see Peluchette and Karl 2008).

9 I am grateful to Anna Kurian for directing my attention to this incident.

10 There has been regional variation in the use of SNSs too. Mixi is Japan's preferred SNS, while Hyves is that of the Netherlands. China's instant messaging service QQ became one of the world's largest SNSs. Orkut, despite being a Google SNS, did not catch on in the USA, but became Brazil's preferred SNS (89 percent of 15- to 45-year-old web users are on Orkut, according to Vogt and Knapman 2008), and now that of India (Madhavan 2007). Microsoft's LiveSpaces is more popular elsewhere than in the USA.

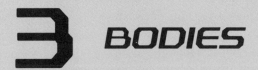

3 BODIES

CHAPTER PLAN

Posthuman Bodies
Aestheticization
Digitization and Informatization
Cryogenics and Transhumanism
Consumer Techno-Bodies

Connected Bodies

Embodiment, Disembodiment, and Re-embodiment

Cyborg Identity and Politics
Citizenship

In William Gibson's cult novel *Neuromancer* (1984), the "hero" Case *escapes* his meat-body by entering cyberspace. With this image Gibson inaugurates what is probably the most enduring theme in cyberpunk fiction: the transcendence of and escape from the flesh-and-blood body.

Human bodies have had a varied relationship with technology. The body is a *source* of technology as much as it is a *location* for technology (Shilling 2005). Prosthetic devices have altered the shape, function, ability, and appearance of the body. In fact, from the use of the first tools, the wheel and fire, technology has been intimately linked to embodiment and the ways in which humans have used their bodies. Thus, today's nanobiology and electronic implants are not entirely radical developments – they extend what technology has always done for and with human bodies.

If machines are external, i.e., foreign, to the human body – as devices to enhance our functions – then what happens when the machine is incorporated into the body? And if the body were to be inserted into cyberspace or VR, is "our" body distinct from the machine? Does the foreign "body" (the machine) become a part of our *natural* body?

These problematic situations that generate philosophical questions about bodies, nature, and technology are more intense in the age of computers.

- What is the ontological status of the cyborg body?
- How are identities and subjectivities of bodies reconfigured or problematized through cyborgization?
- How does cyborgization and informatization alter the social interactions of cyborg bodies?
- What are the political implications – in terms of citizenship, for example – of cyborged bodies?
- How does consumer culture intersect with cyborgization?
- Does the transcendence of the human body/form appeal to all ethnic groups and individuals?

Networked human bodies occupy multiple time zones and spaces – an "unnatural" state. Logged into cyberspace worlds, the body is "left behind" in the chair as individuals explore other regions – an experience that extends that of being "immersed" in the world of a novel or a film.

Donna Haraway (1991a/1985) sees the cyborg as a figure with enormous political potential, breaking the taxonomic barriers between human and animal, the physical and non-physical, and the organic and machine. It thus resists any totalization, which is predicated upon the fixation of identities and cultures. These are always displaced and multiple, and hence symbolize the potential for a reconfiguration of the social itself. When the cyborg is freed of the constraints of (bodily) identity, it also points to the constructed nature of identities and borders: "woman," "black," "heterosexual."

The body is, however, not simply *any* body. Bodies are raced, gendered, and classed, and situated in particular social, economic, and cultural contexts. To speak of "the body" is, therefore, to erase very real differences *between* bodies. These differences are material and discursive, where material conditions of economy, clothing, food, and medical interventions generate, construct, and reinforce the differences between bodies as much as discourses of law, religion, manners, and sociability discursively construct body differences. Contemporary technologized bodies could be (1) bodies that "jack in" to virtual spaces via the World Wide Web, the mobile phone, or video conferencing, or (2) bodies altered through the addition/incorporation of inorganic (electronic, chemical) materials. Cyber- or techno-bodies are human bodies interfaced with machines, mostly via electronic linkages and computer networks where the interfacing is facilitated by surgical, medical, and electronic modifications to the organic substrate that is the human body. They are bodies modified to enable them to overcome disability or to enhance their capacities. These are *cyber-bodies*.

Cyber-bodies are technologically modified or networked bodies that seem to transcend, at least for a time, their immediate physical, geographic locations by being able to *be* or *do* things elsewhere or through other means.

This becomes, I argue, a form of *disembodiment* and a *simultaneous re-embodiment*. These are posthuman bodies where "wetware" (the flesh) merges and interfaces with hardware (the computer or the machine) and the software (code).

A cyborg works in two directions at the same time. The cyborg expands *outwards*, beyond the immediate physical limits of skin and bones. A cyborg can also bring the world *into* the mind directly. In VR environments, neural simulation or sensory stimulation which we would otherwise absorb through our body's eyes, skin, ears, and nose is provided by technologies that can enhance and alter sensations to suit the individual, thereby creating a whole new "reality" (for the duration that one is in cyberspace or VR, it is real). Thus, sensations experienced in the recesses of the mind are *not* connected to the immediate location of the body: you can be sitting in an air-conditioned, sterilized office space and yet smell the woods in the country through VR environments that are directly loaded into your body and consciousness.

In both these movements – outward and inward – what we have is a *disembodied* state where the actual spatial situation of the body has been overcome, or extended, into another space altogether, and a *re-embodiment* where a different kind of body is constructed. This re-embodiment is what I designate *e-mergence*, a portmanteau term signifying the *merger* of wetware (organic) and software (or electronics) but also the *emergence* of a new kind of human.

It is therefore not enough to say that the body is transcended, or that cyberculture facilitates disembodiment. We need to rethink the kind of body that is formed in place of what we have conventionally seen as the human.

Electronic cultures such as the one we live in allow us to invent entirely fictitious and new identities. We can alter age, gender, looks, preferences in food, language, nation, and location. On MySpace or in *Second Life*, no one can ascertain with any degree of assurance whether you are what your computer/digital profile says you are. The poet T. S. Eliot described the modern condition of role-playing as "prepar[ing] faces to meet the faces that [we] meet" (1993 [1917]: 14). Cyber-roles and avatars extend the "preparation" of faces into another dimension. Civilizational processes (as Norbert Elias 2000 has shown) through human history have been about the cultivation of appearances and behavior. Online etiquette and social networking evolve their own standards and norms of conduct.

The body is located within certain social systems – even when online – and discourses. Medicine, the law, religion, the family, and the state all use certain notions of the body and deal with the body in certain ways.

- The fashion industry sees the body as a project which can be sold certain clothes and accessories and thereby generate profits.
- Medicine sees the body as a set of anatomical and physiological features whose exact workings must be decoded – knowledge acquired – and helped to run smoothly.
- The industrialist sees the body of workers as tools that help manufacture and hence as the source of profits, and classifies bodies in terms of their productivity.

- Religion often sees the body as committing sin and requiring absolution through prayer and fasting (with the latter being directed primarily at the body through denial of nourishment).
- The family is a unit of relationships which assumes only certain kinds of relationships – especially sexual – between bodies.
- The law controls the movements of bodies, and penalizes "criminals" by incarcerating their bodies in cells.

What is clear is that bodies are subject to economic, political, epistemological, ideological, and scientific-technological observation and control. Posthuman culture of electronically linked and altered bodies is no exception.

Posthuman Bodies

The posthuman is not merely a temporal marker ("post") but also suggests an advancement and augmentation of the human through technological, surgical, medical, and digital means. The posthuman is an *e-mergence*, a consequence of the convergence of technology and the organic body that results in a human form and functionality that seems to be an improvement of the earlier model.

Bodies have never been "natural." Whether it is a prosthetic arm for the injured soldier or braces to align the teeth, bodies have been constantly modified in all cultures. Tattoos, jewelry, fashion, dressing, piercing, surgery, exercise regimens, yoga, implants, posture and gait correction, grafts … the number of things done *to* the body constitutes an exhaustive list.

> **THE POSTHUMAN**
>
> Another term for cyborged bodies, where organic bodies are modified through surgical, chemical, and technological interventions and networked with software and hardware in order to restore, augment, or modify their "natural" abilities and conditions. The posthuman is an **e-mergence**, a congeries of wetware (organic), software (computer codes), and hardware (prostheses, electronic implants, and computer chips) whose interaction with/experience of the world is mediated through technology.

Nature itself cannot be seen as the binary opposite of culture/technology. Nature is technologized and mediated, and the experience of nature is mediated and made available through technology. The boundary between the perceiving subject and the perceived environment has collapsed.

Body modification includes procedures of aestheticization through tattooing or scarification, medically and surgically induced alteration, and technological intervention in the body's form and function. In the case of cyberpunk, for instance, body modification becomes high tech, and bodies are invariably "techno-bodies."

Techno-bodies are cyborg in a different sense. With the increasing use of genetic engineering and animal transplants, the cyborg is also something that blurs the human–*animal* boundary, not just the human–machine one. Donna Haraway's recent work (2006) on "companion species" expands the very idea of "species" to speak of "respect" and "response" (the etymological roots of "species"), along with the development in the "posthumanities" (Cary Wolfe 2007, 2008) towards other life forms. Thus the notion of the cyborg as human-machine is not an accurate picture of the new forms of bodies in the new millennium.

Aestheticization

Aesthetic manipulation of the body is as old as humanity. Silicon implants, obesity-control modes, gym workouts, and assorted "makeovers" ensure that a particular form is maintained – a form that seeks to fit into the socially acceptable idea of a "beautiful" body. Surgical modification of the body has often been directed at enhancing people's quality of life, especially those with motor or other kinds of disability. Implants, prosthetic devices, and artificial limbs are aids to improving the survival of the body. Tattoos and other body markings are often signs of identity. Communities, tribes, or social groups might adopt characteristic marks to indicate membership. Body modification could be a sign of rebellion in subcultural groups – thus making it an emphatically political move.

Body modification is a *sociopolitical* act because it seeks to redefine the role, ability, identity, and *agency* of the human body, even as it grounds the political in the body.

The new fashion for body modification became more pronounced in the 1990s and has been traced to the tattoo culture of an earlier era (De Mello 2000). Body modification became a subcultural movement with punk in the 1970s. It destabilizes the notion of a coherent body and interrogates established norms about what a body *should* be. Politically, communities of modified bodies constitute a radical subculture.

In the case of women, body modification has been a matter of considerable controversy. Cosmetic surgery, argue feminists (Davis 1995; K. P. Morgan 1991), further commodify the woman as a sexual object. However, artists like Orlan argue that by embarking on body modification through her own choice, she subverts conventions of women's beauty.

Gay, lesbian, and transgender body modification queer the body itself. As individuals whose identities are in any case on the margins of "mainstream" culture, such practices emphasize a radical sexual politics. By showcasing stigmatized body pleasures (such as S/M), they question the norms of sexual behavior.

In technoculture, body–machine interfaces – from the dialysis machine and the pacemaker to implanted chips – are examples of posthuman bodies.

Popular examples of the posthuman arts that reconfigure the body through surgery and technology are represented by Stelarc, Orlan, and the Psymbiote team Isa Gordon and Jesse Jarrell. Australian artist Stelarc wired his body into the World Wide Web so that people keying in commands from elsewhere could get his body to move (www.stelarc.va.com.au). French performance artist Orlan undergoes multiple cosmetic surgical operations to alter her face and her body – the operations are telecast live over the World Wide Web (see www.orlan.net). She called the project

The Reincarnation of Saint Orlan. Isa Gordon wears silicon, latex, and electronic circuitry that seeks to "fully transform the artist into a seductively organic yet entirely unfamiliar hybrid organism, a human/machine chimera with fully integrated control systems" (www.psymbiote.org/).

Stelarc proposes a machinic-somatic integration that radically alters the frontiers of the body's autonomy and *expands the horizons of the body's borders*. Orlan blurs the first border we live within: our skin. Orlan calls into question this border by revealing its constructedness: we can acquire beauty and looks, we can "tone" the body. By altering looks, skin color, and shape, we alter our border with the world, and hence our interaction with and reception by the world.

Other aestheticization projects that have recourse to technology and primitive rituals of scarification or alteration include the community of Body Modification Ezine (www.bmezine.com). Individuals here exhibit photographs of their artwork and offer suggestions. The online magazine brings together people who do this work, often cutting across geographic and political boundaries to form a subcultural community.

One of the key aspects of such aestheticization and modification is the extreme individualism of the "artists." As Victoria Pitts puts it:

> the discourse … denaturalizes the body and endorses an ethic of individualism: we should neither be forced to conform to the dictates of our own culture nor be limited to body modifications that have already been invented. (2003: 169)

There is, Pitts suggests, a liberal emphasis on customization, individuality, and personal freedom. However, like most responses to body modification subcultures, Pitts also presupposes a "natural" body that is then denaturalized. To see body modification as a transgressive act demands that we have some norms about *what* boundaries (of form, function, looks) have been transgressed.

The more significant question is, I believe, to see how such augmentation or creative modification functions to appropriate, say, primitive cultures (most of the modifications are directly inspired by rituals from non-Western cultures, as seen on the Body Modification Ezine website). Here are three questions of this type:

- What does it mean for the *commodification* of non-Western, Third World cultures when practices that carry enormous metaphysical, religious, or emotional significance (frequently all three) become part of a global ethnic chic industry?
- Does personal agency imply the freedom to market ethnic chic whose "original" has a different valence for another culture?
- Does a modified body demand/require a new welfare or voter's ID? What does it mean for medical treatment? And how does modification affect the genders and races?

This individualism and drive to customize identities – as epitomized in many cyber-technologies – deny the social location of all bodies, whether modified or not. Bodies live in social settings and demand a share in the economies of food, politics, and sexuality. These are not questions of individuals alone but *collective, communitarian* and *social* ones: questions of agency, power, and profits.

Digitization and Informatization

Medical technology has played a crucial role in the construction of cyber-bodies. Surgical implants, prostheses, chemical modification, and genetically altered bodies call into question the very idea of a "natural" body.

Digital bodies such as those seen in the Visible Human Project or the Stanford Visible Female enable sophisticated reconstructions of the body on the PC screen. The body is reduced or rendered into thin slices that are then filmed and digitized. The Center for Human Simulation at Colorado has also digitized the human body (www.uchsc.edu/sm/chs). Medical visualization technology and digital human projects are ways of perceiving and representing the body – that is, they are about *images*. When converted into digital format, transmitted, and reconstructed elsewhere to *produce* an anatomy – where numbers represent tissues and cells – the steps of this transformation of the image are lost.

These are examples of "transcoding" (the process of translating something into another format; Manovich 2001: 64; see also Thacker 2004a). In this case the body is transcoded into the language of genetics and computers, with the result that we have digital humans, bioinformatics, computational biology, and, not least, genomic art.

TRANSCODING

Technically, transcoding is simply file conversion – from .GIF images to a video clip to audio files to print. In cultural theory, it is taken to represent the shift between the cultural "layer" and the computer "layer."

The transcoded body here needs to be understood in two ways – as a biological, molecular, species body *and* as a body that is compiled through modes of visualization, modeling, and datasets. A body submitted to and constituted by an unavoidable and empowering technical deterritorialization, a body whose embodiment is increasingly realized in *conjunction with technics* (Hansen 2006). Of these, nanomedicine, genetic engineering, and assisted reproductive technologies (ARTs) are significant.

Gene therapy is built upon the premise that since DNA controls several of our behaviors, aptitudes, features, and even vulnerability to disease, altering DNA would be an effective and permanent way of fighting disease. Bodily processes are recorded and transmitted through biomemes, so that records of brain or heart activity are readily available for the physician to print out in case of an emergency.

NANOTECHNOLOGY AND NANOMEDICINE

"Nano" is one billionth of a meter, roughly six carbon atoms in width. Nanotechnology seeks to engineer and manipulate matter and processes at the level of the atom. Nanomedicine is the medical application of nanotechnology. It involves the repair of body organs at the level of cells and even molecules such as protein.

These are medical interventions at the level of the cell and the molecule. They render the body into increasingly smaller sections for analysis, but also for intervention and modification. This form of medicine that links information technology and medical biology is info-medicine.

Genetic reprogramming enables the body to experience the world differently, especially when that body has been unable to do so previously due to corporeal problems or disease. Prosthesis and genetic alteration are both, finally, technics of the body that augment the body's experience of the world.

Cloning, like gene therapy, treats the body as a manifestation of the code of life: DNA. It is yet another example of the informatization of life where DNA and the genetic code are taken as the essence of human life. There is an interesting paradox about the informatization of the body. The body is "rendered" into code when it is digitized and biologists trope it as a *text* (DNA as the "*book* of life"). DNA is seen as a source code. An obverse of this scene of the body-as-code also exists. A new form of the material body is now visible in genetic engineering when the database or information (the *text* of the genetic code) helps generate actual material objects – from Dolly the sheep to bacteria to drugs. Thus, on the one hand we have a body rendered into information, and on the other information helps generate actual material bodies.

Molecular biology and biotechnology treat biology and the body as technology, where the body labors. The body functions as an economic body and as property (the patenting of genomes is an instantiation of this notion of body-as-property). As Eugene Thacker puts it, there is a continual "transformation" of biological and medical value into economic value, where the body is believed to possess "biomaterial labour" (2005: 47). The organization of genetic information helps classify human beings, their DNA, into databases. This classification system is not medical or biological alone, but cultural, as Thacker (2005) has persuasively argued. This informatization of the body also has other implications. Genetically engineered organisms have been the subject of the patent controversy: are laboratory-manufactured organisms "natural" (and therefore non-patentable, under US patent laws) or "invented" (and therefore patentable)? When in 1980 the US Supreme Court ruled that Anand Chakrabarty's lab-reared bacterium could be patented, it set in motion a whole controversy and debate about the body as *property*. The 1976 John Moore case – when Moore claimed that the cell line (called the Mo cell line) produced from his cancerous bone marrow belonged to him – is another example. The California Supreme Court ruled that Moore did not own his biological materials. In the case of the biotech industry, this debate acquires greater significance when entire communities, tribes, and races can have their genetic material collected and databased (as in the Human Genome Project). Reconfigured bodies in the biotechnological era lead us to ask: which bodies count (Bowen 2005)?

Cryogenics and Transhumanism

A subcultural movement that believes in extending and transcending the human body is Extropians (www.extropy.org). Extropians celebrate the human–machine interface, proposing a "transhumanism" where the human lives beyond the biologically given body, processes, and time. Transhumanism, as stated by the World Transhumanist Association (2002) in its declaration, seeks to "redesign the human condition, including such parameters as the inevitability of aging, limitations on human and artificial intellects, unchosen psychology, suffering, and our confinement to the planet earth."

The politics of Extropians is indeed disturbing, and not because they seek to alter a "natural" process (we know that for centuries now, humans have intervened in natural processes). Their very definition of posthumans opens the debate about their politics: "persons of unprecedented physical, intellectual, and psychological ability, self-programming and self-defining, potentially immortal, unlimited individuals." Extropians assume that only certain kinds of individuals – those possessing the qualities mentioned above – will want immortality or freedom from diseases and aging.

The key questions would be:

- Does the choice of advanced bodies apply to all races, ethnic groups, minorities, women, and the differently abled?
- What about the social and cultural norms that might dictate, as they do now, the choice of bodies and forms?
- Would enhanced abilities be the norm to which many cannot (afford to) subscribe?

The web presence of Extropians and transhumanists seems to consist almost entirely of Caucasian races. Does this imply a racialized dichotomy of transhuman existence and body modification?

Consumer Techno-Bodies

Cyberspace "decks" in cyberpunk are manufactured in Japan. Viruses in William Gibson are often Chinese.[1] Techno-bodies are invariably *consumer* bodies. When Stelarc swallows a camera to film his insides or when Isa Gordon wears titanium gloves and headsets, they remain firmly entrenched in consumer culture and industry that supplies the material.

Social theorists have proposed that young people's consumption represents a postmodern lifestyle in Western cities and urban centers of Third World nations (Miles 2000). Youth also constitutes one of the largest consumer groups of new media technology (Livingstone 2003), although significant differences exist between classes and the genders in consumption and skills (Wilska and Pedrozo 2007). In Miles's argument, these are lifestyle choices that determine, to a large extent, youth's identity. Within the contemporary consumer culture, goods and commodities constitute the individual. Personalization, emotional attachment to one's gadget, and stylization are processes of domesticating and individualizing technology in ways that make it become a component of one's identity.

Social theorists believe that in a world given to rapid changes, consumer identities become a means of stability (Miles 2000). Material culture studies (Miller 1987) demonstrate how goods and commodities are not "add-ons" to an individual's identity but rather *constitute* it in a close relationship. It is not the fragmentation of identity as much as a different *configuration* of identity.

One way of understanding consumer culture and the new media is to locate the role of users. Following David Marshall's (2004) innovative reading, I propose that we need to see consumers as "produsers" or "prosumers." Marshall suggests that the populace is engaged in the very *process* of cultural production. The new media subject that emerges in the use of a device is the result of a series of choices and decisions that in turn determine which game format is popular. However, Marshall does not see the implications of his argument. When users' feedback or repeated use informs further development of the interface or the technology or the game format (in computer games, in the form of patches, for example), what we must recognize is the *co-construction* of technology (even though, admittedly, overall power and profit remain in the hands of the capitalist, monopolistic manufacturer). What we see in such a techno-consumer society is the recursive nature of all new media cultures where the interface or technology is linked to the material user and the practice of usage.

Connected Bodies

When you work at your PC while listening to your favorite music on your iPod as your flight information is updated unobtrusively on your PDA-mobile, these devices are rendered invisible. People engage with the process (email, music, information) even as the medium is rendered transparent. The device becomes an extension of the user's body (Lupton 1998). Bodies in the digital age work at these two levels – (1) of being so mediated that the body itself is the medium and the techno-device disappears, and (2) the body develops a very personal attachment with the device.

Bodies are now, in William Mitchell's apposite metaphor, Me^{++}. There is a biological "core" (which itself has been informatized and data stored elsewhere) that is interfaced with and connected to networks, communities, and systems. This means our bodies' interaction with any physical space is radically affected and altered in the digital age. There are no enclosed bodies or bounded neighborhoods, only connected spaces in dynamic interaction with one another. The city permeates the body's cognitive system as never before as the materiality of the body merges with, is informed by, the streaming data from communications systems. Conversely, the space around the body is alerted to, affected by, the presence of the body. The body alters the flow of information when mobile phones, iPods, PDAs, and other devices log on to networks, download weather and transport information, explore eating places and *other* geographies. This is an extraordinary *deterritorialization* of bodies and places because one can be in a locality while also being elsewhere, say shopping online via the mobile, in a mall "situated" in another city, or a virtual warehouse. This is the experience of being in contact with multiple spaces simultaneously.

Deterritorialization also works as a mode of control. Texting individuals can coordinate their movements from different places, and be led to their meeting points via constant communication on the cell phone. No place therefore needs to be completely new because the soundscapes of information render the place familiar.

The experience of space is also an experience of time. Contemporary research has shown how mobile communications have altered peoples' experience of both space and time (Green 2002).

The mobile as a personal, "anywhere, anytime" device alters the sequence of work, leisure, and family time – from being messaged at the dinner table to personal calls at work. These are the alterations made to everyday *temporal* organization. Mobile computing – laptops, PDAs, palm tops – can ensure that work hours extend into leisure, family, or social time. Perpetual contact is a perpetual realigning and merging of many spaces in this ICT-empowered body.

Service providers for mobile phones ask us to "be in touch" with our loved ones and colleagues via the mobile. And, what is surely ironic is the metaphor of "touch" that all communications technologies use: "touch" is a *proximate* sense. It requires *physical space sharing* for "touch" to happen. The reiteration of the metaphor in communications suggests a continuing obsession with the obliteration of distance. What the technology does is to appropriate the "proper" sense of "touch" to mean communication, correspondence, and connectivity.

Networked bodies and spaces also mean that the distinction between private and public spaces is altered. A new kind of *social* space is formed that alters the very nature of social interaction.

Timo Kopomaa describes the mobile phone as a "third space," *between* the private home and the workplace. The virtual space carved out of the public or private arena when one is on the phone is a "third space." One withdraws into this "third space" when at work, with other friends, or at the dining table (Kopomaa 2004).

Since places are lived spaces, and such technologies alter the body's experience of "living," it also alters the flows of that space. External architecture and spaces are now altered so as to be sensitive to visitors' movements, cameras track material bodies and vehicles – thereby making them spaces of *hypervisibility* – and loop the information back into a database.

This means that bodies and exterior space permeate each other, make each a part of the other when they affect each other. If the incoming information cyborgizes the material body, the body's movements and actions humanize the architecture and place.

Culturally, this networked body has interesting consequences. Take the case of PCTs. Where television and the computer game drove children into the house, mobile phones and "wearable" PCTs enable them to be "outside." They offer young people the chance to explore new spaces without their parents being unduly worried – since they can be contacted and/or located through GPS – or even aware. Children who are more restricted in their mobility – since they do not drive until they're old enough – find the mobile phone a new mode of sociability. New geographies of childhood are therefore emerging (see Jones et al. 2003).

Mobile phones and "wearables" generate a new proxemics where the body carrying the mobile organizes space differently. James Katz (2006a) proposes that the mobile phone demands and creates a whole new "choreography" of the body (head angled in order to hear better, body postures). Such connected bodies mean that the negotiation of spaces by a social group is altered. A social group, where "bodies" are usually "in sync" – walking together, sitting together, speaking to one another – alters when one of them gets up and goes to answer a call on the mobile, or when a person shares a message. Music or podcasts for people to share via one speaker or microphone alter the alignment of bodies, and therefore the negotiation of space.

Clearly, connected bodies augment spaces, and spaces augment the bodies negotiating them.

Cyborg bodies are constituted in and through communication. In an innovative reading, David Gunkel (2000) suggests that the cyborg alters our notions of subjectivity because it is not an autonomous, pre-established subject that engages in communication. The cybernetic loop through which information flows back into the system and initiates responses is perhaps the easiest way of thinking about the cyborg as a subject *in* communication. The cyborg body is somewhere between the biological body and the subject constructed through the flows of information. The technology is not a prosthesis for the "original" body, but helps construct the subject. This is the augmented body, the networked body of the posthuman. The task for cyberculture, then, is to shift focus away from the individual subject that initiates conversations to the *social and material conditions in which various subject positions become visible and possible.*

Embodiment, Disembodiment, and Re-embodiment

The posthuman experience has often been seen as a new Cartesian one, the ideal state where there is pure mind and no body. The body, and therefore embodiment, has been transcended.

Embodiment is the centering of the body as the site of subjectivity, identity, and selfhood. An identity or experience is embodied because it proceeds from the body's interface with the world. It is this experience of the interface that contemporary digital technologies mediate and alter.

Disembodiment is the digitized human body, the reduction or reconfiguration of the human's personality, form, function, and behavior into a set of codes entered into a database. The Visible Human Project transforms a human body into a series of downloadable, searchable, traversable images for public consumption. The digitization of the human body in this project renders the body in a format that can be placed on a desktop, transmitted via the Internet, or added to other files. "Real" flesh-and-blood humans can be turned into a set of numbers that can be stored, transmitted, and then "reassembled" elsewhere to become a searchable image or object on a screen. The Human Genome Project and bioinformatics are both examples of the digitization of the human body.

Disembodiment allows us to "retrieve" another's personality, not necessarily by meeting him or her face to face but through a database. Disembodiment is also the extended sensory experience – augmentation – of the body through wired technologies (but, as we shall see, it is not an adequate explanation of what happens with the cyberspace experience).

Katherine Hayles argues that posthuman culture is not about leaving one's body behind, but about "extending embodied awareness in highly specific, local, and material ways that would be impossible without electronic prosthesis" (1999: 290–291). This is what I see as a new form of *re-embodiment*. On the one hand Hayles suggests that the "meat" body limits our sensorial and other abilities and we need to transcend this limitation (*disembodiment*). On the other, she proposes that extending the body's abilities through electronic and other processes remains embodiment with a difference (this would be *re-embodiment*). Re-embodiment is a convergence of technology and the body that facilitates the extension of the body into other dimensions, even while remaining meat. I termed this re-embodiment of the corporeal in technology *e-mergence*: the merger of the body with electronic technologies and the emergence of a new networked human form.

Posthuman identity is emphatically *not* an escape from the body but a foregrounding of the body within new conditions of technology. To put it differently, the posthuman is the e-mergence of a human form whose experience of and interaction with the world is mediated by technology. This means the human must now be reconceptualized as a body, self, and identity that exists in close alliance with machines and other life forms, some of which have been integrated into the body of the human. We have to see the human as an *assemblage* of wetware (organic materials), software, and hardware.

In the posthuman, the human is embedded in/connected to the device in a mutually looping relation. The human *responds* to the machine and the machine *responds* to the human in a feedback mechanism, where the organic and the inorganic are in constant *communication* with each other. The posthuman is therefore a system of communication.

The posthuman exists in a symbiotic relationship with technology where technology is not simply a functional/instrumental device but a component of the posthuman's identity itself. The posthuman is a *congeries* of software, hardware, and wetware (the organic body). The posthuman is the augmented human body. Such an augmented human is *not*, however, a universal category, as we shall see.

The utopian discourse of cyberspace (Rheingold, 1994; Turkle 1995) suggests that the transcendence of the body is to be eagerly looked forward to. This transcendence – the apotheosis of European Enlightenment ideology of the separation of the earthly, material body from the rational, intellectual, abstract mind, as Lupton (1998) points out – might not be (1) necessary or (2) advisable for all bodies. That is, transcending the body for the white race is not the same for the

African or Asian body, for whom rights, privileges, and welfare depend on the body. In the same way, transcendence of the body does not mean the same things for women as for men.

Each of the above examples suggests that the material body of the minority, the queer, or the differently abled remains in one place and retains the *corporeal* markers of identity while being able to experience a different order of reality via technology. This is a *reconfiguration* of the human rather than transcendence.

This reconfiguration of the body is the posthuman, the cyborg. With the cyber-cultural turn, we are able to store, retrieve, and alter human form, structure, and interaction (e.g., asynchronous communications such as email that allow us to be "linked" to another person, but not face to face, and mediated via text) as never before. Cyborgization today is thus only a culmination of a process of the organic–technology interaction. The *e-mergent* body is itself a medium for various technologies. It is a

- biological body (organic);
- a body compiled through visualization (X-rays, scans);
- a body compiled through simulation and modeling (the CHS or VHP);
- a body compiled through databasing (HGP).

A posthuman body – the site of the organic–technology interaction – is what Mark Hansen (2006) calls a "body-in-code." This is not the same as Gibson's famous "data made flesh" (1984: 16) or an informational body. Rather, it suggests a body whose very embodiment is constituted by its conjunction with technics. The body's primary constructive and creative power is expanded through the new interactional possibilities opened up by digital media and artificial reality. In this view, virtual reality spaces are not just a technical simulacrum engineered by technology. They are "*mixed reality*" where the virtual is "simply one more realm among others that can be accessed through embodied perception."

MIXED REALITY

The "mixed reality" paradigm as identified by Mark Hansen (the term was coined by artists Monika Fleischmann and Wolfgang Strauss) rejects the theme of bodily transcendence in virtual realities. This paradigm suggests that the body is the interface to the virtual, playing a crucial role in crossings between virtual and physical realms. It thus reinstates the body at the center.

This "mixed reality" paradigm is attractive because it refuses a simple embodiment/disembodiment binary. It rejects the real-embodied versus simulation-disembodied opposition by treating the means of access to other (virtual) realms as central in rethinking the body. We need to see the present configuration of the human body: one has to "construct an extended operational system that functions beyond the biology of the body and beyond the local space it inhabits" (Stelarc 2002: 122).

What I call re-embodiment is precisely this "extended operational system," a "mixed reality" paradigm where the (embodied) modes and means of perception – which, it must be emphasized, are also socially informed – are more significant than the contents of cyberspaces and VR environments. Re-embodiment and e-mergence return us to the body, but the body-in-technics, whose convergence with technology facilitates augmented perception, but does not reject the body. Re-embodiment or the "mixed reality" paradigm do not split the body and identity between a real-material self and the virtual one. Instead, the virtual is experienced through the real, just as the material-real is mediated by the virtual. This is the *recursive* identity formation of cyberculture.

This view, I believe, remedies the transcendence-of-the-body paradigm and tilts it in favor of retaining the social, cultural, economic, and libidinal body even in cyberspace. In order to illustrate this recursive location of the digitzed body, consider the Human Genome Project (HGP) – the project to map the human genome in its entirety.

The HGP is funded by the US government's Department of Energy. Its stated goals are the identification of the 20,000–25,000 genes in human DNA to determine the sequences of the 3 billion chemical base pairs that make up human DNA and to store this information in databases.

The body is this convergence of human and non-human/machine, of the material and the non-material, personified. And yet, this databasing is not the mere rendering of an organic body into numbers and code. It is essential to keep in mind that bodies are not neutral bits of data: they are raced, classed, gendered, and "coded" culturally. Thus, a project such as the HGP serves, as I have argued elsewhere (Nayar 2006a), as a mode of colonization – in fact, the rhetoric of the HGP (www.ornl.gov/sci/techresources/Human_Genome) uses the tropes of exploration, discovery, and conquest, all of which once constituted the language of colonialism. Originally African Americans were *not* included in the genomic survey of the human race. It was only after persistent demands that DNA samplings from African Americans were also included as part of the *human* genome (the question remains: does the initial exclusion signify a belief that the African races were *not* part of humanity?). It is crucial whose genetic make-up is being used as a baseline or standard because medical and health research will use it as a model. In fields like pharmacogenetics (where medicines will be prepared according to genetic make-up), there will be no medicines designed for the African American genetic profile. Commercial drugs based on genetic profiles will, therefore, not be designed for African American or Chicano/a people. Norton Zinder, who chaired the HGP advisory committee, had in fact mentioned social anxieties that "having the human genome at hand might provide an infinite number of new reasons for genetic discrimination by employers and insurance companies; it might even inspire Nazi-like eugenic measures" (cited in Wilkie 1993: 77; for critiques of HGP see Amani and Coombe 2005; Cross 2001; F. Jackson 1999, 2001). Bodies in databases are not simply numbers: they possess "characteristics" that, if ignored, can lead to disturbing effects in terms of medical, health, and ethical areas. The company that controls the database may choose not to be involved with "other" bodies (minority or African American). It is therefore crucial to ground the body in specific physical, cultural, racial, and ethnic terms, even in cybercultures.

Cyborg Identity and Politics

The key question in posthumanism (for an exemplary critique, see Badmington 2004) is: are we "body" or are we "mind"? The Cartesian subject – split between mind and matter – is further complicated by the interface technologies of today where both matter and mind are wired into an *external* entity that conducts thinking on its own (the computer). Since both body and mind are reconfigured with technology, where is the "essence" of the human? Where is the "real" human in this networked, digitized, and modified body–mind? Three points can be made right away.

First, the human–machine linkage in the case of cyberspace or the PC is *not* a simple human/non-human binary. "Cyborg identity" emerges precisely because we do not experience our mobile phone or the PC as a different entity. Rather, we experience the PC, cyberspace, and our act of communication through a phone as an extension of our bodies and our selves ("this is *me* speaking on the phone"). Thus, what we have is a "mixed reality" context where bodies, machines, and virtual spaces are merged into a complex entity, one supplementing the other in a symbiotic relationship. This is the new "psychotopography" (Lupton 1998: 98–99; Seltzer 1992: 19) of human bodies where the psychological and geographical spaces cross natural and technological borders and where interior and exterior states merge. This is augmented psyche, body, and experience where the borders have blurred between cyberspace and my "self," my mobile phone-generated space of communication and entertainment, and my senses.

Second, following from the above, identity in the posthuman age rests in, or is disseminated *across*, organic bodies and inorganic machines, bodies and tools, selves and cyber-entities. The "mixed reality" paradigm and the e-mergence of the posthuman suggest that identity is no longer localized in or restricted to a body.

Finally, at the very moment when bodies are increasingly retreating into cyberspace and ghettoized from communities and social interaction (except via electronic communications), the private body also becomes connected more than ever before. This dual move of privatization/disappearance and publicization/connection is a characteristic of the digital age.

Cyber-identities and cultures – to reiterate the central thesis of this book – are recursively linked to the real. The "mixed reality" paradigm does not privilege one reality over the other, but proposes that access to one form of reality is always mediated by the other.

Cybersubjectivity does not ensure the erasure of racial, sexual, or gender identities in the material world. Reactionary movements such as neo-Nazism or racist organizations such as National Alliance simply carry over their ideologies from the material world into cyberspace. Caroline Bassett (1997), for instance, found that even in virtual cities, online gender performance remained faithful to gender norms and exhibited a remarkable degree of conformity to ideals of the body. For women and minorities, who have sought rights and privileges based on their bodies, transcendence of the body is a curse rather than a blessing for the simple reason that for them the physical body is *political*. It is based on the color, ability, and ethnic identity of the physical body that welfare, employment, medical services, voting rights, and citizenship are made available to the individual. There is no "virtual citizenship" possible without a physical body.

Also, online interaction might temporarily transcend "real" identities and bodies but, as studies of computer-mediated communications (CMCs) and Usenet have shown (Boler 2007; Burkhalter 1999), *people in cyberspace use their real-life experience to make sense of, evaluate, and respond to online ones*. Online interaction – where people masquerade in terms of their gender, racial, or sexual identities – often works in such a way that users feel deceived when they discover the masquerade, that people are not what they claimed they were.

Since we can now conclude that (1) cyberculture cannot be treated as an independent entity, devoid of any connection with the "real," and (2) we live in a cyborged society, it stands to reason that we need to see how cyborgization affects identities and politics in the material, social world. Our relationship with some form of machinery – from the television to the computer – or the other alters our functioning in society. For many individuals body modification, prosthesis, and surgical interventions affect their mode of functioning and determine their employment, place of residence, and social life.

Politics is primarily about *embodied* identities. Identities are not immanent but social. Identities are not stable entities but shifting, altering and realigning on a regular basis, and situated within multiple discourses of gender, race, ethnicity, and sexuality. Identity is always a social practice, informed by other social practices. Therefore, the nature of identities generated through cyborgization is a crucial factor in determining (or predicting) the kind of politics that is possible. In this final section I look at select body identities in the posthuman age.

Aging often brings along a different pace of life, communication, sociability, and community interaction. Decay, disease, and disability are not uncommon to aged bodies.With new forms of computer and cyberspace connectivity, individuals with minimal sensory mobility can communicate. Augmented senses and limbs, for example, can enhance the individual's mobility and communication where the PC, software, and networks mediate between the (slower, weaker) body and the world. Technology enables disabled bodies to carry out routine tasks *and* helps them escape the body (into virtual worlds). Thus, in the case of aging and identity, we need to see cyborg bodies as working at two levels: the *restorative*, where the basic functions and actions of the body can be facilitated, and the *extensible*, where the aged, slow body can be escaped from into virtual worlds. In the case of the aged, cyborgization enables a different order of identity itself.

Particular kinds of cyborg bodies have been "criminalized" in the cybercultural age. The hacker's body, for example, portrayed as soft, given to inertia and junk food, is treated as a travesty of the human form in popular culture (see D. Thomas 2002). Such representations of the nerd or the hacker often suggest that their physical characteristics are attributable to their obsession with cyberspace rather than human society, inert postures (slumped in the chair in front of their PC) rather than vigorous physical activity, communication only through email and text rather than face to face. They are individuals who lack control over their bodies (Lupton 1998: 102–103).

Changing roles of men and women in families and the increasing mediatization of home life have resulted in new configurations of domestic space. Modified humans, who have acquired whole new identities through, say, transsexual surgery (men and women who undergo surgery to become the opposite gender) constitute cyborgs. With ARTs, cloning, and transnational adoption, the notion of family itself as proceeding from a family tree through sexual reproduction needs to be rethought. As Chris Gray points out, such technologies call into question the conjugal (sex) and consanguine (blood) relationships that have traditionally defined families (2001: 144).

These technologies raise interesting questions about children and parenting, and therefore about families:

- Does a cloned "sibling" or a child "created" for the purpose of stem-cell harvesting have a different role and position in a family?
- Does a lesbian, gay, or transgender couple's lab-created child acquire a different valence?
- Does a lesbian or gay couple, whose childbearing "function" is technologically determined and mediated, constitute a "family"?
- Is kinship always only heterosexual (Butler 2002)?

Clearly, families are increasingly mediated by technology, whether it is the domestic space of the house, intra-family communication, or reproductive functions.

Cyberspace is created by thousands of workers across the world, often low paid, with little chance of accessing the freedoms or utilizing the fluid identities of cyberspace. Call center and outsourcing work that depends on and informs much electronic economic and other transactions has altered the biological clocks of laboring bodies in Asia with their time schedules. Finally, informational labor acquires a higher value than manual labor in the knowledge economy. The digital divide is a real one, and, as Castells (1989, 2000) points out in his work on the informational society, technologically driven informational cultures now influence the ways in which economic and political power circulate.

In Greg Downey's (2002) terms, Internet workers are molders of (digital) technologies, but are technologies themselves. The "digital economy" is built upon the work of new technologies and "digital artisans" (Barbrook 1997). Even consumers who contribute to the expansion and development of the digital economy do *cultural* "work," an instance of what Tiziana Terranova calls "free labor," "the knowledgeable consumption of culture [that] is translated into productive activities that are pleasurably embraced and at the same time shamelessly exploited" (2000: 37). Even subcultural practices – Napster, patches developed by gamers – are absorbed into capitalist business practices, thus demonstrating how cultural "labor" undertaken as consumption or voluntary activities tie in with the "digital economy." Activities like public opinion, fixing cultural artistic standards, fashions, and taste that help the "digital economy," constitute "immaterial labour" (Maurizio Lazzarato 1996, in Terranova 2000: 40–41), but it is the *labor of bodies and real people nevertheless*.

The bodily transcendence myth reinstates the older ideology where the Westerner/upper class is envisaged as all mind, and the laboring class/Third Worlder is matter. The VR or bodily transcendence paradigm is a mixture of the virtual and the material, and one cannot critique cyberspace without understanding this particular dimension. The virtual worlds of global finance, high technology, electronic governance, and sophisticated weaponry are rooted in, derived from, sustained by, and dependent upon materials, labor, and bodies in a symbiotic relationship. Even with e-mergent bodies, politics, welfare, and rights will require a physical body.

The cultural industry thus dovetails into the software and other industries even though the "labor" of the cultural and knowledge workers is unrecognized. This linkage once again grounds cyberculture in the real and material. Are such cultural workers contributing "labor"? Do they control what they "produce" in their very act of consumption?

Cyberculture, like all forms of technological development, invariably has a connection with war. The Internet itself began life as a US Defense Department-designed mode of survival in the event of war. The experience of viewing war through the eyes of cameras "on the field" began with the Gulf War. Nanotechnological developments seek to "improve" the soldier's body with flight simulators (basically VR), to measure pilot stress and offer advice via onboard monitors, and to control behavior and improve efficiency though implants. The warrior is now a "cyborg warrior" (Gray 1997). Intelligent, remote-controlled nanoweapons and robot warriors can become perfect killing machines because they do not involve human bodies on the part of the attacking forces. A new form of conflict is now visible: information war. Infowar is usually a bloodless conflict, consisting of hacking and attacks on vital networks and databases. However, hacking has moved beyond propaganda hacking into the realm of cyber*terrorism* (see Chapter 4), where an attack that begins as infowar could cause extensive, real/material damage and death (the basis for the newest film in the Bruce Willis *Die Hard* series, *Die Hard 4*).

Citizenship

Citizenship is based on the consent of the individual to be governed. This implies that an individual has to be *able* to make rational choices, where the choice depends on *knowledge* leading to *informed* consent. The issue of citizenship or political rights is about *embodied* individuals.[2] Rights, privileges, and duties are always centered on the body – just as racism, sexism, and other such discourses first impinge upon the body.

The state, the guarantor of citizenship, increasingly loses its powers to corporations and transnational agencies and decisions. But citizenship is conferred by the power of the state, and the absence of a state signifies a certain flaw in the political machinery.

As for the individual, does a database – of his or her life, personality, loves – represent that person? Is a cyborg, whose mind is at least partly run by a computer program, an individual in the full sense of the term? Does a disembodied intelligence such as seen in cyberpunk, for example, constitute an individual?

Finally, if democracy and governance are based on the informed consent of individuals, the database and the information it contains have to be open access. Who controls this database – the state, a corporation? Are access to and knowledge/control of new technology disseminated across social strata? Or do they remain in the control of a few? Does contemporary technoscience generate new forms of racism and discriminatory moments where African American citizens or minorities lose control over the database that informatizes their bodies to private corporations (Nayar 2006a)?

If an "individual" is defined and marked by the possession of agency (the ability to determine one's course of action), then part of our agency now is facilitated and even influenced by non-organic machinery.

How is citizenship to be defined and determined in the case of cyborgs, and often in cases where massive power rests in organizations outside the nation-state?

What is needed now is a new definition of the individual and of citizenship.

In the age of shifting spaces and of multiple locations and variables, the very notion of citizenship as tied to a territory-state becomes irrelevant. Building on the thesis that cyberspace is recursively linked to material conditions, political practices, and corporeal bodies, we can rethink the notion of citizenship.

Simultaneously, local-specific rights are subsumed into larger discourses and global movements for human rights. Claims and entitlements, once the feature of citizenship, are now made beyond the state. Migrant populations participate in these demands for rights (now coded as a demand for *human* rights). Borderless migrant workers' programs, borderless market conditions, and global flows of capital entail a different status for workers – who, critics argue, possess limited civil rights even if they are not citizens (Soysal 1994). In Aihwa Ong's (1999) influential argument, flexibility, migration, and relocations are desired over stability and lead to what is called "flexible citizenship." Building on this notion of "flexible citizenship," Ong (2006) proposes that in the neoliberal theories of governance that have emerged in the context of global capitalism and ICT-dominated culture, governments are no longer interested in governing every individual. Such a neoliberal theory places the onus of development, security, and agency on the individual. Self-enterprising and self-responsible individuals – who are also flexible, mobile, and economically productive – are true citizens. The increasing withdrawal of the state from welfare mechanisms meant to cater to all citizens suggests that Ong's theory is correct (Ong 2006: 502). In such a context, cyberspace, argues Ong, becomes the space for political and citizenship activism.

The Internet facilitates a particular form of "flexible citizenship": "cultural citizenship." Cultural citizenship is the use of cultural artifacts and practices to define and regulate the relationship with the state. For some thinkers, this relationship is one of subjection (T. Miller 1993). However, the relationship between the citizen and the state, even when subject to regulation, is never completely totalitarian, especially not so in the cultural realms (Fiske 1989; Hermes 2006: 302). It is in the spread and consumption of the mass media that the digital age makes its presence felt in very powerful ways.

Mass media, including genres such as soap operas and the news report, help disseminate ideas and build communities. They build identities, create and erase differences, and help emotional linkages. In the age of Internet popular entertainment, the "informed consent" of citizens occurs on an entirely different plane. A greater knowledge of activities, experiences, identities, and differences is now possible. The screen is the "space of appearance" (Silverstone 2007), where the Other becomes visible to us, where the thus far absent Other appears to us. Thus the media constructs and expands our imaginary, where the elsewhere and the Other are also *here*. This enables a cultural citizenship where experiences and identities are more easily disseminated.

What we can argue, following Hermes, is that we may not be creating new citizens as much as *new forms of citizenship practices* through a greater participation in cultural "encounters" and practices. Cyborged citizens – those that are privileged to have access – receive news, entertainment, and information 24/7, on the move, anywhere in the world. Networks and communities are scattered across the world and their activities available to their members all the time via the World Wide Web. This makes for a different order and quality of "informed consent" on the part of its citizens. It is in this sense of the new "mediapolis," where the Other in Abu Ghraib or Bosnia can appeal to people and communities across the world, that a cultural citizenship is formed.

Such a cultural citizenship is also about increasingly mediated transnational populations. Diasporic and migrant populations maintain their dual "connections" via the Internet, email, and the telecommunications infrastructure. What also occurs is a multiple positioning of national and cultural identity across the world where migrants from, say, India connect with Indians across the First World, thereby distributing a kind of "Indianness" globally (for a study see *Global Networks*, 6/2 (2006)).

Yet, even as we valorize the possibilities for cyborged citizens we need also to be alert to the other side of cyber-citizenship. Does cyborgization apply to all segments of the world's populations? Studies, for instance, of the "Arab Internet" have revealed the inherent divides within Internet cultures (see Warf and Vincent 2007). Will the world provide only for the technological haves and abandon the technological have-nots? Would ethnic minorities also acquire – or require – cyborg citizenship? These are not questions of technology but rather of political economy and culture.

It is possible that advanced technologies become *discriminatory*, excluding large sections of people from the benefits of medicine, welfare, and political rights. The authorities and organizations that control the database may choose not to be involved with minority bodies, as argued above. Posthuman bodies, acquirable only by the wealthy, run the risk of creating a new ghettoization. Cyber-bodies are not simply information-bodies (to return to Eugene Thacker's argument cited above): they retain a large component of the organic-material. Thus cyborgization and genetic manipulation are not simply about informationalization; they have concrete consequences for physical bodies. We need to hold on to this thought as a necessary corrective to the ebullient hagiography of cybercultures.

NOTES

1   I have elsewhere detailed the various forms of posthuman bodies in the fiction of William Gibson (Nayar 2008b).
2   Chris Hables Gray thus suggests a new Bill of Rights for the USA where "business corporations and other bureaucracies are not citizens or individuals, nor shall they ever be" (2001: 27).

4 SUBCULTURES

CHAPTER PLAN

Blogs

Webcams and Women

Cybercrime and Hacking

Tactical Media, Hacktivism, and Cyberterrorism
Tactical Media and Infowar
Hacktivism
Cyberterrorism

Fans and Fan Communities
Individual and Community
Informational Space
The Private and the Public
Fandom and Politics
    (i)   Consumerism
  (ii) Identity
 (iii) Agency

Cyberhate

Cyberfeminism
Feminist Cyberpunk
Cyberfeminist Art

In every age, dominant classes and groups seek to control technology in order to reinforce their interests. However, subordinated and marginalized groups also appropriate the same technology for purposes of political resistance and subversion.

The Internet and the new communications technologies are no exception and subcultural practices have flourished in cyberspace.

Subculture, as Sarah Thornton defines it, is "subordinate, subaltern or subterranean" (1997: 1). Subcultures are often – but not always, since there could be formations *within* a mainstream community (say, the Goth scene within punk) – the marginalized, oppressed, or illicit groups that share a common ideology and cultural practices. Punk, as Dick Hebdige's (1979) work demonstrated, is the finest example of subculture, where punk's clothing, music, and attitudes were in sharp contrast with mainstream cultures of the opera, formal clothing, and museum arts. Subcultural practices often evoke moral panics, anxieties, and even oppressive measures by mainstream cultures and the state because they are seen as being subversive, antisocial, and malicious. Finally, membership and peer recognition in subcultural groups is a guarantor of identity.

Subcultures are social groups that possess or deploy specific cultural forms and characteristics where these forms/characteristics are used for the political purpose of opposing high or dominant culture.

Cyberspace enables the existence, indeed proliferation, of subcultures, countercultures, and politically edged cultural movements. Electronic or cyber-subcultures are a different use of the new ICTs, for purposes recognized and categorized as illegal or antisocial by the society and state.

SUBCULTURE

Usually a group of practices occurring on the fringes of mainstream culture, and frequently in opposition to it. These could be cultures formed around particular political ideas, fashion, or taste in music. Subcultures are unofficial cultural formations that seek to escape or subvert state and corporate power, often through the use of similar technologies. With the advent of ICTs, subcultures have taken to online lives and communities that work at breaking the corporate stranglehold of information, software, and cultural meanings.

Electronic network cultures are essentially a set of *social practices* that use computers and digital technology. Networks, PCs, and technologies become what people make of them – the purposes they use these for, the consequences and modes of use, and so on. That is, we need to rethink technology as technology-in-action, taking on the form, shape, and function of its use by people: "legitimate," subversive, "terrorist," or emancipatory. Further, treating information technologies as a system of social practices also helps us see how categories such as the cybercriminal, the hacker, "subversive" use, or "legitimate" user are *socially constructed*. That is, the "criminal" is a social category where the criminal nature of an action is not immanent but attributed by norms, the law, and a culture.

Subcultural uses of technologies are very often outside the purview of businesses and governments. They are often unregulated and are positioned as marginal to the mainstream use of such technologies. What I am calling "subcultures" expands the semantic scope of the term significantly to include social practices that are not simply counter to mainstream culture, but also deemed illegal and threatening. They might use what is called "alternative media," media "produced outside the forces of market economics and the state," such as those used by protest groups, political dissidents, and even fans (Atton 2004: 3). Or they might use "mainstream" media for their purposes and thereby subvert the latter's statist, market-driven agenda. (However, it is also commonplace to see what was once subcultural becoming a routine phenomenon.)

Thus cyber*crime* – ranging from hate speech to credit card fraud – is also a subcultural practice where mainstream technology is appropriated for ends deemed illicit by governments, society, and structures of corporate capitalism. While this expansion of the meaning of the term might seem to treat crime and a subversive *cultural* practice as similar, I believe it is justified because both "crime" and "subversive cultural practice" are socially constructed categories. Cultural practices in different regions and cultures often seem bewildering and objectionable to others. They thus lay themselves open to political intervention – human rights campaigns and social reform movements in history are examples here – because cultural difference often translates into political action.

Secret societies and fringe organizations with a web presence now attract greater membership across a broader geographical territory. The propaganda and information exchange on which their conspiracy theories, cult beliefs, and cultural practices depend are easily transmitted. For example, the Grand Encampment of the Knights Templar of the USA (www.knightstemplar.org/) – a subcultural group that acquired greater visibility after the publication of Dan Brown's *The Da Vinci Code* (2003) – shares space with the CIA (since the latter is a "secret service") on www.theinsider.org/resources/orgs/, a website that provides information about secret societies. The Extropian Institute closed in 2006, although its material at the time of writing was still online (www.extropy.org/). Its belief in cryogenics and posthuman life was explicitly identified as a subculture on project.cyberpunk.ru/idb/extropians.html.

Collective subcultural forms, especially in a country where ICTs are beginning to transform social life, include anti-state protests and activist groups. The massive anti-dam movement in India, the Narmada Bachchao Andolan (NBA), constitutes just such a subcultural form. The Friends of River Narmada group (hosted at www.narmada.org, but not a part of the NBA) is, in its own words, "an international coalition of organisations and individuals (mostly of Indian descent)."

Central to this subcultural project is the collection of alternative forms of development. Reports, scientific studies, opinions, and personal comments about alternatives to the big dam syndrome archived on this site constitute a massive resource for those who are opposed to present development trends in India. This kind of linkage of sub- or countercultural groups has been facilitated by ICTs, and is therefore a significant phenomenon in India's cyberculture.

Global coalitions against the Iraq war (e.g., www.moveon.org; www.unitedforpeace.org) would be subcultural in the purely technical sense that they are against the state. However, ironically, their popularity and large memberships suggest that they are not on the fringes of mainstream society but very much a part of global political culture. Another online global organization, www.oneworld.org/, looks at anti-globalization movements, human rights campaigns, and poverty alleviation efforts across the world (from 1,600 organizations). Subcultural forms can be mundane and unintended uses of high tech. They can be individualist, communitarian, or global. They could be simply about the everyday life of an individual or they could be major threats to institutional structures. We shall move from relatively "innocent" subcultural forms to more "dangerous" ones in the following discussion.

Blogs

Blogs are perhaps no longer subcultural, considering their sheer heterogeneity, numbers, and expanding use on the World Wide Web. Their enormous popularity and proliferation suggest that they have become a folk cultural form (Pareles 2006, in Bell 2007: 5).

Blogs are essentially a form of online life-writing. Autobiographies and personal essays are traditional forms of announcing one's self, constructing a persona for the world to consume, and presenting a particular face to the public. Structurally, the blog consists of *textual* elements (diary notations, hobbies, quotes, favorite online sites), *visual graphic* elements (photographs, icons, weblinks), and *interactive* elements (online discussion, email IDs). The postings could be either self-focused or other-focused (Hevern 2004).

If there is a logic and "spirit" for blogs, it would be that of *perpetual change*. Here "perpetual change" refers to the endless construction and reconstruction of the private self for potentially unlimited public consumption. Further, blogs also represent *augmented* communication because of their high degree of interactivity and potential global spread. This is the *spirit* of blogging. It underwrites how the presentation software alters (for greater visibility, attention, and attractiveness) how we write, and how we judge other blogs.

As an active, organic form, blogs represent life-writing that is never complete. There is, as a result, a certain unfinished and indefinite structure to the blog. Blogs are a means of constructing the subject for public consumption. In terms of autobiography, the blog is a "celebration of the self-aware subject" (Kitzmann 2003: 52).

BLOGGING

Blogging is the construction of online diaries or blogs, which often include personal webpages that are available for public reading and response. Blogging has been defined as "reverse-chronological posting of individually authored entries that include the capacity to provide hypertext links and often allow comment-based responses from readers" (Bruns and Jacob 2006: 2–3).

Blogging assumes, like life-writing, that the subject is *aware* of himself or herself and that this subject is worth knowing. But blogging constructs the self even as it enables this construction to forge a community link. Blogging is therefore an interesting negotiation of the private and the public where to announce one's private thoughts/fears/desires or to record one's home is to be a part of the community. The community is in fact constructed through this sharing of the private space.

Blogs *extend* personal homepages, inviting the viewer to meet the self, whose public face is the homepage. They advertise the self, or rather those aspects of the self the individual wants advertised. (Studies have shown that most homepages do not necessarily reveal the author's personhood at all; see Killoran 2003. Empirical studies such as that by Qian and Scott 2007 have suggested that bloggers who *know* their target audience – especially offline – are more likely to reveal themselves in their blogs). Thus, blogs may not carry any visual representation or information concerning the author (visual anonymity), and texts might not give away more private details than the author thinks necessary (discursive anonymity).

Blogs generate a *hyperlinked self* where every self/author is a node in a rapidly proliferating, non-linear, fragmented rhizome: a whole universe of linked personal blogs/selves.

Politicians have increasingly taken to online lives as a supplement to their speeches and manifestos. Journalists use blogs to publish those stories that their newspaper did not/could not carry. Academic debates and exchanges and politically significant interventions may not find a print life, but could very well appear online in blogs. Juan Cole's controversial Informed Comment blog (www.juancole.com/) with its anti-Iraq war opinions was perhaps instrumental in Yale's denying him tenure – thus demonstrating the public–political consequences of life-writing. Political blogs such as Cole's or a politician's mark the democratizing dimension of blogging, as Stephen Coleman (2005) has argued. This democratization is made possible through three key features of blogs. First, blogs constitute a bridge between private and civic spaces. Second, unlike speeches and formal expressions, blogs allow the articulation of incomplete thoughts and ideas. Finally, blogs allow access – if access to a PC is possible – to local, national, and global debates for everyone. Unlike debates in parliaments or special forums, where credentials rather than opinions govern the legitimacy of speech, blogs allow anyone and everyone to hold and articulate political opinions. More importantly, according to Coleman, blogs enable politicians and parties to "listen" to the groundswell of subjective but politically significant opinions.[1] For academics, it allows them to comment on areas outside their immediate areas of expertise but still run informed and widely circulating debates about these (Glenn 2003).

The scale of self-expression for public consumption in blogging is considerably different from any other form of communication. This is the logic and spirit that drives blogging: that there is possibly unlimited freedom to express oneself, just as there is *potentially* an unlimited number of readers/listeners. Blogs also allow the dissemination of information that mainstream media leave out. For example, military blogs like Milbloggers provide detailed accounts of US military action in various parts of the globe. BlogLeft (www.gseis.ucla.edu/courses/ed253a/blogger.php) provides critical views of the former Bush administration, especially its war "policies." In Iran, journalist Sina Mottallebi was one of the first bloggers to be arrested on charges of "undermining national security through security activities" (Kahn and Kellner 2007: 528). China has insisted that blogs register with the government. All these examples illustrate the power of blogs as social media, where an individual converses with the world about real matters that occur in the real world, even if the conversation is between people who may never meet.

Blogging is inherently dialogic. Unlike the traditional autobiography, the blog elicits opinions and responses. It is a conversation with the world, it accounts for the Other, and writes in *response to the response of the Other*. Blogs are private expressions that are imbued with the *spirit* of public reception/hearing (the latter being the case with cell phones). The blog is written *anticipating* a response, and this makes it dialogic. However, it is also possible that blogging becomes an example of "phatic culture" where "conversations" serve the purpose of social networking but without the informational or dialogic intent (V. Miller 2008). In this sense, blogging becomes an instance of media culture where substantive content is subordinated to the effort and purpose of simply maintaining a network. It becomes an end in itself, and does not constitute the full scope of "communication."

Blogs are not necessarily truly "subcultural," since they now constitute a mainstream use of the Internet and ICTs. However, blogs enable the expression of intimate details in online personal diary form – details that would not find print expression in many mainstream cultures. The confessional diary that the blog enables reaches out to many people because it is online and free. In certain cases, the intimate blog constitutes a subcultural form in a mainstream culture where the intimate is shut out, religiously, from the public gaze. For example, *Belle de Jour*, a novel published anonymously in 1999, was supposedly adapted from the blog of a London callgirl and became instantly sensational. A blog by an Indian woman journalist (thecompulsiveconfessor.blogspot.com/) made her sex life a matter of public consumption. Her revelations about her promiscuity attracted over 400 hits a day (the blog became controversial and famous enough for the UK's *Telegraph* to run a feature on her; see Dhillon 2007). In the Indian context, such a blog was a subcultural form (it gave inspiration to others, like the bisexual blogger at closetconfessions.wordpress.com/) because it was attempting to do something that print and mainstream cultures in India refused to do: transform the intimate life into a public document.

Within new forms of cybercultures, mobile blogs (moblogs) are an increasingly common application of software and communication technologies. What makes this now legitimate "program" (Nokia has its Lifeblog software, for example, and there are dedicated platforms like www.orfay.com) fascinating is that it did not come out of the tech or R&D labs but was created by the social software community and general users existing on the World Wide Web. Thus, the blogosphere is a world created almost entirely by the users of technology.

Moblogs contribute to the democratization of news, and thus break the monopoly of media corporations and the state when individuals can photograph/film and upload events from anywhere in the world. Increased communication and networking transform the mass and the crowd into a "smart mob" (Rheingold 2002). In 2004, the University of South Carolina distributed camera phones to amateur reporters and designated them as election observers, providing them with a platform, the Wireless Election Connection Moblog (www.wec-textamerica.com), and thus significantly altering the nature of the election and the student community's role. When

US Speaker Trent Lott made some racist remarks in 2003, the main newspapers had only minor coverage. It was the blogging community that spread the details and created a public awareness campaign that eventually led to his removal.

Moblogs are thus a part of the *social* media, where the content is not always produced by one person but is created through links, other blogs, and reader comments. In this it also serves as a community platform, building an audience of readers and viewers through *augmented* communication.

Moblogs may be topical, personal, or political (see Döring and Gundolf 2006). They may serve as social networking tools or venues for the expression of serious, politically significant opinions. In most cases, however, they are records of everyday lives and the ordinary. It is therefore interesting to note that one of the most popular of the everyday personal blogs came from Iraq in July 2004, uploaded logs by American soldiers posted there (then at www.yafro.com and "CrashtheSoldier" at www.blueherenow.com). Here the question is of mass media communication and *agency*. Individuals now can be alert to social settings – their ecology – and record them with little or no help from corporate media houses.

As an example, journalists' reviews of products or movies no longer constitute the only word on the subject. Bloggers write in with their responses, which might very well contradict what has been printed in the public domain. Blogging thus adds a new dimension to the theme of "truth" itself by filling in the gaps and correcting the errors in public domain documents and discussions. Blogging must be treated as an extension and alternative to dominant public discourses and therefore constitutes subculture.

Workblogs share information about particular professions and have been a major success. In fact, corporate offices now seek to convert blogs into profit, using popular blogs to transmit information about new products (Power 2006).

Webcams and Women

Webcams became popular as a means of broadcasting one's self with accompanying visuals, telecasting the mundane and everyday life of ordinary individuals and offering a chance to be *seen*. These are technologies of *self-representation for public consumption*, a cybercultural form that combines amateur video filming (the home video), theater, autobiography, and spectacle.

Commentators have argued that such a form of representation extends and expands the spectator's role, resulting in excessive voyeurism (John Dvorak 2000, cited in White 2003: 10). Its biggest selling point is its "liveness" – webcams can telecast 24/7. Thus webcams bring the spectator as close to the real as possible with no apparent intervention or mediation by technology.

Webcams are generically linked to autobiography, even as webcam realism parallels the documentary movie. Reality TV shows such as *Big Brother* are mediated versions of the webcam subcultures.

What webcams represent is a subcultural form of converting the everday into a spectacle. They empower the ordinary (wo)man-on-the-street to place her-/himself on the airwaves (though s/he cannot ensure viewership). Individuals are free to indulge in recording what nobody else might find worthy of recording. Unlike the soap operas, dramas, and film documentaries of the media conglomerates, webcams have a different relationship with the everyday material world of the individual. The webcam makes a hero/ine of us all. It transforms the mundane details of our everyday lives into the subject of a soap opera that is out there for people to see. In other words, it allows us to transform our everyday life into theater and invites us to be *performers*. Its linkage to the real world is that it goes one step further in the mediatization of the world: it converts our everyday into drama for public consumption (or, as I have argued in Chapter 2 on popular cyberculture, transforms a private act like shopping online or surfing into a spectacle for surveillance by search engines, service providers, and others).

Webcam sites run by women represent a subcultural form that has found large-scale popularity in recent years. Women's webcam sites present a complex negotiation between identity, self-representation, gender, and spectatorship. While the camera places the woman's image as something ready for consumption, it is not the "pure" objectification of cinema. Webcams do not allow unhindered access by (male) spectators into the woman's private domain.[2] The difference here is that in the case of women's webcam sites, the woman controls her representation.[3] Most webcam sites run by women are clear that, despite the overwhelming view that webcam girls offer up salacious and/or pornographic material, they do *not* intend to serve spectators in this way (White 2003: 16). In this way, the women assert their control over the technology, their self-representation, and, most significantly, the spectators. This subcultural form therefore becomes a mode of altering the gendered power equations within the technological realm and of empowering women.

Cybercrime and Hacking

If blogs and webcams represent a relatively safe subcultural use of cybercultural technologies, then cybercrime and hacking represent a distinctly more "dangerous" form. The computer, the Internet, electronic networks, and new information technologies have generated novel threats to individual, corporations, and nation-states.

- Personal details may be stolen from your PC and sold or delivered to third parties.
- Email messages can end up corrupting your hard drive through the deliberate spread of viruses.
- Defamatory messages and information may be placed on government or corporate websites.
- Denial-of-service crimes involve flooding a computer resource (e.g., a web server) with more requests than it can handle. This causes the server to crash, thus denying authorized users the service it offers.

- Masquerade is a frequent phenomenon where, by stealing a password, someone can steal an entire identity.
- Locating and intercepting online financial transactions can result in actual theft.
- Cyberstalking has resulted in well-publicized cases of pedophilia, where children are "groomed" through online interaction as a preliminary to offline encounters with perpetrators.
- White supremacist and extreme right-wing groups run hate campaigns using the Net (often called "cyberhate").

These are some of the most common forms of cybercrime in the last decades of the twentieth century, reported with alarming frequency in newspapers, government statements, and surveys (Dowland et al. 1999). With the progress of the "information age" (Webster 2003), the darker side of electronic networks and the Internet began to be revealed through the 1990s. Businesses and governments cite threats to their profits, national security, and social structures. Post-9/11 cyberterrorism has acquired new significance with the discovery that terrorists are also now "Net-savvy." Threats to the family, to children, to profits, and to the nation-state are all increasingly linked to electronic cultures of the digital age and are accompanied by calls to tighten security, regulate the Internet, and frame laws regarding cybercrime.

At this point it is important to note the distinction between *crime* and *deviance* because not all activities on the World Wide Web or using computers are classifiable, with any degree of certitude, as "criminal." *Crime* describes a set of actions prohibited by *law* and which therefore constitute recognizable offenses entailing penalties by the state. *Deviance* includes actions that contravene, contradict, or are in antagonistic relation with informal – that is, not necessarily codified by law – *social* norms or codes, established moral values, and cultural practices. The problem with cybercrime is that nations have different definitions and views on what constitutes crime or deviance.

With the rise of ICTs a new form of criminal emerged. Technologies such as computer-mediated communication (CMC) and networking that constitute the vital cogs in the wheels of multinational business are also, ironically, the modes of cybercrime. The global nature of the Internet enables crime to be transborder too, where victim and perpetrator need not share the same geographical space.

Cybercrime is defined as "computer-mediated activities which are either illegal or considered illicit by certain parties and which can be conducted through global electronic networks" (Thomas and Loader 2000: 3). These "illicit" actions are classified as criminal by the *law* in various cultures and countries. Thus, electronic cultures *facilitate* certain kinds of crime because they *enable certain kinds of social interaction* (mass connectivity, group talk, anonymity, instantaneous communication, non-spatial locationality, dispersion of "users"). While the actions – violence, stealing, stalking – are themselves not new crimes or are no less shocking than earlier forms, they have taken on new significance precisely because of the facilitating role communications technology plays in their execution. That is, while theft or violence are not in themselves new, what is novel are their modes of operation, extent of reach, degree of damage, and the increased visibility facilitated by the new technologies.

At the individual level, cybercrime includes invasion of privacy, child pornography, and bank card frauds. Porn, soliciting, sexually explicit material, or euthanasia advocacy need not necessarily be legally prohibited in specific cultures, but these are actions that might be deemed to be socially unacceptable and therefore would constitute "deviance" rather than "crime."

At larger, national and global levels cybercrime includes hacking into military and economic databanks, misinformation, and activity that cripples a state's operations. Indeed, by the 1990s cybercrime became widespread enough to warrant a separate cell in the UK – the National High-Tech Computer Crime Unit (NHTCU) – which subsequently merged with the Serious Organized Crime Agency.

The Center for Strategic and International Studies' *Report of the CSIS Homeland Defense Project* in May 2001 identified the following types of threats in the "new environment" of globalized ICTs:

- The threat of disruption of communication flows, economic transactions, electric power grids, and political negotiations.
- The threat of exploitation of sensitive, proprietory, or classified information.
- The threat of manipulation of information for political, economic, military, or troublemaking purposes.
- The threat of destruction of information or of critical infrastructure (Borchgrave et al. 2001: xvii–xviii).

David Wall provides a useful classification of cybercrime.

(i)   Cyber-trespass: entering into other people's property/databases and causing damage (including viruses, defacement of websites, hacking),
(ii) Cyber-deceptions and thefts: stealing money or property and intellectual property violations (including credit card frauds),
(iii) Cyber-porn: violating norms and laws of obscenity,
(iv) Cyber-violence: causing violence – psychological and/or physical – to the person (including cyber-rape, stalking, hate mail). (2001: 3–7)

HACKING

Hacking is the unauthorized entering of a computer database for any purpose. Now treated as a new form of crime, hacking has also led to the glorification of the hacker as a person who breaks security codes when he – it is invariably a male – penetrates computer systems. The **hacktivist** is a hacker who uses his computer skills for political ends in order to effect social change.

The nerdy college boy or software engineer hacker is probably the most publicized criminal of the informational age. Extremist groups and political dissenters also use the Internet for their purposes. But arguably the most "glamorous" form of cybercrime is hacking.

Hacking has aroused two very different kinds of cultural response. One treats the hacker as a social misfit, a criminal, and a data thief. The other sees the hacker as a hero who is able to subvert and crash the security systems of profiteering and ruthless corporations whose profits are built on exploitative labor and secrecy. We shall examine both views here.

Classifying hacking as crime and demonizing the hacker ensures that the state or the corporation controls the definition of "normalcy" in CMCs while also justifying control, surveillance, and punishment. In many cases, as Nissenbaum (2004) suggests, demonization and criminalization are to do with vested (corporate) interests in information and the digital media. A social ontology of cyberspace emerged in the 1980s and 1990s where a variety of social institutions and social agents – web masters, web surfers, vendors, cybercrime specialists – were identified. These are *defined* roles. But there are also agents whose roles are not within these defined and therefore legitimized spheres. Such agents are the hackers. They represent anarchy, lawlessness, resistance – especially to private *property* (copyrighted software) – and decentralization. Nissenbaum's argument locates hackers and hacking in their *social* contexts of laws, institutions, profits, and criminality, and thus shows how online work finally connects and feeds back into the real and the material. This is of course made clearer when the hacker is arrested in widely televised news reports: the *body* of the hacker, who lived all his life in a virtual world, is taken off to courts and prisons (on the hacker body see D. Thomas 2002).

The hacker is driven less by the aim of profit – though he or she might stand to gain financially from the operation – than by the intricacies of computer technology and security settings. It is the technology itself that drives the "innocent" hacker or the techno-brat. However, "malicious" hackers set out to spread damage (extracting information and corrupting networks). Hackers become figures of subcultural resistance to technology because they symbolize, as the definition suggests, "unauthorized" access.

Hackers who break into systems and networks to steal data in order to sell the information are of an entirely different order. This kind of hacking is espionage, specifically corporate espionage, where information translates into money. Stealing IDs, illegal fund transfer, or sale of information to business rivals constitutes the work of such "information mercenaries."

Finally, there are political groups and their sympathizers who use computers, electronic networks, and information processing to further their political ends. Illegal political activity, hate campaigns, fund raising by separatists, and parallel social movements that subvert the state, with or without accompanying real-time military operations, are now facilitated by ICTs. Electronic insurgency and information terrorism – often known as cyberterrorism, defined by Dorothy Denning (2000) as "the convergence of terrorism and cyberspace" – both appropriate the state's own networks and structures to further subversive political ends.

However, hackers are not simply techno-savvy criminals. The virulent fear of and aversion to hackers, Douglas Thomas (2000) painstakingly demonstrates, masks a fear of technology itself. Contemporary technology is built upon a logic and culture of secrecy. Passwords and codes rule the domains of cyberspace. As Thomas points out, the hacker frequently can only be caught in possession of such passwords and codes: to possess the code is to perform the act of hacking. The password, which is supposed to be secret and which identifies the user as legitimate, is stolen and used to enter systems illicitly. Within this process of verifying identity, anybody with the password becomes legitimate: the hacker gets into the system irrespective of who he or she really is. In other words, to possess a password is to possess a virtual identity for the electronic network or database no matter what the real-life identity of the hacker is. Hacking is built upon this separation of the body from the identity of the hacker. This leads us to two specific features of hacking and cybercrime.

First, for law enforcement agencies, crime needs a body, a local place, and a spatial specificity. As Majid Yar (2006: 18) points out, cybercrimes are located in a *non-spatial environment*: identifying and policing locations with crime-inducing characteristics – as is done with the usual forms of law enforcement – is impossible. Further, there is no "where-did-the-crime-take-place?" kind of question possible because, as noted earlier, the perpetrator and the scene of the crime do not have to share the same geographical space.

Second, unlike in "traditional" crime, it is people with greater access, income, privileges, and education and occupying middle and even upper classes of the social order who are the perpetrators. The usual patterns of criminal behavior – poorer socioeconomic backgrounds, deprivation, lack of resources, below-average education – do not apply to hackers (Yar 2006: 19).

Hackers, as represented by films like *War Games* (1983) and *Hackers* (1995), possess certain characteristics: they are usually very young, from the mid-teens to late twenties, male, underachievers in other areas, lacking social and interpersonal skills, and fascinated by technology. Anxieties about subcultures as symbolic of the "fragmentation of the social" (as Chris Jenks's 2005 work on subculture is subtitled) translate into anxieties about brilliant but unethical and intelligent individuals whose social responsibility is conspicuous by its absence. Here the breach of corporate databanks or resistance to state authority is seen as a breakdown of the social rather than as resistance to an authoritarian, exploitative regime. The brilliance with technology might seem threatening to many, but the hacker also elicits an admiring response for his or her unique abilities (Dowland et al. 1999: 720).

Hacking can be treated as a form of *passing* and *masquerade*. In an environment where identities are free-floating and vague, the hacker assumes many faces and identities with a purpose. Hacking is regarded as antisocial, ironically, in an environment which encourages the creation of false and/or unverifiable identities.

These abilities are not simply about being able to illegally access databases. Hackers have also been at the forefront of the computer revolution because they write codes that are just as good as any "legitimate" one. Thus, computer programs that enable people to enter government or corporate websites are also codes like, say, Microsoft software – but the consequences of using these programs are very different from running Internet Explorer. Hackers have developed sophisticated programs (BO2K, L0phtCrack, Floodnet; see Furnell 2002: 119, 123, 178–181) that enable "denial of service" attacks and password stealing (technically called "phishing"). If the legitimate program writer develops codes for socially and legally acceptable uses/users, the hacker develops them for a different, illicit purpose. This does not detract from the fact that, despite their illicit use, hackers also help move the computer or the software technology forward. It is the social perception of their work that renders their innovations "illegal."

Hacker groups in the 1980s and 1990s (Legion of Doom, Masters of Deception, Chaos Computer Club) represented a *new social configuration* enabled and empowered by technology. Here, rather than the view of the solitary, antisocial hacker, we see a new form: a group of hackers who resist authority and breach security systems. Like punk bands and subcultures, hacker groups constitute a micropolitics at the level of computer users. Hacking conventions bring together these gifted individuals, just as any "legitimate" form of socializing.

Hackers, at least according to the Hacker Manifesto (first published under the title "The Conscience of a Hacker," 1986) by Loyd Blankenship (available at www.phrack. org/archives/7/P07-03), argue that monopolistic, capitalist corporations should not control services such as the web and the phone. The Manifesto presents the hacker not as a criminal but as an intellectual explorer who defies and breaks into the systems devised by profiteering capitalists. The Manifesto depicts the hacker as a gifted individual who threatens the "system" that seeks to control knowledge and data. Finally, the Manifesto also sees hackers as contributing to social causes and global justice because they are often part of anti-racist and anti-war protests.

Hacking has received a great deal of attention from intellectuals and software researchers for other reasons. Refusing to treat hacking simply as a criminal trespass into databanks, researchers at MIT, for instance, produced the Hacker Ethic (a term coined and popularized by Steven Levy in *Hackers: Heroes of the Computer Revolution*, 1984). The Hacker Ethic argued for six main principles in hacking:

- Access to computers ought to be free, unlimited, and total.
- Information ought to be free.
- Decentralization is to be preferred over authority.
- Hackers cannot be defined in terms of their educational qualifications or career graph.
- Computers can be the source of great beauty and art.
- Computers can improve your life.

Here the computer becomes a source of a better lifeworld itself. This transforms the perception of technology – the computer and now the World Wide Web are sources of individual and collective security, pleasure, and sociability.

Social theorists building on ideas of subculture formations suggest that hacking, like other forms of juvenile delinquency, is located in a social context. Peer association, group pressures, the need for recognition, and mutual exchanges about programs are sustained forms of interaction and behavior among the hacker subculture (Rogers 2000). Dorothy Denning's description of the hacker and *his* culture (the masculine pronoun is deliberate, considering the fact that studies have revealed the predominance of men in hacker cultures; see, for instance, Yar 2006: 35–36) captures the social ethos of hacking:

> Most hackers do it [hacking] for the challenge, thrill, and social fun. Although the stereotype image of a hacker is someone who is socially inept and avoids people in favor of computers, hackers are more likely to be in it for the social aspects. They like to interact with others on bulletin boards, through electronic mail, and in person. They share stories, gossip, opinions, and information; work on projects together; teach younger hackers; and get together for conferences and socializing … By sharing the secrets they learn, hackers also gain recognition from their peers and entry into exclusive hacker groups. (Denning 1991)

Thus hackers see themselves as participating in a cultural formation, albeit an unauthorized or unacceptable one. This is why hacker culture can be classified as subculture: it reconfigures technology and social relations by subverting the rules, laws, and social norms regarding the use of technology. It works in opposition to monopolistic, capitalist, statist regulation and perception of the new technologies.

Tactical Media, Hacktivism, and Cyberterrorism

Cyberterrorism can be described as an extreme form of political hacking, where extremists, terrorists, and activists appropriate computer and information technologies for violent, subversive, or protest purposes directed against specific bodies, organizations, dominant groups, or states. In order to see it as a form of political hacking, we need to locate cyberterrorism on the same plane as *hacktivism* (activist hacking, see below).

Other forms of technological activism are not quite "criminal" but constitute an important component of the political realms of cybercultures. Net activism is the use of software and the Internet to spread propaganda, campaigns, and protest.

Tactical Media and Infowar

The term "tactical media" draws upon an earlier term, "tactical television," coined during the first Next Five Minutes (N5M) conference in Amsterdam in 1993. The idea was to explore the tactical potential of consumer electronics, especially the video camcorder, as a means of social mobilization. In 1996 a group of media activists in Rome formed the "tactical media crew" (www.tmcrew.org) to cover Chiapas and the Zapatistas, Noam Chomsky, feminism, and free radio.

TACTICAL MEDIA

Tactical media are based on temporary alliances provoked by an immediate issue or event that utilize media forms to protest, campaign, and organize opinions for anti-government or anti-corporate purposes.

Tactical media, writes Geert Lovink, are mainly the "media of campaigns rather than of broadly based social movements" (2002: 255). Tactical media, as defined by the Critical Art Ensemble (CAE), refer to:

> a critical usage and theorization of media practices that draw on all forms of old and new, both lucid and sophisticated media, for achieving a variety of specific noncommercial goals and pushing all kinds of potentially subversive political issues. (2001: 5)

They involve diversionary tactics, false propaganda, and anti- or non-copyright regulations (on its copyright page, CAE's *Digital Resistance* carries a legend "Anticopyright, Critical Art Ensemble"). Lovink lists the following modes of tactical media: getting access to buildings, networks, and resources, hacking the power, and "disappearing at the right moment" (2002: 260). Tactical media are temporary, shifting, and unorganized. A good example would be the anti-World Trade Organization (WTO) protests in Seattle in 1999. The independent media came together for that time, started their campaign, and left afterwards (though residual petitioning continued; see www.indymedia.org.uk). The Electrohippie Collective (ehippies) created a software that was embedded in a webpage. Anyone who went to the webpage could download this program – which repeatedly loaded pages from the official WTO network. Thus when sufficient numbers of people downloaded the software, the WTO network would be overloaded with requests and would simply crash. Activists appeared against McDonald's (www.mcspotlight.org) and Lufthansa (now at www.noborder.org/archive/www.deportation-alliance.com), and independent media sites like www.indymedia.org (with local versions across the world) developed.

In many cases, these virtual protests are not isolated or simulations. This "mass virtual direct action" (MVDA) accompanies protests on the streets, thus marking the merger of the virtual with the material. They are the electronic equivalents of protesting bodies on the streets. As the Netstrike for Palestine puts it, its aim is "to add our virtual bodies to the presence of the physical bodies of people who are taking to the streets around the world to denounce the Israeli Occupation" (www.geocities.com/netstrike4palestine).

The crashing of a network's mainframe (as in the case of the WTO above) results in massive financial losses, and can be treated as an instance of the linkage between the virtual and the material.

CAE coined the term "electronic civil disobedience" (ECD) to describe its use of tactical media in the electronic age. We need to see media propaganda as possessing the power to alter material conditions (CAE cites the example of Orson Welles's radio dramatization of H. G. Wells's *The War of the Worlds*, which triggered a real social panic; CAE 2001: 19). ECD often consists of what is now called "infowar."

False propaganda during wartime is a very old tactic to demoralize the enemy. The age of ICTs takes misinformation to a new realm: cyberspace and electronic communications. Geert Lovink (2002: 308) correctly points to the rise of the "military electronic complex" during the first Gulf War (1991), with its resistant (tactical) "viral" propaganda within global media. Infowar includes the use of open source software (as opposed to monopolistic, copyrighted software), public access, and decentralized systems. Lovink lists Linux as a "positive infowar strategy" against Microsoft (2002: 309). A website like www.disinfo.com carrying texts such as "You Are Being Lied To" would constitute an excellent example of infowar. The Italian Netstrike (first created in 1995) asked users to insert their "target" URL and click Reload continuously, which jams the selected URL with requests. Now Netstrike campaigns both against the Israeli occupation of Palestine by sending requests to the Israeli government in order to crash the servers, and against the NATO Conference on Security Policy (www.india.indymedia.org/en/2004/02/209036. shtml). Campaigns against censorship, "denial of service" (DoS) attacks, spreading free software and alternative interfaces, building communities around political issues, alternative search engines, peer-to-peer networks, listservs, "subvertisements," and open source movements are all part of infowar and represent, along with hacktivism, the main interruptions in the otherwise hegemonic and tyrannical movement of global technocapitalism. Net activism and tactical media suggest that cybercultures are a contested zone where different practices and applications rooted in differing political, social, and cultural ideologies and agendas in real life are played out.

Hacktivism

Hacktivism is a form of activism for social change that appropriates computers and electronic networks for this purpose. Also called electronic civil disobedience, hacktivism is geared to political ends.

An early example of hacktivism and political hacking came from the Electronic Disturbance Theater in 1998. Using its Flood Net software, it invited artists, ordinary individuals, and intellectuals to come together in cyberspace in support of the Mexican Zapatistas. What they did was a virtual sit-in, flooding Mexican government and official websites and thus overloading the servers, sending them crashing. In the same year, Tamil separatists sent between 800 and 1,000 emails every day for several weeks to Sri Lankan government offices and websites. Protests against the Iraq war (www.stopwar.org. uk) have been made online almost continuously since 2003, and online opposition to a possible war against Iran is already underway (www.stopwaroniran.org/petition.shtml). Hacktivism is clearly here to stay.

HACKTIVISM

Hacktivism is electronic activism that takes apart databases, hacks into mainframes, and creates electronic disturbance for political purposes.

Hacktivism is political action located between public protest (marches, strikes, and other similar acts in the public sphere) and computer-mediated communication (CMC). More accurately, it generates a public sphere in cyberspace via the use of CMC. If governments and administrative bodies use CMC and cyberspace to elicit citizen responses or advertise themselves (see Chapter 6), activists use them for protest. Hacktivism advanced the earlier stage when hackers broke into systems and networks as a challenge. The social, cultural, and political implications of such abilities or acts began to be exploited only in the late 1980s and 1990s.

Hacktivism can be studied in very different ways, depending on one's own location.

Within democracies like the USA, hacktivism and CMC-driven political debates constitute a widening of the public sphere, leading to greater democratization where more citizens can respond to, approach, and even interrogate the government. They can be seen as a means of a more participatory political ecology in which a communicative process between citizens and the state is facilitated through online work.

In global terms, indigenous groups, anti-globalization activists, and peace activists *as* hacktivists protest US neo-imperialism, war efforts, and economic policies. Environmental groups use the same technology in order to draw attention to the dangers of mining, deep-sea fishing, CFCs, and other predominantly First World lifestyles. In such cases, hacktivism is closely aligned with the new social movements that emerged in the later decades of the twentieth century.

One of the greatest advantages facilitated by the new communications technologies is that activists situated across spaces can come together for a cause, and virtual sit-ins can be performed wherever one is located. Unlike earlier forms of activism, which required specific spaces – preferably public spaces in the city – for activists to gather, cyberspace activism does not limit anybody from protesting just because he or she is situated far away from the culture/space of protest.

Cyberterrorism

Concerted action against computer and communication networks can cripple governments, especially since many financial transactions are now reliant upon the electronic transmission of data. While the term "terrorism" itself has never been satisfactorily defined, it is mostly used to describe violent criminal activity targeting persons, nations, and spaces. Cyberterrorism is the action by a group of people using computer networks to vandalize and destroy a nation's or group's electronic, financial, and physical infrastructure for a political purpose. Dorothy Denning, a leading expert on the subject, provides a detailed definition of cyberterrorism as:

> unlawful attacks and threats of attacks against computers, networks, and the information stored therein when done to intimidate or coerce a government or its people in furtherance of political and social objectives. (Denning 2000)

Cyberterrorist attacks could result in:

- breakdown of electric power grids, transportation, and disaster management networks;

- breakdown of financial transactions leading to stock exchange crises and economic collapse;
- breaching of defense and national security mechanisms.

Recognizing the threat from cyberterrorism, the US government prepared a comprehensive plan, *Defending America's Cyberspace: National Plan for Information Systems Protection*, in 2000. Most First World budgets for securing information systems have increased astronomically since 9/11.

Today the structure of state or corporate electronic networks – dispersed and dependent on wide-ranging connections and nodes – leaves them open to cyberterrorism. Any one of these can be compromised and attacked simply because keeping a large network under surveillance is much more cumbersome than keeping a building or a centralized vault secure. Thus the very technologies that have increased the capacity and speed of communications, governance, and financial transactions weaken their security and open them up to possible attacks.

Terrorists can operate at a distance, thereby making their detection and capture much more difficult. Surveillance by security agencies is much more problematic when the perpetrators are not within proximate distance. The complete anonymity offered by ICTs empowers the terrorist because identification by security agencies becomes more complicated. The Internet also enables terrorist groups and subgroups to coordinate their activities with little chance of being caught in the act of communicating messages or plans. Encryption technology helps coded messages between outfits to escape surveillance, and the sheer volume of traffic makes the task impossible for any state or agency.

Fund-raising and propaganda are more easily achieved through ICTs. Terrorist groups can reach a greater number of people in various geographical territories by accessing listservs and other databases, without the necessity (and concomitant risk) of personal appearance or appeal. In fact, as we have seen above, much Internet activism is worked through anonymity even in the public sphere because fellow activists do not ever meet.

ICTs enable even a small group of terrorists to achieve maximum damage. With computers and suitable network technology, a handful of people can achieve devastation – as opposed to conventional terrorism, which demands larger infrastructure and personnel. Also, the very nature of the networks – interlinked, interdependent – makes for a cumulative or cascading effect. Penetration and destruction of one network enables the cyberterrorist to generate an exponential level of damage.

The cyberspace environment is almost completely unregulated. While governments can keep tabs on the physical and financial resources of terrorist groups, electronic surveillance of such groups becomes more difficult because no governance of cyberspace is possible. The decentered network and the multiple locations of terrorist outfits in cyberspace cannot be kept under surveillance by any one organization or state, and require a massive cooperative effort by many.

One of the multiple consequences of the threat of cyberterrorism is increased state control and regulation of the Internet. Regulations to monitor emails and private networks have been proposed, and even made law on the pretext of "national security" (see Vegh 2002).

Fans and Fan Communities

Fans constitute a community, a subculture that builds on their collective adoration of a star. Fans are a response to the media-driven system that constructs "stars." Fan culture constitutes subculture by virtue of being a process of meaning generation that may or may not be "legitimate."

Fans generate their own meanings of the star-text. This is fan-text, something that may be derived from the star's persona/role/achievement, but is not necessarily the construction of the media industry that surrounds the star. The term "fan," also connected etymologically to "fanatic" and "fancy," originally referred to an excessively enthusiastic man at the temple. "Fancy" was used to refer to the patrons of prize-fighting. The term thus gestures at both an emotional attachment to particular icons or beliefs and a sense of collectivity. Long before the web became a part of everyday life, fans communicated through print. Fan clubs met on a regular basis and exchanged notes about their icon. What the World Wide Web has done is to make fan distribution independent of geography. Social networking among fans is now truly global, where one fan sitting in India might "connect" with another in Canada.

Fansites are a form of subculture because they work in peculiar and sometimes in oppositional relation to mainstream culture. Fans of X-Men or Buffy (the Vampire Slayer) see themselves as people whose identities are intimately linked to the TV series or the characters. It is their common love for the series that unites them, even if this relationship might seem excessive or derivative. Fans generate their own meaning from the cult texts. Thus fan fiction and fanzines where readers create their own plots for Harry Potter (see the fan fiction at fanfiction.mugglenet.com) or *Star Trek* (whose fans have themselves achieved cult status as "Trekkies," but also include lesser-known film parodies such as the Finnish *Star Wreck*, 1992–2005, and *Star Trek: The Pepsi Generation*, 1989) constitute a subcultural community where the cult text helps people come together to develop their own meanings that may or may not be legitimized by the "original" one. They are subcultural because the fan fiction may not achieve the same kind of financial, cultural, or social capital as the cult text.

In the case of slash fiction (fan fiction based on homoerotic relationships between male characters), yet another niche is carved out within fan subcultures. While there is a distinct tendency to slide into gay porn, slash fiction – for instance, *Star Trek* slash fiction revolves around a possible relationship between Spock and Kirk – subverts the "original" storyline and adds elements of sexuality (for an archive see www.fanfiction.net/ or slashfanfiction.com/).[4] Henry Jenkins (1992) has demonstrated how the creations of fans contribute to the celebrity's identities and can be seen as a mode of community building.

Individual and Community

Fansites are communities linked by a common icon and are therefore a mode of social interaction. Fan communities online enable fans to overcome their geographical and temporal limitations and interact with fellow fans or even the celebrities themselves. They thus bestow a certain amount of social membership, a collective sense of identity.

Online fan communities are an example of a *cultural intimacy* despite the geographical and temporal distanciation.

For women fans in particular, the World Wide Web allows greater freedom to communicate and establish connections with other fans. Susan Clerc (2002) points out that almost all fan fiction is written by women, and this suggests that it is the women who do the communication work to forge and sustain the community. Contemporary technology here enables women because, for most women confined to the domestic sphere, there is little incentive to acquire knowledge of modems or web links unless they help them "meet" their friends. Thus fansites help women get in touch with one other, and mark the creation of communities of women.

Online fan communities open up the space of communication among fans, creating conversations and exchanges that revolve around their chosen celebrity (Pullen 2000). While fans have always exchanged news, photographs, and gossip about their chosen celebrity, cyberspace enables a greater extent of dissemination. It is the sheer scope of the Internet that enables the creation of large online fan communities (Pullen estimates that there are at least 1,200 *Star Trek* sites).

Informational Space

Fansites provide vast amounts of personal information about celebrities and are a parallel, even unofficial, source of information about them, where both private and personal information about the celebrity is a *necessary* component for fans. This is "second-order information," not because it is unimportant, but because this information has no official sanction and receives no confirmation or denial. That is, the information is assumed to be true in the absence of any proof on the fansite.

Fans everywhere commodify the object of their attraction, invariably constructing their icons as highly stylized yet real, mysterious yet knowable, distant yet intimate. The icon occupies multiple positions in online fan communities.

Fansites such as the European Free Improvisation Home Page (www.efi.group. shef.ac.uk/) or the *New Gibraltar Enyclopedia of Progressive Rock* (www.gepr.net/)

may be seen as encyclopedias that incorporate information outside the scope of or marginalized by "standard," commercial reference works (Atton 2004: 149–150). They thus represent an alternative storehouse of knowledge, and thereby subvert market economy-driven knowledge sites and spaces. This form is clearly indebted to ICTs for information gathering, classification, and dissemination.

Fansites are therefore informational spaces, official or vernacular (i.e., unofficial), that are built around a particular celebrity.

The Private and the Public

The online fan community, therefore, is a strange mixture of the private and the public. It empowers the fan through the construction of a collective identity and creates a space where he or she can articulate personal aspirations, desires, and sentiments about the star. The latter aspect is particularly facilitated by the degree of anonymity bestowed by the construction of an online avatar. Individuals can be adoring fans without publicizing their true identity.

In the case of marginalized communities such as queers, an online fan community serves as a space that is at once private and public (as part of a like-minded community space). Judith Franco (2006), studying lesbian fan communities, locates a high degree of intimacy and involvement in the early stages of community building, where fans exchange personal information in the form of photo albums, cultural identity, and personal details. Online fandom also enables many individuals to transcend their political, social, and cultural backgrounds to come together as a community united through a common focus of adoration that may have nothing to do with their "true" community.

Fan communities have been seen as "alternative communities" because they rebel against mainstream culture and norms (Bell 2001; Pullen 2000). Gossip, anti-fan work, extra and sometimes embarrassingly private information constitute fan "work" – which may not be officially approved by the celebrity around whom the fan community revolves.

Fandom and Politics

Fan culture has definite political dimensions, not least because, like all political culture, it involves the making and work of collectives.

(i)   Consumerism

Fan communities *extend* the celebrity-consumer culture into a new realm (cyberspace). In so doing, online fan communities represent new forms of older activities. In cyberculture the act of meaning production is carried out through new media, but it is not essentially different from "regular," offline fan work.

(ii) Identity

The fluidity of identity and the option of anonymity ensure greater freedom for the shy, the marginalized, and the diffident to be a part of the fan community, to adore their chosen icon, and to articulate their feelings. Female fans who might otherwise find it difficult to be accepted or to articulate their opinions/desires *vis-à-vis* the celebrity text can do so in cyberspace. Thus cyber-fan culture opens up the public space of articulation for women fans, and might eventually lead to smaller private networks that could then very well function as support groups for the women (Clerc 2002).

(iii) Agency

Fansites regulate what can be written or posted on the site. Fans describe how they met their idol, and thus seek to enhance their reputation/status *as a fan*. Such fan production can be treated as the agency of the individual. It constitutes a subcultural agency when fan writing moves beyond what is sanctioned and approved. Fanzines clearly co-construct narratives (plots, characterization) in their fiction, and thus bestow on the fan something more than a merely passive consumer role. Communities of fans (e.g., www.tintinologist.com) construct parallel narratives about their favorite characters and stories, and thus significantly alter the "original versus derived" paradigm, for, if fans can produce original plots based on "original" characters, what makes these plots secondary?

Private posts online include fan productions like poetry or fan fiction (what John Fiske 1992 terms *enunciative* fan production). In some cases, as Judith Franco (2006) has shown, fans move out from the online world into the real when they purchase the best seats for their celebrity's show. Here the contacts and power centered around the virtual fan community are instrumental in altering social-public arrangements in the material world, once again demonstrating the linkage of the two worlds.

Cyberhate

White supremacist, extreme right-wing, and radical groups have acquired greater visibility for their ideologies and hate campaigns by means of ICTs. Neo-Nazis, the Ku Klux Klan (of which at least 40 groups now exist), racialist groups, and homophobes all build communities with a greater degree of ease on the World Wide Web. Individuals can now share their beliefs more or less securely through listservs and mailing groups without necessarily going "public." Access to such material – the basis for community building via communication – is rendered easier, and all from the privacy and comfort of home.

The National Alliance, a US-based organization, declares its primary belief as follows:

> Our world is hierarchical. Each of us is a member of the Aryan (or European) race ...
> We have an obligation to our race as a collective agent of progress. Nature has refined
> and honed the special qualities embodied in the Aryan race so we would be better able
> to fulfill the mission allotted to us ... (National Alliance 2007)

The Alliance, as I write, seeks deployment of the Iraq troops on the Mexican border. Their (undated) pamphlet ironically titled "Amnesty" suggests that the biggest threat that the USA faces is from Mexicans, not from blacks (National Alliance n.d.).

The web facilitates the circulation of violent images – which are raced – and, for most of these organizations and groups, demonstrates a fixation on war (Zickmund 2002: 240–241). The resort to myth and debatable history – such as the National Alliance's narrative of the progress and evolution of the Aryan race cited above – provides the necessary iconography for the community to bond around.

In such discourses of cyberhate, Jews, colored races, and homosexuals become the Other. This ties in with the anti-immigrant feeling that has become a hallmark of Euro-American societies (the National Alliance's rhetoric is one of many). The Other is also located as the source of contamination and conspiracy and the source of the white race's grief.

According to at least one report, the Ku Klux Klan's activity "spiked noticeably upwards in 2006, as Klan groups have attempted to exploit fears in America over gay marriage, perceived 'assaults' on Christianity, crime and especially immigration" (Anti-Defamation League n.d.). In its write-up this report explicitly lists the following as the "media" component of the organization: "Mass mailings, leafleting, and the Internet."

While cybercultural technologies open up spaces for activism, they also open spaces for hate crime and race-related attacks. Cybercrime is also, in many unfortunate cases, reflective of genuine social problems and tensions – racism, sexism, exploitation, pedophilia, among others. Thus discourses of cyberhate could have very material and physical consequences for their victims.

Cyberfeminism

Cyberculture's discourses "figure" women in specific ways (gender and sexuality in cybercultures are discussed in greater detail in the next chapter). Feminist critiques of cyberculture, a component of the feminist critique of technology itself, theorize a different role for women in the age of cybertechnology.

Cyberfeminism has three principal aspects: *theory* (rethinking the relationship of women and cybernetics/digital cultures), *artistic work* (artists with an explicitly feminist agenda using ICTs), and *activist work* (social and political action, propaganda, and movements). The theoretical aspect of cyberfeminism will be discussed in Chapter 5. In this section I am interested in the ways in which subcultural forms with a feminist politics appropriate and redeploy cyberculture.

Sadie Plant's now classic formulation of the web as a weave presents a different appropriation and representation of the digital age. Building on the early feminist work of Mary Daly (1990/1978), Plant, in her essay "The Future Looms" (1995), argues that the computer is a simulation of weaving, "joining women at the interface between man and matter, identity and difference, one and zero, the actual and the virtual" (p. 63). For Plant, programming is feminine weaving. Donna Haraway, writing a few years before Plant, sees weaving as the strategy for "oppositional cyborgs," an act of resistance in the face of networking by capitalist corporate bodies (1991a/1985: 170). Weaving is, in such interpretations, a code for female creativity.

Of the many forms of cyber-subculture, cyberfeminist cultural work is arguably the most fascinating. Two forms of cyberfeminist cultures are dominant: feminist cyberpunk and cyberfeminist art.

Feminist Cyberpunk

As we have already noted in Chapter 2, cyberpunk represents a countercultural appropriation of cybertechnologies. Yet, despite its oppositional character, mainstream cyberpunk retains the gender biases and patriarchal ideologies of SF and technologies. Women writers like Pat Cadigan and Marge Piercy therefore rewrite cyberpunk from a feminist angle.

A prominent feature of this rewriting is the refusal to treat the computer age and its technologies as merely emancipatory. Feminist cyberpunk sees an inherent link between cyberculture, technology, capitalism, and patriarchy. That is, cyberculture for feminist cyberpunk is the product of an unequal system of finance, technology, labor, and cultural stereotyping where

- women's contributions are ignored or undervalued;
- the emphasis on reason and scientificity ignores emotional responses to and relations with technology;
- the female body is still sexualized for male consumption; and
- women's relationship with technology is never seen as primary.

Mainstream cyberpunk, they believe, ignores these crucial aspects of ICTs. The overemphasis on hacking and jacking in, they suggest, represents the male desire for power and control, this time via electronic circuitry and computers. Feminist cyberpunk therefore seeks to foreground women's contributions to and appropriation of ICTs.

First, feminist cyberpunk seeks to be more inclusive in terms of its demographics. Therefore, there are more colored people, more differently abled people, and more queer people – categories, they argue, that have been marginalized within mainstream cyberpunk. Second, feminist cyberpunk sees technology as rooted in a specific social and cultural context. ICTs emerge in the age of globalization, transnational labor, and financial flows. The "wired" world is predominantly "First World." Colored people's access to such technologies remains low, even in the First World.

Third, feminist cyberpunk redefines technology in terms of its *use*. It includes magic, spirituality, and emotions as equally important responses to and modes of appropriation of ICTs. Pat Cadigan's fiction, for instance, renders cyberspace and its attendant features as a shamanic, quasi-mystical space.

Fourth, feminist cyberpunk problematizes the "alien" theme so common to SF and mainstream cyberpunk. Building on the work of feminist theory, feminist cyberpunk sees the woman, the colored, and the queer as always the alien Other. The discourse of the alien and the foreign in mainstream cyberpunk, they suggest, reinforces in the literary realm and in cyberspace such *realities* of everyday life where these categories are irreducibly alien to/for white cultures. The cyborg in feminist cyberpunk calls attention to the constructed nature of all categories of the human, animal, and machine. It suggests that social and cultural (as well as economic) discourses and realities construct and empower certain categories as mainstream and dominant, and others as negative or subordinate. The cyborg identity of transgender, transracial, and transethnic characters is thus treated as a source of freedom from categories.

Fifth, writers like Cadigan, Piercy, and Melissa Scott consider the theme of bodily transcendence that is so central to cyberpunk as an escape. For the woman (white *or* colored), the body remains central to structures of exploitation and freedom. The transcendence of the body once again privileges mind over matter – a stereotype that, since the early modern period, has been gendered (the male as mind and the female as matter). Hence the escape from the body is a *male* fantasy, the search for a realm of "pure" consciousness, whereas for the woman the body is at the center of the search for identity and emancipation. Hence feminist cyberpunk sees computers, ICTs, body modification technologies, and cyberspace not so much as a means of escaping embodiment as an augmentation and regrounding of the body. Emancipation must proceed from the body, must account for the body. To reject the body in favor of the mind is to willfully ignore that material lives are lived through the body. This is especially so in the case of colored women. The body is raced and gendered, and all subjectivity proceeds *from* the body. For the black woman, therefore, *cyberspace foregrounds the black body's subjectivity in technology*. Technology itself must be experienced as/through a black, female body.

Cyberfeminist Art

Contemporary cyber- and digital art influenced by feminist theory – especially Luce Irigaray and Hélène Cixous – first manifested online as the VNS Matrix, a group of four Australia-based artists: Josephine Starrs, Francesca de Rimini, Julianne Pierce, and Virginia Barratt. The VNS Matrix's agenda, politics, and slogan were as follows:

> We are the modern cunt
> positive anti reason
> unbounded unleashed unforgiving
> we see art with our cunt we make art with our cunt
> we believe in jouissance madness holiness and poetry

we are the virus of the new world disorder
rupturing the symbolic from within
saboteurs of big daddy mainframe
the clitoris is a direct line to the matrix
VNS MATRIX
terminators of the moral codes
mercenaries of slime
go down on the altar of abjection
probing the visceral temple we speak in tongues
infiltrating disrupting disseminating
corrupting the discourse
we are the future cunt.

(VNS Matrix 1991)

The idea was to shock, even as their feminist appropriation of technology received enthusiastic support from theorists like Sadie Plant (who used the VNS Matrix's line "the clitoris is a direct line to the matrix" as the epigraph for her 1996 essay "Feminisations: Reflections on Women and Virtual Reality"). Sexual difference, identity, and the question of women's "weaves" and networks were assimilated into techno-art forms here by the VNS Matrix, and thus marked a departure from the masculinist-capitalist technology.

Building on this feminist appropriation of cyberspace, more subcultural forms emerged in the 1990s. *Ambitious Bitch*, a CD-ROM art piece created by Marita Liulia (1996), for instance, deployed the image of the bitch as the centerpiece (Donna Haraway's more recent *Companion Species Manifesto*, 2003, replaces the cyborg with the dog). In 1994 VNS Matrix was back with a CD-ROM, *All New Gen*. Combining the video game with SF, this parody once more focused on the slut (now called "cybersluts"), with a play on "Gen" (taken to mean both generation and genders), and used extensive vaginal imageries. The idea was to replace, or at least offer an alternative to, computer games that were exclusively male-centered (soldiers ripping up spaces, male explorers, city builders, images of masculine conquest and penetration).

Central to this feminist "turn" to cyberculture was the role of terminology and the roles essayed by the women in cyberspace (on their websites, in groups). The emphasis on *being* sluts or bitches (a routine term in cyberfeminist writing practices) and the in-your-face sexuality and anatomy ensured that the art forms were woman-specific. Thus, rather than being reduced to a sexual object defined and described by the male techno-user, cyberfeminists transformed cyberspace into the realm of the decidedly, irreducibly female. Where pejorative terms like "sluts" had been used by men as categories of disparagement and marginalization, cyberfeminists reclaimed and turned them into *positive* identity categories to describe cyborg/wired women: the "bitch" or the "slut" becomes a term of *self-definition*. "Bitch" websites foreground the female form and sexuality: these practices treat such terms as signs of empowerment. In some cases, cyberfeminist websites and groups even invoke a mystical or quasi-mythic ethos. For example, the "Bitch From Hell" (www.yoni.com/bitch.shtml)

uses goddesses like Kali, Hecate, Lilith, Morrigan, and Ereshkigal as icons for feminism. Fulfilling the stereotype of the woman-as-nag and bitch, the site declares:

> It is in the energy of the dark goddesses that a vast storehouse of feminine power lies. Often suppressed and denied she will eventually leak out in hostility and sarcasm, with sly cutting digs, nagging, gossip and put downs. (www.yoni.com/bitch.shtml)

Another similar online cyberfeminist project asks a series of questions, including:

> Do the words "If you REALLY loved me …" turn your heart to ice? …
> Do you want to SMACK women who play "helpless" just to gain male attention and stroke male egos? …
> Have you HAD IT with people telling you that you are TOO LOUD, TOO ASSERTIVE, or TOO OPINIONATED? (www.heartlessbitches.com)

Like second-wave feminism and French theory (Irigaray, Cixous), which built an entire language of the woman's body – what is called *écriture féminine* – and its physiology, cyberfeminist art appropriated the body and its metaphors as its starting point.

However, in and of itself, cyberfeminist work was not startlingly new in its ideology or agenda. Feminist films and visual art forms had been a part of the counter- and subcultural movement since the 1970s. Riot Grrrl and female punk bands had created a feminist niche within even subcultural forms, protesting against the stereotype of the "cute" woman in popular representation. Unfortunately, the art form also privileges the body, and thus runs the risk of reinforcing the old paradigm: woman = matter/body.

To locate theory and resistance within the body alone does not free women from the earlier paradigm. While the appropriation of mystic icons and spirituality serves the purpose of making the feminist project more open, feminism's location within poststructuralism or Marxism often results in an uncomfortable direction for those inclined to spirituality. Finally, the racialized nature of many of these projects once more calls into question the race divide in cyberculture. While certain projects (Riot Grrrl Is, 2002) have a determined anti-racist stance (alongside its anti-heterosexism), most cyberfeminist projects are white-centered.

Cyberfeminist art links high tech with the material world by demonstrating how technology predetermines women's roles, and the possibilities of subverting them. Like women's webcams that used technology to represent women without the interference of (patriarchal) corporations, cyberfeminist art underscores how technology can be appropriated by women to empower themselves. Cyberfeminist art suggests that in order to reverse the masculine technology–non-technological woman paradigm, women need to shape the design and use of technology.

Cyber-subcultures are not radically new. They extend into another realm, and with a greater degree of connectivity, community, and visibility, systems of thought, beliefs, and practices that have existed for a long time. Subcultural forms such as fan fiction or cybercrime constitute obsession, deviance, or criminality in their appropriation of technology. However, in order to understand the true significance of these forms, detailed ethnographic studies remain to be done.

NOTES

1   However, political and politicians' blogs and blog campaigning are not entirely demo-cratic. Studies have shown how control exists even in such so-called campaigns so that the discussions suit the campaign's agenda (see Janack 2006).
2   Webcam pornography, however, thrives on this aspect. "Hidden" cameras that follow a woman in her everyday life allow spectators to "access" her through the camera's eye, and appear to deliver the woman up for consumption.
3   Jennifer Ringley is credited with having launched the lifecam trend in 1996 with her Jennicam, which ran until 2003 (archived at www.arttech.ab.ca/pbrown/jenni/jenni.html).
4   For studies of slash fiction see Jung (2004), Shave (2004), Thrupkaew (2003), and Woledge (2005).

5 GENDER AND SEXUALITIES

CHAPTER PLAN

Gender and sexualities in cybercultures include multiple sites of inquiry, from the sexualized body in cyberspace to the gendered use of cell phones.

The theme of "gender and cyberculture" addresses particular questions about ICTs and PCTs.

- Are there significant differences in the ways in which men and women appropriate or are appropriated by technology?
- Is a technological artifact gendered in terms of design, functionality, and use?
- If so, what are the mechanisms by which one gender is marginalized or exploited in the process of design, production, and consumption of technology?
- How does digital technology facilitate repressed sexualities?
- What is the connection between sexuality, technology, and capitalism?
- Finally, does digital technology provide spaces for thus far marginalized sexualities?

Any technology emerges in a social context and is mired in contemporary social relations and structures. As feminist studies of technology have demonstrated (e.g.,

Cockburn 1985; Wajcman 1993), technological developments have, historically, been used to limit the woman's sphere. Social studies of technology show how women have played a significant role in the development and design of what we now take as commonplace technology (Bijker 1995). These technologies not only ensure a gendered division of labor but also demarcate specific spaces (that of the house/home) as "woman's space" and limit women's movements to that space (Cockburn 1985).[1] Thus, the woman's *projected* and *real* role in the use of that particular technological artifact has prompted the artifact's development in particular ways.

The augmented human, the cyborg (arguably the most potent metaphor and symbol of the digital age and cybertechnology), has meant very different things for women. In "A Manifesto for Cyborgs: Science, Technology, and Socialist Feminism in the 1980s," Donna Haraway (1991a/1985) treated the cyborg as a metaphor for new alliances and political affiliations. Haraway rejected the older notions of technology's masculine biases that only reinforced gender inequalities. Instead, she proposed, the cyborg with its indeterminate human–machine "form" could possibly function as a new taxonomic order itself, one that did not easily fit the available binary categories of human and machine or nature and machine. The cyborg confounds categories because it *includes* many categories; it disturbs identities because it *includes* many identities: male/female, human/machine, and white/non-white. The cyborg is therefore a politically potent image where a new form of politics – one that is more inclusive, that refuses to accept essentialist binaries of identities and seeks multiple identities – is possible. Since the woman has traditionally been reduced to the body/matter (and where, concomitantly, the man is "mind"), the new body of the cyborg presents a fragmentation of the category of woman itself. The cyborg also breaks down the barrier between self (the sentient human) and Other (machine). The cyborg represents a new route out of gender and identity determinism. It is from Haraway's theoretical point and trope that the gendered reading of cyberspace and cybertechnology takes off.

A second key trope in this reading is that of the weave. Mary Daly in *Gyn/Ecology* (1978) first used the image of weaving to describe and define female creativity. Daly argued that spiders, women, and spinsters weave webs of connectivity among themselves. Women and nature are themselves linked through webs. Daly writes in a particularly evocative passage:

> There is an ineffable difference between Crones' creative weaving and the contrived combinations, the inorganic sticking together of things which is the "genius" of andocratic art, technology, and professional -ologies. Unspeakable also is the contrast between Crones' creative unraveling and the virulent/virile violation and tearing of nature's webs. (1990/1978: 400–401)

For Daly, weaving suggests an alternative, female mode of thinking, epistemology, and creativity.

The reading of cyberspace as a "weave," building on Daly's work, was initiated by Sadie Plant in her key essay, "The Future Looms: Weaving Women and Cybernetics" (1995), in which the trope of "weaving" achieves several ends.

First, it ties in neatly with the image of the "world wide *web*": the WWW as a series of networked points. Second, it builds on the traditional stereotype of weaving as *woman's* work ("weaving is always already entangled with the question of female identity," Plant 1995: 56), but is here, in cybercultures, expanded to include communication and community building among women. It suggests a web woven as an act of *agency*, where women consciously "connect" as an assertion of selfhood and identity.

Third, in sharp contrast to masculine, patriarchal views of cyberspace troped as a new *frontier* to be conquered and *territory* to be explored (again a traditional image of male conquest and control of "virgin" landscape), the feminist "weave" suggests linkage, mutual dependency, and community. Weaving as an innate strategy for women signifies mutuality, where the web is less an augmentation of masculine exploration than the augmentation of community.

Finally, weaving suggests a parallel between handicrafts and cybernetic technologies. From the poeticity of women's handwoven artifacts to high-speed cybernetic networks composed by and linking women, the image proposes an alliance between art and technology, a *technē* in the true sense of the term, but one which offers women *agency*.

Clearly, Haraway's and Plant's visions of cybertechnology are about agency and empowerment for women. With its emphasis on power, identity, and agency, feminist studies of cyberspace explore the *material* (or "real"), the *symbolic* (representations), and *virtual* (cyberspace) worlds without privileging any one. To eschew the material conditions in which women work with new technologies – the gendered division of labor or the sweatshops in Third World nations, for example – in favor of the ecstasy of fluid identities in cyberspace is to miss the crucial point: that despite online work, women continue to live in conditions that are exploitative and unjust.

This chapter looks at sexualities on the Internet. It explores the ways in which the Internet is gendered, the phenomenon of the "sexual Internet," and the queering of cyberspace.

Women and Cyberspace

ICTs are also gendered technologies.[2] From the role of women entrepreneurs in software engineering to the gendered terminology of cyberculture ("matrix" from the Latin *mater*, meaning "mother") and the design of the interface in Windows ("office" rather than "kitchen" or "home"), contemporary feminist readings of the digital age present another dimension of the new technologies.

Feminist cultural theory has been both fascinated and repelled by the prospects offered by the digital revolution. The alteration of time and space, the potential for community building, the hope of cyberspace "freedoms," new forms of identity and surveillance, and the threat of stalking and exploitation are features of the new technology that have very concrete material consequences for women.

Two key dimensions of the gendering of cyberculture, focusing on the female gender, that come in for attention in this section are women's bodies and the gendered nature of cyberspace. As usual, debates about these topics are informed by questions of power, identity, and agency.

Embodiment, Gender, and Technology

Does cyberspace free women from their bodies? Does the possibility of multiple and different identities mean that the problems of embodiment in real life – oppression, harassment, exploitation, pain – are resolved in cyberspace? While hagiographies of cyberculture celebrate disembodiment in cyberspace as an escape, feminists who see emancipation, equal rights, security, and identity as truly *embodied* find this recourse to *virtual* bodies and *digital* identities severely problematic.

Representations of gender, sexuality, and embodiment in cybercultures are riddled with contradictions, mainly to do with the fascination for and revulsion to questions of enhanced bodies and their identities and reproduction. Science fiction privileges technology as a means of augmentation of the body or an escape from it. Anxieties about technology, however, also exist – and these are often displaced onto the woman, in particular the twin themes of motherhood and reproduction. We are dealing here with *representations* of cybercultures and technology as gendered.

Bodies are the first points of interface with a technological artifact, whether it is adapting to an escalator or learning to operate a joystick. Identities begin with the body. This means that a study of the role and impact of technology must begin with the way in which bodies interact with the technological device. When social, material, and cultural contexts are "digitized," then bodies that are embedded in these contexts are also altered in significant ways.

Cult films such as *Alien* (1979) and *Blade Runner* (1982), and fiction such as Mary Shelley's *Frankenstein* (1818), demonstrate an anxiety about the reproduction of the human race and of technological "alternatives." Since reproduction is what ensures continuity of the human race and history, an alien takeover of this process (*Alien*) or the replication of monsters/clones/cyborgs/computers (*Frankenstein*, *Blade Runner*, *Neuromancer*) suggests the end of human history itself. In an innovative reading of such films, Mary Ann Doane (1999) suggests that these themes are essentially about the machine-woman anxiety. The fascination with non-woman-centered reproduction – in the laboratory that functions as a womb – indicates both a nostalgia for and terror of the maternal. The laboratory or machine represents an artificial woman, and the cyborg, which contains elements of the human, complicates the distinction between human and machine in this crucial area of reproduction. Accompanying this anxiety is a crisis of masculinity. Claudia Springer (1999) has argued that the hypermasculine body in the *Terminator* and *Robocop* films results from an anxiety about maleness: the cyborg body is an improvement upon and threat to the "natural" human male's. The narratives also treat the augmented cyborg body as hypermasculine but as lacking in mind. The programmed nature of the cyborg – and the attempt to humanize it in the later *Terminator* films – suggests this tension in the physically strong, hypermasculine cyborg whose agency is governed entirely by the machine/software and the "natural" human.

However, representations of the anxiety of "augmented" mothering are also shot through with an erotic element of transgression and penetration. The interface and virtual embodiment are "seductive" because they promise an escape from the body and its limitations as well as a free play of desire. In such representations, Zöe Sofia (1999) argues, cyberspace itself is female, seeking exploration, discovery, penetration, and control by the male software engineer/code writer/conquistador. This is at least partly the consequence of the genealogy of cybercultures – in masculinized military and corporate sectors.

The debate about embodiment and gendered technology also leads us to a crucial moment in the study of cybercultures: identity and self-representation. Homepages and blogs, for example, are strategies of self-representation in cyberspace. While "home" suggests a space of embodied existence where certain routine actions are carried out repetitively, the home*page* complicates this idea. Homepages and online identities (including membership of online communities) are sites of self-representation from where the individual goes out and meets the world. Homepages enable the individual to possess a different kind of spatiality and embodiment.

Cross-dressing and switching gender identities and roles online enables heterosexual women to "enact" lesbian desires in cyberspace, engage in transvestism, and alter stereotypical roles. The problem with these new forms of embodiment, as Lori Kendall (1996) points out, is that for them to be acceptable and recognizable they need to fit in with established norms and stereotypes. An entirely new order of identity and embodiment is not possible because, as Kendall argues, there is a lack of fit that users themselves recognize between the cyberspace "role" and what they can believe/identify with (which is based on experiences in "real" life).

Embodiment remains central to identity even in the digital age. Portrayals of women soldiers in computer games such as Lara Croft draw upon stereotypes of the woman's body even as users/players assert their agency over this "female" body (Flanagan 2002: 433). Virtual worlds, like the "real" one, also construct female bodies for purposes of domination and manipulation. Add the theme of race to the equation and we have one more layer of complexity: raced gender embodiment in cybertechnologies.[3]

It is in this context of the (social, economic, political) centrality of the organic body with its markers of race, ethnicity, gender, sexuality, and class that we need to analyze the reverence for bodily transcendence.

The celebration of pure thinking coded in cybercultural tropes of the disembodied mind rejects the body as the site of subjectivity and identity. This shift is a gendered one since traditionally the woman has been equated with matter and body, while the man is all mind/rationality. This is the new gendered logic of identity in the information age, one that retains the mind/body dualism coded as male/female. It is for this reason that feminist critics of cybertechnology (Balsamo 1996, for example) object to the "transcendence-of-the-body" metaphor.

The triumphalist rhetoric of disembodied consciousness in Hans Moravec (1988), the leading exponent of the download-your-consciousness-and-transcend-your-body program, and other hagiographers of cybertechnology reinforces this distinction of female body and male mind. Moravec writes:

> Body-identity assumes that a person is defined by the stuff of which a human body is made ... Pattern-identity, conversely, defines the *essence of a person*, say myself, as the pattern and process going on in my head and body, *not the machinery supporting that process*. If the process is preserved, I am preserved. The rest is mere jelly. (Moravec 1988: 116, emphasis added)

The emphasis on thinking as something that ought to be preserved at the expense of the "jelly" is a privileging of the mind over the body. This distinction ignores the contexts in which the mind grows. Cybercultural rhetoric privileges the mind's processes. This clearly places the woman at a disadvantage even in the era of digital technologies because she is anyway only body/jelly! To oppose information and rationality to the material is to ensure that conditions of labor – women in factories producing the very drives and chips that allow Moravec and Co. to download consciousness – and their attendant exploitations remain "invisible." These bodies that labor are material, raced, and gendered. Their welfare, medical services, and wages are based on the color of their skin, their skills, and their location in the organizational hierarchy. Since consciousness cannot be detached from material bodies in the real world, virtual worlds and pure consciousness do not help women. The body, as I have argued elsewhere (Nayar 2006b), cannot be transcended because identity, agency, politics, and justice continue to be predicated upon the body.

Embodiment, in other words, cannot be done away with. In Allucquere Rosanne Stone's words, "virtual community originates in, and must return to, the physical ... Even in the age of the technosocial subject, life is lived through bodies" (Stone 2002: 525; see also Walton 2004). Resymbolizing the cyborg as a transgressive, political "performance" does not change economic, legal, and material conditions. Changes in representation – which work basically only in the symbolic realm – do not quite alter the political futures of real women in the real world.

What can be done, however, is to locate gendered bodies within new technologies in ways such that the body is articulated within institutions, culture, power structures, economy, and other bodies. This requires treating the body not as a self-contained system but as located at the intersection of material, symbolic, and discursive structures. Cyberspaces must be gendered differently.

Gendered Cyberspaces

Research and critiques of the gendering of cyberspace often take two forms (Gajjala 2003). One focuses on development aspects, analyzing the growth of ICTs and their role in women's lives. The second comes from cultural and media studies and focuses upon the representational, discursive, and what one might call "rhetorical" dimensions of webpages, ICTs, and cell phones. What is clear is that neither of these approaches can be subordinated to the other, for the simple reason that questions of access, structural inequalities, and demographics are central to discourses, representations, and uses.

Feminists looking at the structure of cyberspace have proposed that women need not only to be involved in the "building" of cybercultures, but also to ensure that the new technologies further human interest and well-being rather than reinforce existing power relations, injustice, and inequalities (Arizpe 1999). This means not only using the Internet to disseminate feminist ideas and politics (a *discursive* appropriation), but also reconfiguring the very medium for women to use (a *material* appropriation).

As a technology based on the gathering, collating, and dissemination of information, it is important to ask whether the catchphrase "Information is Power" applies equally to men and women.

If, on the one hand, cyberspace and online communication help women connect and develop an identity, cyberstalking and cyberporn make the space an unpleasant, even threatening one (Rogerat 1992). Unequal wage distribution in the software industry, patriarchal industry structures, a gendered division of labor (requiring a detailed statistical account of the demographics of women involved in the industry, at lower levels of programming, as entrepreneurs, and as corporate bosses), the number of women students in the computer sciences (studied by Spertus 1991), and even the physical location of computer terminals (e.g., in remote, dimly lit sections of a university campus; Pearl 1990, cited in Light 1995) are *material* factors to be kept in mind before categorizing cyberspace as favorable/unfavorable to women. It is not enough to look only to virtual environments and communities as providing greater freedom to women; these environments must be located in actual material, social practices within which women live. This approach rejects the vision of an empowering virtual world, since it does not alter conditions in the real one and agency is limited to the virtual alone.

Writing at an early stage in the "Internet revolution," Jennifer Light (1995) argued that online message and bulletin boards, community links, and computer-mediated communications (CMCs) recast the traditional notion of the computer's relation with women. Thus, the key questions concern women's application and use of the new technologies:

- Does the new technology reinforce gendered divisions of labor and conditions of work?
- Do women use ICTs as technologies of freedom? Has the PC been "integrated" into male or female worlds? (The video game, as Wajcman 1993 demonstrated, was integrated into the male pinball arcade and thus became masculinized.)

Contemporary research on the gendered use of ICTs has focused on such questions.

For instance, Rakow and Navarro (1993) discovered that many women used cell phones for purposes of "remote control mothering" to monitor the actions of their children and family. The mobile phone thus reproduces the traditional division of labor where women take their private space and duties with them into their public/ work space. Other studies have demonstrated that women, especially younger women, find the mobile phone provides them with a means to a new identity, offering greater independence and control over their lives, sociability, and links to home, work, or relationships (Döring and Pöschl 2006). The mobile phone gives women greater confidence to negotiate public spaces and unrestricted access to their friends even when alone in a strange area, thus connecting them to familiar social and physical spaces. These are very material consequences for women. The mobile phone transforms an otherwise intimidating public space into private space where they can chat with their friends (virtual space) when occupying a new/threatening/unfriendly (physical) space (Foley et al. 2007).

Cyberspace is increasingly "cybernetic space" (as seen in Chapter 1), even as cities are transformed into "networked cities." Women, argue feminists, need to see cyberspace not as some fantasy world of high-tech wizardry that they may not understand or enter, but as one which is central to their "real" lives. This demands a creative use of technology so that computers and cyberspace are reconstructed and reconfigured to suit and empower women. Clearly, such an approach emphasizes *creativity* and *creative action* as constitutive of female agency and subjectivity (a theme explored by MacNay 2000). In one study, a researcher reported how women website designers were encouraged when users wrote back to say they liked the design, would like to revisit the site, and offered to link up sites to form a community of women's sites designed by and for women. This encouraged women designers to improve their computer skills and others to start their own sites (T. Kennedy 2000).

Women's networks constitute a means for women to enter the public sphere. Computer literacy and networking thus provide women – as traditional education once did – with a means to "leave" the circumscribed space of the home for the world. If the telephone (as Fischer 1988 has shown) served this purpose once, email and social networking sites achieve this end today. For this reason, liberal cyberfeminists, in their positive welcome of cybercultures, have seen cyberspace as enabling and the digital age as promising new forms of freedom for women. Thus Wendy Harcourt, of the Society for International Development, treats the Internet as "a unique medium in that it seems to give expression to both the personal and the political" (Harcourt 2000: 693; see also Harcourt 1999).

This reading of women in cyberspace is woefully inadequate, however, because it pays insufficient attention to the differences in access and the racialized politics of agency in the digital age.

Madhavi Mallapragada (cited in Gajjala 2003) notes that the very idea of an Indian identity on Indian diaspora websites is stereotyped and coded as upper-caste, middle-class Hindu *male*. In effect, gender stereotypes are carried over into cyberspace in the very material and socioeconomic contexts of globalization, diaspora, and technological "modernization." Mallapragada also looks at the machismo image of the Indian software worker in Silicon Valley as on the one hand addressing the older, colonial stereotype of the effeminate Asian male, and on the other cleverly eliding the gendered nature of ICT development: of women in low-paid sweatshops and the lower rungs of the industry.

Outsourcing in the new economy of the 1980s and 1990s meant that white men in First World nations lost jobs to lower-paid women in South and Southeast Asia, who in turn became the main breadwinners for their families.[4] This constructed a new relationship between women and technologies. Cybertechnology is experienced very differently by women of different races and classes. The call center worker in India who deals with First World clients, the factory worker who labels the computer chip, and the entrepreneur in California experience cyberspace very differently. It could indeed be argued in the age of business process outsourcing (BPO) and call centers and sweatshops that the digital revolution is not really a revolution for Third World women, whose subordinate status and oppressive work and living conditions have only been perpetuated and reinforced with the new informational economy. In Rosi Braidotti's (1996) words: "Hyper-reality does not wipe out class relations: it just intensifies them."

Braidotti's declaration and the work of critics discussed above point to the gender, racial, and class contradictions at the heart of ICTs and cybercultures: cyberspace as a counter- and feminist cyber-public sphere with augmented identities, freedoms, mobilities, and agency is made possible by women workers who will themselves never have (access to) such identities, freedoms, mobilities, and agency. While liberal cyberfeminists might see cyberspace as empowering women, they ignore this crucial and very material racial difference. Critical cyberfeminism, as exemplified by the work of Gajjala (2003) and Nakamura (2002, 2005, 2006), locates agency and empowerment within the highly differentiated geographical, economic, and social contexts of globalizing ICTs.[5]

Therefore, while Plant's "weaving women and cybernetics" is an interesting feminist vision, it (1) relies on gendered myths that themselves present problems and (2) elides the raced nature of cyberspace and the institutional structures and their political economy. By suggesting that weaving and cybernetic technologies are alike, Plant romanticizes and naturalizes both a mundane chore – which might even have been forced upon women – and a technology (a criticism that has been leveled against Plant by Faith Wilding 1998). Thus, the question of agency itself is problematic when women programmers, workers, and artists are forced to weave artifacts and programs for corporate bodies. While the emphasis on recognizing the woman's role in the creation of new media is welcome, it is a moot point, as Wilding points out, whether the woman is a free agent. Secondly, Plant's trope of handicraft weaving and computer programming elides very discursive and material distinctions:

- the local, small-market, individualized handicraft "industry" *and* the multi-billion, copyrighted, programming and ICT one;
- traditionally/informally educated weavers *and* women in technical universities and ICT professions;

- the orientalist/colonial search for and subsequent exploitative marketing of "authentic" native traditions and crafts *and* the exploitative raced, conditions of Silicon Valley and Third World labor;
- the irreducibly vast difference between *mathematical* computer language and software (codes, weaving together Zeros and Ones, as Plant notes) *and* subjective, personal women's writing (*écriture féminine*).

If the public sphere, as theorized by Habermas, is the site of "*rational*" debate, then it automatically excludes sentiment and affection (this critique of Habermas's sense of the "rational" public sphere was initiated by Nancy Fraser 1992). This means that women who wish to articulate their feelings will not find the space to do so because the very nature of public debate disallows emotion! Once more this renders cyberspace masculine, rational, and logical while marginalizing women and sentiment. Feminist appropriations of cyberspace allow counter-publics based on such "rejected" or rational aspects as sentiment to be formed (Travers 2003). More importantly, a reconfiguration of the very meaning of the "political" and the "public" would allow an inclusion of the politics of domestic labor, the family, and the question of the private. This becomes a gendered cyberspace with a feminist political edge.

What emerges from the above discussion is that while disembodiment might be a good thing, it is not necessarily so for women (or for the aged, children, differently abled, or minorities). Differential experiences of cybertechnologies, material conditions of labor, and the problem of access are central to understanding the effects of the new ICTs. The question of unequal power structures that determine women's experience of ICTs and digital worlds and the possibility of reconfiguring agency remain the focus of feminist studies.

The Sexual Internet

Sex sells. If the Internet is the quickest way of finding information today, then sex is the most frequently searched-for subject, as empirical studies have shown (Griffiths 2001: 333). Online sexual activities (OSA) or, more popularly, cybersex, is also an extremely lucrative domain – some analysts have reported that Americans have spent $200 million on fee-based adult sites, and some report $1 billion in revenues (cited in Ferree 2003: 385). Sex tourism on the Internet is a billion-dollar industry, and one which grows exponentially every year. A related phenomenon is the appropriation of sexuality for glamour. Official celebrity websites, as Jacqueline Lambiase (2003) has shown, *rely* on sexualized images to increase the celebrity's appeal. Suggestive clothing and provocative poses add to the glamour, and the celebrity's appeal is at least partly dependent on this sexualized visual material.

However, the definition of "sexually explicit content" itself has not been clarified, which leaves the sociolegal domain of "Internet sexuality" or Internet porn" murky at best.

In order to discuss the triangulation of cyberspace, gender and sexuality, and capitalism, we need to first distinguish between erotica and pornography. *Erotica*, a respected form of art dating back to ancient times in practically every culture, is the depiction of consensual sex that does not degrade participants. *Porn*, on the other hand, is often degrading and dehumanizes people, especially women. A subcategory of porn is *violent porn*, where in addition to dehumanization there is also accompanying sexual violence, mostly directed by men towards women (Fisher and Barak 2001: 313). Social psychology studies have demonstrated that there is a clear link between sexually explicit material content, sexual arousal, and sexual behavior (Fisher and Barak 2001).

Cybersex

Datamonitor reported that over 50 percent of the money spent on the Internet is related to sexual activity (cited in Griffiths 2001: 333). The "sexual Internet" is not simply about cybersex. The Internet facilitates multiple forms of sex-related activities. One form of activity includes search for material for educational purposes, commercial acts like sales and purchase of goods from online sex stores, material for entertainment, sex therapists, and finally online relationships. Other sexually related activities include escort services, swinger lifestyles, Internet versions of porn magazines, both commonly available ones (e.g., *Playboy*) and hard-core types, discussion groups devoted to fetishes, paraphernalia, and the bizarre, picture libraries (including video, both free and commercial ones), and live shows (including webcam porn). The more violent and disturbing uses include cyberstalking, online pedophilia, child porn, and celebrity porn (which includes morphing and transposing images of celebrity faces over other bodies).

The Internet *facilitates* particular forms of sexual role-playing. Cyberaffairs and cybersex are examples of such online role-playing for the purpose of sexual "gratification" (the term needs to be qualified since online sex does not always involve the physical except in masturbatory situations). Al Cooper (1999) identified a "Triple-A-Engine" as contributing to the success of the "sexual Internet": *accessibility* (24/7), *affordability* (low-cost sex toys, subscriptions, and porn-site hosting tools), and *anonymity* (disguised identities online). What is missed out here is that cybersex also allows a strange kind of *emotional* link, even in the absence of the physical (Cooper et al., 2000). Online sex can provide a great deal of information about the sexual possibilities open to any individual, thus transforming the Internet into a source of information *as linked to* sexual pleasure.

Emotional attachments, arousal, and psychological pleasure can often lead to visits to virtual sex shops or subscriptions, thereby "rounding off" the online sexual experience. Thus cybersex has both a *psychological* element that demands research and study and a definite *ideological* one.

Cyberaffairs are sexual relationships initiated and sustained *predominantly* (but not necessarily only) in online environments. There are various types of online relationships (Griffiths 1999):

- those that are exclusively in cyberspace, between individuals who (will) never meet (virtual online relationships);
- those who start online relationships but who, with increasing intimacy, wish to take it offline too (developmental online relationships);
- those who meet first offline and then take their relationship into virtual environments as extensions of the "real" one (maintaining online relationships).

Erotic dialogue and text messages, often dealing with sexual fantasies and accompanied by masturbation, constitute what is popularly called *cybersex*. Programs such as *Second Life* enable users to "don" roles, change their physical characteristics, and enjoy online sex. Cybersex must be seen as a new form of social and human interaction facilitated by digital technology. In fact, an early definition of cybersex was "erotic interactions through cyber discourse" (Blair 1998, in Ross 2005: 342). A later definition ran: "carrying on via computer proxy sexual activity through rich description with accompanying sexual arousal, often to orgasm" (Ross and Kauth 2000, in Ross 2005: 342).

Cybersex can be *VR-based* sex, where users in bodysuits with visual, aural, and tactile stimuli or computer-mediated remote-controlled sex toys engage in sex with another user in similar "gear." This form, often called teledildonics, is still in the future and there is little information on actual use. A more popular form is *video-based* cybersex. Users disrobe in the presence of cameras, which transmit the images/video to the other "participant(s)," and masturbate, enabled by software like Cu-SeeMe. This is more voyeuristic, dialogue-based (participants can talk to each other via live feeds), and exhibitionist. Then there is *text-based* cybersex. This is almost entirely verbal, and is at the center of the chat experience.

Cybersex is built on a simple context: *anonymity via cyberspace*. Anonymity in chat rooms and online communication serves as a "disinhibitor" and augments sexually explicit behavior. Intimacy, researchers have noted, develops faster online for precisely this reason: what Michael Ross terms "accelerated intimacy" (2005: 346) and what I call "augmentation" – the spirit and logic I find intrinsic to the design and structure of cybercultures. Related contexts that encourage online infidelity and cybersex include *accessibility* (anytime, anywhere), the absence of evidence, the freedom from sexually transmitted diseases, and the chances of "escaping" from liabilities, obligations, and commitments. If we assume that sexual intercourse is a form of intimate *sociability* and *interaction*, cybersex radically alters the nature of this interaction with the complete absence of face-to-face meetings and ensuing "effects." Cybersex therefore does away with "social sexuality" itself (Ross 2005: 343).

These factors allow repressed fantasies and socially proscribed sexual preferences to surface and to be indulged in cyberspace. Individuals are more likely to indulge their fantasies and experiment because the anonymity and identity-confusing structure of cybersex allow them to do so.

Of such users, some become sexual compulsive users. These are individuals who use the Internet as a forum for their sexual activities because of their propensity for pathological sexual expression (Griffiths 2001: 336). It is a moot (and unresearched) area as to whether the addiction is to the *medium* (the Internet), the *structure* (anonymity), *information* and/or titillation (hard-core porn, fetishes), types of *activity* (stories, games, swapping), or a mix of all of these (Griffiths 2001: 337). In cultures where homosexuality, promiscuity, fetishes, or even overt expressions of sexuality are frowned upon, the "sexual Internet" provides a reasonably affordable avenue for individuals.

The very structure of computer-mediated communication – text, audio, video, graphics – facilitates sexualized expression as never before. The "text" is the language of articulation of desire and fantasies and the Internet is the medium where the fantasies are "enacted." In an innovative reading that foregrounds the social, Michael Ross (2005: 344) has suggested that the Internet is an "intermediate step between private fantasy and actual behavior." While fantasies are private, solitary affairs, the Internet enables their articulation and takes them a step further: "doing" the fantasy online without actually doing it.[6]

Studies reveal that men more than women are likely to be addicted to online sexual activity. However, there appear to be other kinds of gender variables. Women turn to online sexual activity because it enables them to escape the stigma of being sexually "interested." (A Swedish study from 2002 showed that 35 percent of men and 40 percent of women first met offline sex partners online, with 10 percent reporting the occurrence to be over six times. See Daneback et al. 2007.) It also allows them to be less inhibited and provides the chance to be more articulate about what they like. Men turn to online sexual activity because it is a space where they are "perfect" men and have no dysfunctional traits or performance anxiety (studies cited in Griffiths 2001: 337–338).

However, despite the advantages that such anonymous pleasures offer, online sex communities on, say, *Second Life* are restricted and buried deep in cyberspace. One cannot enter them without "proper" introductions (Biever 2006). The particular problem of access has been to some extent mitigated by the widespread availability since 2000 of multi-user sex game sites such as *Naughty America* (www.naughtyamerica.com). The latter is an interesting mix of online and offline dating and cybersex. Subscribers take in biodata, meet in cyberspace, and can then meet offline for sex. Here sex is closely tied in with game playing, and thus shifts sex from the realm of the merely physical to the level of entertainment (*Naughty America* advertises itself as "good, wholesome, American adult entertainment" and as "never degrading") while allowing the possibility of entertainment becoming flesh-and-blood physical.

Transforming sex into game playing and entertainment brings us back to the theme of gameworlds. Sex in the form of "immersive" avatars in specific environments of choice becomes interactive cinema. It shifts the domain of sexuality to one of entertainment, especially community-based entertainment in the case of multi-user worlds. This calls for new definitions of intimacy and privacy (in its privacy policy, *Naughty America*, like several other sites, acknowledges that it tracks IP addresses). The fact that sex has always been a saleable commodity is never clearer than with the creation of online games such as these, where the added attraction of anonymity and access generates greater participation and therefore profits. Technosexuality in the gameworlds of *Naughty America* and *Second Life* is inextricably linked to a new "care of the self" in terms of spaces of freedom, but one that serves the purpose of technocapitalism.

Responses from feminists to cybersex have been of two kinds. One sees cybersex as liberating for women. In cyberspace, controls of social norms, behavioral norms, and bodily risk do not exist. Women who have little success in "real" life, or who have been rejected as unattractive, can ignore their body's imperfections and be as beautiful as they wish in cyberspace: in cyberspace they are ideal women. But the most appealing factor is the control women can have over their own bodies, desires, and sexuality. The second response sees cybersex as intimidating and exploitative, as the realm of male, heterosexist practices that continue to victimize women, albeit in cyberspace (Döring 2000). The predominance of heterosexist and male presence on the Net suggests a gendered structuration of online sexuality itself.

Cybersex presents a series of illusions: of perfect bodies, of non-messy sexual encounters, and of impersonal intimacy. Psychological studies have suggested that cybersex is a mode of recovery and survival for trauma victims. Abused women, for example, who find it difficult to form real intimate relationships find it easier to get into an online romance and cybersex because of this "dissociative" nature (Schwartz and Southern 2000: 129–131).[7] Cyberspace and its technologies allow greater "play" and imagination than would be possible or safe in real lives and, in some cases, argue Monica Whitty and Adrian Carr (2003), might even have therapeutic value.

Pornography, Capitalism, Culture

Pornography is the production, circulation, and consumption of materials that depict, support, and fulfill the sexual fantasies and needs of people. It is thus seen not only as a discourse that is very strongly gendered and raced, but also as a service or product akin to, say, tourism.

In this section, the focus is on pornography not simply as a discourse but as an *industry*. The reason for rooting cyberporn in a materialist critique is very simple: it is one of the largest industries of the digital era, even though it is only one component of the global sex industry (which includes the billion-dollar sex tourism industry).

In fact, the amount of revenue cyberporn generates is nothing short of staggering. Juniper Research put revenues at US $500 million in 2004, and expected it to reach $2.1 billion in 2009. A 2005 Wordtracker report found that the first six of the top ten and ten of the top twenty search terms on a majority of web metacrawlers were pornographic in nature (Coopersmith 2006: 4). Companies like Private Media Group (www.prvt.com), the first adult entertainment company to be listed on Nasdaq, and New Frontier Media generate profits worth billions every year (Internet sales for Private Media Group for the quarter ending September 2007 were 1.4 million euros, an increase of 12 percent, and total new media sales recorded an 8 percent increase at 4.5 million euros; see Private Media Group 2007). In terms of users and revenue, therefore, cybersex and cyberporn merit study as perhaps the most widespread and commercially profitable use of digital technology.

Electronic and digital pornography expands the user base: more people than ever before can access porn with just an Internet connection from the privacy of their own home. In terms of economics, it is an excellent venture: the costs of production and distribution fall with each passing here. Similarly, the costs of *accessing* porn also fall, thereby opening up the space of cybersex to far more people. The booming economy of cybersex – a different sense of libidinal *economy* if ever there was one – has also spurred infrastructural developments: from streaming video content (Video on Demand transmitted over the Internet by broadband, VOD IP), to interactive video conferencing to cell phone cybersex to high-definition DVDs. Ancillary developments include the sale of advertising space, sex toys sold online, credit cards, software and multimedia devices, and pornography-related services (including instructional software and advice on how to construct your own porn site; see www.hosts4porn.com).

Sex tourism mediates between online porno-capitalism, entertainment, and cybersex. Sex tourism websites offer advice, practical steps, and the possibilities of fantasy-fulfillment in various parts of the world. They become the preliminary steps to real-life commercialized sexual encounters. Sex tourism websites rely on stereotypes and myths about sex workers – stereotypes that are raced (the "oriental" woman, the "ebony" woman, and so on). They also facilitate experimentation with transgressive sexualities (Chow-White 2006).

Blaise Cronin and Elisabeth Davenport (2001) and Jonathan Coopersmith (2006) usefully locate the phenomenal growth of cyberporn within a context of marketing, technical innovation, and user-driven development. The significant difference from old-fashioned pornography is that cheaper and DIY technology allows anyone to produce porn, what Coopersmith terms a "democratization" of porn.

Internet sex carries with it the potential to become an addiction. Mark Griffiths (2000a, 2000b, 2001) has proposed that it is not an addiction to the Internet *per se* that is the issue, but the fact that the Internet provides a supposedly safe space for people to indulge in their addictions. Individuals can now upload their intimate moments on the Internet and transform their sexual act into public pornographic content. Webcam sites offer precisely this facility for producers and consumers of porn. This alters the very notion of private acts, even though the option not to upload remains. The boundaries between the private moment and a public spectacle become blurred: viewers are even allowed to "follow" the individual on a day-to-day basis. As noted in the case of women and webcams in Chapter 4, this converts the everyday into *spectacle*.

Webcasting offers an option to publicize the private as never before, and perhaps transform it into commercial profits. Thus, it is not surprising to note that in 2001, over 70 percent of porn sites were developed by individuals *outside* the industry (Cronin and Davenport 2001). Technology here is shaped by consumers' lifestyles, trends, and uses, which further the demand for better graphics, sound, and video and thereby fuel the development of these techniques.

Variations and experimental forms have grown with the aid of digital technologies. The magazine *Fleshbot.com*, for instance, showcases the latest forms of pornography that can be generated by changing innovations in technology.

Pornography in the digital realm must be treated as a *service* and *product* shaped by social contexts. Cyberporn is a digital formation constituted as much by social values (including obscenity norms and laws) as by technologies (webcasting, streaming video). Adapting the theoretical framework suggested by Cronin and Davenport (2001: 35), we treat cyberporn as

- the commercialization and normalization of acts/behaviors that have been stigmatized in traditional markets (the latter led to porn thriving as an underground commodity);
- an emergent phenomenon that is linked with liberated self-expression and group validation (what can be termed the *augmentation of expressive sexuality*);
- a new relationship between producer and consumer where feedback loops (coded as "what consumers want") inform future techniques and content;
- the redefinition of pornography itself as entertainment, education, and lifestyle choice.

The above framework foregrounds the role of the user-consumer at every level, treating pornography less as an independently manufactured product than as a *co-constructed* one. When the consumer asks for a specific product or service or sexual interaction in cyberporn, he or she contributes to the producer's knowledge base as to what is desired and therefore saleable. This "constructivist consumption" (Cronin and Davenport 2001: 36) informs the services and products offered in the future. It is in this sociodigitization that the commercial success of adult sites and online porn lies.

Sociodigitization also has other consequences. Just as consumers generate and drive content and form in online porn, the very accessible presence of all forms of sexuality online, and therefore in the *public domain*, means an increasing legitimation and validation of these forms. Interest groups with specific sexual tastes find it easier to connect and communicate online, and therefore a community of users is built up. The *interactive* nature of much cyberporn – interactive chat, multi-user adult sites, and games sites and live cams (as opposed to print porn almost always consumed in isolation) – also ensures that cyberporn becomes a *community* of users who always have the possibility of meeting offline. Cyberporn has now become mainstream. As Cronin and Davenport put it, it is difficult to ignore an industry that caters to basic human instincts and generates this kind of revenue (2001: 42).

However, the profit- and user-driven electronic porn market has had its downside and elicited strong responses. Yahoo! was forced to shut down several of its adult, *user-formed* chat rooms in 2005 when they were suspected of being used to lure minors to meet potential rapists and pedophiles. Earlier in 2001, Yahoo! had taken a decision to remove all ads featuring sexual items and porn when the American Family Association and other organizations registered strong protests (Anon 2001).[8] The anti-pornography movement treats porn as sexual discrimination and a practice of exploitation based on sex that constantly targets women, but where the harm of the civil inequality of the sexes is rendered as sex difference. Erotica is sexually explicit material but it does not, according to Catharine MacKinnon, generate or derive from the *subordination* of women (MacKinnon 1987: 163–197). Thus porn, in this definition, is aligned with coercion, force, defamation, or assault – all of which center around the *woman as victim*. This distinction, which calls attention to the social and cultural subordination of women that porn exploits, and perhaps even assists, is crucial to understanding the nature of responses to cyberporn, pedophilic activities online, and cyberstalking.

With increasing scares and moral panics over stalking and kidnapping of children, the social outcry against Internet porn and child access to adult content became widespread. Debates about porn became what is termed "public reason" debates, where citizens sought to arrive at a set of *shared* reasons (Watson 2007).

In 1996, Adult Sites Against Child Pornography (ASACP) was formed by over 5,800 adult sites. Legislative measures were introduced and adult sites introduced statutory warnings about their content. In 2004, British cell phone operators and service providers adopted a self-regulated code of conduct for adult content. Thus, while adult sites continue to function and make profits, greater social and political action against specific forms of porn has also emerged, especially in the 1990s.

The financial success story of online porn apart, pornography remains, from an ideological standpoint, the representation of sexual activity that degrades particular individuals, races, or communities, mostly women. If digital culture is marked by a sociodigitization that works within the framework of the material structures of everyday lives, then unequal gender relations and patriarchy also inform cybersexualities. Pornography's objectification of women, stalking, and workplace harassment – features of everyday life in the "real" world – are also features of online life and relationships. In fact, such sexually offensive acts and behavior might even be exacerbated by the availability of email and chat. Ironically, research with limited test groups has demonstrated that, in contrast to expectations about relatively relaxed standards of behavior in cyberspace, women and men held more stringent standards as to what constituted sexual harassment online (Biber et al. 2002; Boies et al. 2004). Virtual rapes have been reported by women users of multi-user domains (MUDs) and other online adult interactive sites (Dibbell 1993; Döring 2000: 869–871).

There exists another dimension to online pornography. Studies of rape sites have discovered that rape representations on dedicated Internet sites are often so structured and stylized that it is impossible to discover the location of the rape, or the class or ethnicity of the perpetrator, while the *victim* is clearly marked (Japanese, Chinese, etc.). Information about the victim is almost always available, though the perpetrators remain anonymous, suggesting that not only can rape occur at any place (hence the anonymity of the location), but that all men are potential rapists.

It is also significant that such violent pornography or rape sites are clearly *raced*, with ethnorape being a common topic (Gossett and Byrne 2002). This suggests a link between sexual violence, wider dissemination of technologies of representation and access (it is easy to find rape *sites* but harder to find rape *print* porn), and race.

In the case study cited above (Kennedy 2000), women website designers who used cyberspace for their own purposes often received negative feedback for their work (including abuse, threats of physical violence, and hacking). This was especially true of women who designed sites with feminist content – an action seen as threatening to patriarchal control of both social space and cyberspace. Women who use online resources have been victimized at some point or other, according to studies. For instance, women who sought help and advice on health matters online often became victims, suffering harm due to loss of privacy, inaccurate information, stalking, online harassment, or inappropriate online behavior. Pagejacking might redirect a woman visitor seeking information from a website on mental health to pornographic material. As Finn and Banach (2000) point out, women are more likely to face such negative effects – online attacks and threats – because this is the case in the larger society itself. This means that women continue to be the victims of male sexual desires, fantasies, and domination.

In addition to the question of civil sexual inequalities becoming the engine of the "sexual Internet," other related ideological issues arise. Sex shops, a constituent of the "sexual Internet" as noted earlier, sell sex toys but not contraceptives. They showcase pleasure but not medical and other "safeties." They sell partners, but not necessarily consenting partners. They sell sexuality but not its ethics. Finally, they sell non-reproductive sex, but they do not sell the stability, emotional support, or even the tensions – especially for children – of the family (Fisher and Barak 2000). Other appropriations of porn for activist purposes – including PopcornQ (an activist site that produces gay and lesbian porn; www.planetout.com/popcornq), the World KISS Project (which uses Japanese dolls to make intercultural erotica; www.kiss-wkp.com), and Nakkidnerds.com (which encourages traditionally shy or reclusive sections of the student population, or nerds, to showcase their bodies; www.nakkidnerds.com) – reveal a creative use of porn and erotica that resists the simple commercial exploitation of ICTs and the "sexual Internet."[9]

Cybersex and the "sexual Internet" clearly must be approached from psychological (individual, group, cultural), economic, and ideological-political positions. The "sexual Internet" is thus a space where multiple economies – commercial, political, and libidinal – intersect (Nayar 2008c).

Queering Cyberspace

Does sexuality in cyberspace include non-mainstream, marginal, and what are often called "deviant" sexualities? Does the digital age accommodate the sexual Other?

Feminist and queer geographers have noted the existence of heterosexual spaces and geographies of other sexualities (Binnie 1995; Rothenberg 1995) in urban spaces. But does *cyberspace* embody a new geography of sexuality?

The anonymity of identities in cyberspace enables the queer to find a space where he or she can communicate and form a community without fear of discrimination or "discovery." The Internet allows personal preferences to circulate without revealing the physical address or identity of the advertiser. It is thus a space of refuge too. Nina Wakeford (2002) identifies several kinds of cyberqueer spaces: newsgroups, chat rooms, and websites.

Marginalized sexualities find spaces of articulation and expression. With access to the Internet and computers, lesbians and gays can look for sites where they can articulate their problems, publish their work (art or poetry), and address political concerns. It is important to note that in many cases, lesbian and queer movements in cyberspace are embedded within larger real-life movements and the social context of communities. Thus, cyberspace activism by queers supplements social activism in real spaces (see Elisabeth Friedman 2007).

These sites can serve as *spaces of resistance* to heterosexist cyberspace, where pockets of queer art can alter the nature of cyberspace representations. They are *spaces of identity formation* in a context where the "real" spaces of heterosexual, patriarchal technocapital have denied the queer his or her identity – the queer can begin the performance of identity (at least) in cyberspace.

Queer communities formed in cyberspace are not only sites of articulation and expression. They can become sources of support through help and advice groups where individuals might go without fear of stigmatization. They can also serve as important spaces for health matters and advice (a theme that has been extensively studied in specific contexts; see Bolding et al. 2004; Poon et al. 2005).

The extensive use of spatial metaphors in queer sites seems to suggest a queer spatial architecture in the virtual world (Woodland 2002). Moreover, they are safe spaces for queer folk to meet without fear.

If identity is performative (Butler 1990, 1993) demanding repetition of roles and role-playing, then cyberspace allows, within the technical limitations imposed by computer/software systems, the performance of queer identity. Detached from the body and fluid in nature, cyber-identity seems to fit queer identities – always marginal, shifting, and unstable in a heterosexist world – perfectly (a little too perfectly, as Wakeford 2002: 412 points out). In many cases, personal ads by lesbians and gays enact such roles. Studies have shown that personal ads are often fantasy narratives – they are not only expressions of self-identity but also "explorations of life-choices advertisers want to make to become who they have the potential to be" (S. Burke 2000: 595). In a heterosexist world where men masquerade as women online, most of such ads had as their ultimate aim face-to-face meeting to minimize such deception about gender and sexuality.

One could expand the notion of "queering" to include those categories of sex and gender that fall outside the schema of male/female: intersex individuals. Adapting

Judith Butler's (1993) contention that bodies "matter" only within socially acceptable roles, it could be argued that intersexed individuals need to undergo medical intervention and alteration so that they can fit into one of the two socially recognized genders: they cannot exist outside this scheme. The intersex movement (at the forefront of which is the Intersex Society of North America) argues for recognition of intersex as a "third sex," outside and beyond the male/female binary, but a gender in its own right (see S. Turner 1999). The movement gains momentum and publicity through its petitions and online advocacy mechanisms, thus transforming the discursive structures of cyberspace into something more representative (see www.isna.org/). As with queer identities, intersex work on the Internet is the construction of a space for identities that have been socially marginalized.

However, as Sue Ellen-Case (1995: 340) points out, even access to such liberating lesbian (the subject of her essay) or queer sites demands location of the woman (or queer) within institutions that can afford the computers and connections, and a degree of education. This material dimension to queering cyberspace is something we cannot afford to ignore when we see the Internet as an empowering space of representation and articulation for the marginalized.

NOTES

1 In a fascinating study Strasser (1982) demonstrated how the washing machine transformed washing from a more community-based activity to a solitary one. Women washing clothes in the open air in their backyards and exchanging news across clothes lines meant that even grinding labor enabled some socialization. The washing machine took the labor into the space of the house, and thus erased the possibility of female community.
2 While "gender" does not mean only "female," the dominant focus in this chapter remains the female gender.
3 However, even when women are aware that the role essayed in cyberspace may not be "real," they (like all users of ICTs) act *as if* they were meeting *real bodies*.
4 For a study of the gender aspects of the new economy in European nations, see the journal *Gender, Work and Organization* 14/4 (2007).
5 Recent NGO and development work by Gajjala and Mamidipudi in Hyderabad, India, therefore seeks to locate e-commerce for handloom weavers that empowers the weaver without loss of autonomy. Such work marks the construction of electronic spaces – "digital formations" – that is attentive to local social, economic, and cultural structures while appropriating ("localizing") transnational networks and ICTs. See Gajjala and Mamidipudi (1999, 2002).
6 This, of course, leads to other questions: does cybersex constitute "real" sex? (See the incident cited at the beginning of this book.) Following on from this, does a cybersex act constitute infidelity? Is typing out a fantasy (including chat) the same as sexual intercourse? Such questions call for a more detailed elaboration of what constitutes the sexual act. Women, especially those who are married, according to some studies, see online sexual affairs and relations as being more serious than men. See McKenna and colleagues (2001) and Parker and Wampler (2003).

7   These individuals, however, run the risk of becoming compulsive cybersex users leading fragmented lives, playing roles, and even causing pain to others (in cyberspace), as the authors point out (Schwartz and Southern 2000: 130–131).

8   Incidentally, this move was applicable only at the US Web portals of Yahoo!, an interesting insight into another kind of digital divide!

9   See Katrien Jacobs (2004) for a reading of such web spaces.

6 PUBLIC SPACES

CHAPTER PLAN

"Cyberspace" is literally "navigable space," and the term gestures at both territory and direction. Since space, as geographers have argued (Lefebvre 2000; Soja 1993), is constituted by the actions taking place in it, it follows that cyberspace too is the product of social interactions and relations, generating its own forms of identity and politics, and embedded in local, historical, and global cultures/contexts. In this chapter we turn to the construction of a public sphere – a space of community and social interaction – in and through cyberspace. Before moving on to issues of community, governance, and networking, we need to locate cyberspace itself within larger geographies of the late twentieth century.

Cyber-public space is the augmentation of existing public spaces and an extension into another realm of the communities, sites of political action, and agency that exist in the real public sphere. This also means, as pointed out in Chapter 4 on subcultures, that cyberspace is a fiercely contested zone, where ideological battles are played out between commercial interests and justice movements, neo-cons and radicals, businesses and environmentalists, the state and civil society. Even with radical and subversive movements in cyberspace, control is exerted by commercial interests. Even as the latter push for state governance of the Internet, alternative media escape legislation and hackers disrupt the profiteering narrative of mainstream technocapitalism.

The theme of cyber-public space can be broken down into questions such as:

- What is the link between global restructuring, global geopolitics, and cyberspace?
- How does one map cyberspace?
- How is the space of the home, the everyday, the office, and public space affected through ICTs and personal communication technologies?
- Do ICTs significantly alter resistance, political participation, democracy, and social movements?
- Are larger "territories" like nation and region affected by transnational and global electronic linkages?
- What forms of control and surveillance exist and are facilitated by ICTs?

Cyberspace

Cyberspace is the consequence of global communications technology – the space of a phone conversation to the VR environments of computer games. Cyberspace can be read at various "levels," from the location of a VR system to its internal spaces, from spaces of surveillance on CCTVs to entire informational cities.

While enthusiasts of cybertechnologies (e.g., Negroponte 1995) rave about the transcendence of space with the creation of virtual universes and parallel worlds, it is salutary to note (as Stephen Graham 1998 does) that cyberspace co-evolves with very material, bricks-and-mortar spaces. Thus, cities are increasingly structured to accommodate cabling, wired sections, transmission towers, and transport that, in turn, generate cyberspaces. Even as people communicate across spaces and with no physical, face-to-face interaction, they continue to inhabit real buildings and bodies.

Global Cultural Spaces

The later decades of the twentieth century are marked by global communication networks that unite far-flung spaces and bring the unknown into the realm of the known (or at least the *knowable*). Global media and communications render the distant, proximate.

Diasporic communities can connect to their "homelands," families, and communities via ICTs, and thus remain culturally, emotionally, and intellectually both in their adopted cultures and in those they have left behind. ICTs facilitate a simultaneous deterritorialization (losing their homeland) and reterritorialization (staying attached to their homeland through different mechanisms).

Increasingly, however, the cultural texture of cyberspace is American, with the predominance of English and the dominance of American corporate-invented software, employment, and network providers (Microsoft, AOL). Cyberspace, as critics (e.g., Sardar 2002) have pointed out, is Americanized.

Another mode of such globalization of cultural spaces is religion. Religion the world over has begun to negotiate with new technologies. When printing first appeared in Europe in the early modern period, Christianity benefited enormously through cheaper printing of the Bible (Eisenstein 1979). Religious discourses traveled as never before, altering the very nature of faith. In the age of computer networks and digital technology – with computer "gurus," shamans, and mystics – faith returns in different forms. Dubai-based Ilkone (whose name means "universe" in Arabic) has introduced an "Islamic phone," the i800. The company promises to connect believers with their beliefs wherever they are (www.ilkonetel.com/). Select temples in India allow the devout to SMS prayers. PilotYid.com is a Judaism-based service that allows users to download prayers into their mobile; the service is called, appropriately, "Psalms in His Palm" (Biddlecombe 2004).

Cults too use computer networks to present their arguments, just as mainstream religions seek to expand their reach. Virtual gatherings in designated "conference rooms" exist for various religious beliefs and faiths. Stephen O'Leary (1996) argues that virtual rituals could be seen as "attempts to fulfill authentic spiritual needs now unmet by the major institutions of religious tradition" (p. 803). He concludes that they reintegrate the minds and emotions of the participants – and that this is a major new dimension of the public space.

"Cultural spaces" also include the space of commerce. The Internet as an advertising medium has grown exponentially. Banners, pop-ups, streaming audio and video, and increasingly dynamic ads have converted the Internet into a new *space of consumption*.[1] Studies have shown that the Internet constitutes about 2 percent of advertising expenditures in the US media (Leckenby 2005: 11). It constitutes, also, a new configuration of cultural space because Internet advertising (or *Netvertising*) is a whole new form of consumer communication.[2]

The interactive model of Internet advertising means that the consumer searches, selects, and follows through (in a series of clicks). It places the consumer at the center of the process of communication because it is the consumer who determines the degree of interaction with the advertisement. This is a major shift in the cultural space of consumption and has warranted an entire journal (the *Journal of Interactive Advertising*) to study its development.

Global Restructuring

What is more insidious about cyberspace is the ways in which it restructures the material world. Cyberspace exists because structures like engineering, labor, markets, and technological constructions enable it to exist. The expansion of cyberspace is driven not by its immanent nature but through the proliferation of these structures. Cities are reorganized to enable new technologies and new corporate entities to emerge, and differential salaries alter consumer patterns, rents, real estate markets, and social relations.

Network cities are metropolises linked to the world through ICTs. ICTs disperse the production and consumption of products across the world. This includes the dispersion of the software, communication, consumer, and, most importantly, *cultural* "dimensions" of cyberspace. This dispersion leads to a homogenization where most wired cities resemble one another and thereby lose their local distinctiveness (Castells and Hall 1994 term them "soft cities" because they have lost their unique sense of place).

However, not *every* part of the world becomes a part of this new geography of "global cities." Sections of the world remain excluded from the informational networks due to differential access, poor technology, and geopolitics. Thus the Euro-American use of ICTs is in no way comparable to that of South America or the interior of Africa. Restructuring does not always ensure greater or cheaper access to new technologies, as noted in Chapter 1 in the section on the "digital divide." Countries like India are a part of the restructuring of the globe through ICTs because they serve the purpose of providing back-office support. India is thus drawn into the informational society, not as an equal player that decides on policy but as a supplier of cheap, perhaps lower-skilled labor. In a process of deracination, call center workers are given "Western" names, have to acquire American accents – it must be remembered that the imposition of the invader-foreigner's language was a key aspect of colonialization – and go through a rigorous 6- to 8-week course in "American culture" (see Shome 2006). Restructuring here often translates as a one-way exploitative connection to the informational economy.

> **GLOBAL CITIES**
>
> Global cities are cities linked to global flows of finance, data, and ideas, often working as nodal centers for the transmission of these flows and possessing an urban architecture that is delocalized, containing the same chrome/glass/hardware structures as any other city.

As Manuel Castells points out, the main labor issue of the informational society is not the end of work but *the condition of workers* when even low-paid child labor is inducted into the force (Castells 2000: 153). This exploitative restructuring of the world and its increasingly ghettoized, socially excluded labor force –the "black holes of informational capitalism" (Castells 2000: 165) – to generate profits for a few is a point to be kept in mind when we read a Negroponte. Global restructuring cannot be read in isolation from the kinds of changes the ICT "revolution" engenders *within* various cities. Cities in India and South America that have gained much from the informational society's outsourcing business exhibit particular kinds of tensions.

Everything from transport systems to banking and finance, the making of business parks and gated communities becomes geared to serving the informational economy rather than any other system. Changes in rents and the lifestyles of younger professionals in the IT field, as well as different work approaches and cultures, ensure turbulence in the social sphere of these cities (the most prominent being the demand for and dominance of the English language). James Heitzman's study of the city of Bangalore sums up the poignant situation where beautiful virtual worlds are built upon and alongside the seriously poor and damaged "real":

> Perhaps it is here, in the grotesque distancing of the gated urban enclave from the barefoot boys cleaning dishes behind the tea stalls, that we see the mark of the global, the resemblance of Bangalore to other world cities. (2004: 209)

This is also "restructuring," one where the invisible but powerful world of virtual spaces and global finance is located in and alters the nature of the material world of such cities.

However, restructuring also includes the forging of new connections between political and interest groups, creating *transnational classes and publics*. Thus, the linking up of NGOs or human rights organizations worldwide through ICTs marks the creation of new political spaces in cyberspace. This restructuring opens up newer political affiliations, alignments, and zones of action. Political mobilization and campaigning, information networks, and activist propaganda that now reaches out globally indicate that politics will no longer be place-bound but will take on a dispersed structure that might have local effects – a clear augmentation of the political.

NETWORK SOCIETY

A term increasingly used to describe the wired nature of cities and societies across the world. Network cities are linked to global flows of commerce, consumer culture, and even politics. These are wired, hyperconnected cities where public debates, essential services, leisure, governance, and commerce are all technologically mediated with software, computers, and the Internet.

Spaces of Surveillance

CCTVs, webcams, electronic tracking, and digital traces are technologies of surveillance. Personal and intimate details can now be tracked, recorded, and coded into databases for somebody else to access. The private is no longer fully private. Employers access employee email and CCTVs track the movement of individual bodies in malls or parks. The Human Genome Project maps the DNA of whole communities. This kind of monitoring has also turned inwards, with probes installed inside human bodies to measure levels of insulin, medication, and changes in specific body conditions. ICTs mark new forms and new degrees of surveillance. They serve the purpose of *extensive social control*.

Concerns about "identity theft" can be mapped on to this increasing surveillance. Passwords, IP address tracking, security codes, and firewalls are security measures that seek to protect data and the user's identity. Searches on the World Wide Web also become spaces of surveillance. Martin Zimmer's work on Google as a technology of "dataveillance" (the use of personal data in investigating or monitoring one or more persons) warns us of the potential for abuse of searches. Zimmer (2008) argues that we must expand the investigation of search-related privacy problems from "concerns over the personal information about other people that can be found via search engines, to include critical exploration of the personal informal that is routinely collected when users rely on search engines for their information-seeking activities" (2008: 83). Google, for Zimmer, is a near-perfect collector of information from its users: all its users get drawn into a "larger infrastructure of dataveillance" (2008: 93), thus showing how the surveillance society has expanded in insidious ways.

Credit card frauds and "identity thefts" are crucial elements in a culture of technological anxiety and greater insecurity. Surveillance is thus also about one's self: what information leaves my PC/home.[3]

Mapping Cyberspace

Since cyberspace is articulated with and within social and material spaces, it cannot be read as an entirely new geography without connecting it with the material.

Cyberspace can be "read" as constituted by and in other spaces. These could be the spaces of Internet infrastructure (such as bandwidth or user traffic) or information spaces (which includes spaces of information exchange such as email or chat). In addition to these cyberspaces that are linked to the material, ICTs generate new forms of spaces within the material. They change, or augment, notions of home and community, for example.

Infrastructure Spaces

A useful mode of dealing with cyberspace has been proposed by Martin Dodge and Rob Kitchin (2001). This involves mapping the global, regional, or local Internet infrastructure. Global media atlases prepared by companies like PriMetrica (TeleGeography at www.telegeography.com/products/map_internet/index.php) map the dispersion and diffusion of Internet infrastructure and use patterns, with specific regional data about bandwidth, IP addresses, host density, and Internet traffic. Martin Dodge's Cybergeography research site (1997–2004) included an atlas of cyberspace that mapped cables and satellites, website maps, user-path maps, MUDs, and virtual worlds (www.cybergeography.org/atlas/atlas.html). These could be interactive maps that enable a user to examine the Internet's backbone structure, dispersion, and concentration through the ICT mapping tool, Mapnet. Internet activity mapping tools like Palantir enable Web users to monitor traffic from several sites or over a period of time.

These are mainly efforts at mapping the material infrastructure of cyberspace and its use. They are often *topological* maps, and the map may not correspond to any particular geographical space. That is, these maps reveal other kinds of information of use, dispersion, and infrastructure that may have nothing to do with geographical spaces as we know them.

Information Spaces

Information spaces are spaces of information exchange. Listservs, email, and newsgroups constitute spaces of information. Even site maps on company websites, which lead you along specific paths or let you search randomly, are spaces of information. These are spaces of social processes, since communication is about sociality.

Email is surely the most widely used aspect of digital technology and was its first application (it came into use in 1970). Like all forms of communication, email is a social process, a mode of interaction. Email constitutes asynchronous communication, where people need not be online simultaneously: messages and letters can be responded to much later. Email has transformed communication because it is cheap (indeed, free), efficient, can be archived, and can address multiple respondents at one click. Increasingly, people can communicate on the move with iPhones and Internet-on-the-mobile technology. Email has altered linguistic skills, with emoticons and new forms of phrasing emerging with the medium.

EMOTICONS

Emoticons are facial icons meant to convey emotional states. Derived from "emotion" and "icons," they represent a new language that has evolved with cybercultures and SMS communications.

Mailing lists extend the scope of email communication. They are one-to-many forms of information exchange. Newsgroups provide information on specific topics. Protocols govern the use of this space and are usually set in place by the users themselves. The Netscan project at Microsoft, which was updated until May 31, 2007, provided statistics on the number of posters (those who post messages) and articles in various newsgroups and thus built a database of popular newsgroups. Newsgroups are a social space where the commonality of opinions and interests brings people together online despite their geographical dispersion.

Internet Relay Chat (IRC), often abbreviated simply as chat, is synchronous online communication. It could be one-to-one or one-to-many, and people's responses appear as text on screen. The correspondents are only identifiable by their usernames, and their real-life identity does not ever have to be made known on the chat. Chat therefore is seen as a major space of freedom where one can articulate desires, fears, fetishes, and quirks without attracting real-life opprobrium. Chat Circles (alumni.media.mit.edu/~fviegas/projects/chatcircles/index.htm), developed by Fernanda Viégas and Judith Donath in 1999, uses graphic interfaces for chat, and gives colored circles to all participants – the more the participant "speaks," the brighter the circle! This means users can enter the chat room and know at once how many people are there (an advance over earlier forms of chat where users were not aware of lurkers who only watched and did not contribute to the chat). Online social networking sites like Facebook, Orkut, and MySpace extend chat into another dimension.[4]

Expanding the possibility of social spaces of information are multi-user domains or MUDs. These are parallel worlds where "players" engage in role-playing. MUDs are navigable spaces, with different kinds of rooms, walkways, and connecting paths. Users literally move through the world of the MUD. It is therefore interesting to see the online spaces of MUDs being created along the lines of fictional worlds in novels. Popular examples include the online game Discworld MUD, based on Terry Pratchett's fiction (discworld.atuin.net/lpc/), or MUME (Multi-Users in Middle Earth, (www.lordotrings.com/artmedia/mume.asp) and LOTRO (Lord of the Rings Online, lotro.turbine.com/), based on J. R. R. Tolkien's *The Lord of the Rings*.

We now have Massive Multi-Player Online Role-Playing Games (MMORPG), with entire cities and civilizations (in *Civilization*) and universes. VR gameworlds such as *Second Life* (www.secondlife.com) are commercial projects where people can create avatars, party, buy and sell property, or socialize. What is important to note is that all of these VR worlds are *social* worlds, creating spaces not only through "constructions" of rooms and walkways but through social interaction. Routes of conversations, clusters of discussions, and exchanges of details constitute a social space of information. Users build online communities, rooms, and spaces through the sharing of information, even if they use available templates to do so. As theorists of space like Henri Lefebvre (2000) have argued, space is made *through* social interaction.

However, as noted in Chapter 5, cyberspace and virtual worlds are gendered. They carry over gender and power inequalities from the material world into the virtual one. Feminist critics (e.g., Travers 2003) have proposed that cyberspace's gendered nature can be altered significantly by women users. Just as the public space has traditionally excluded women, cyberspaces continue to treat women as marginal. A feminist reclamation of cyberspace as a more open public space requires not an escape from but a return to embodiment.

The public space itself demands neutrality, rationality, and objectivity. Partiality, emotions, and relationality are consigned to the private sphere. This automatically excludes women's concerns (family, relationships, emotions) as being unfit for the public space. Similarly, cyberspace as social space excludes such "feminine" aspects when it functions as a public space. Increasing numbers of women users, online support groups, and political activism alter the public space as a feminist counter-public space (an argument against the Habermasian public sphere made by theorists like Nancy Fraser, 1992). This would of course be further refined to suit women in particular regional, ethnic, and racial groups and contexts.

Cyberspace is also mapped around other "spaces": home, diasporas, and communities. The question of the public space in cyberspace involves, in addition to issues of diasporas and communities, that of netdemocracy and e-governance.

Home and Cyberspace

(i) Wired Homes

The space of the home is being increasingly transformed. Workstations enable users to link to the workplace. Shopping can be done from the comfort of the home, and debates about a community matter discussed via email. Mobile phones enable users to get in touch with their children from outside the home. Through GPS and monitoring of their child's mobile phone, parents can keep an eye on their offspring's movements in the city. People working from home use the space designated as "personal" or "familial" to reconstitute that space. "Smart" homes, wired, networked, and always online, enable children to "leave" home without really leaving it, just as information exiting the home through social networking sites can cause possible invasion of the space by strangers. Undesirable information may enter the home and crucial information may leave it. Internet ICQ ("I Seek You") chat often rests on self-disclosure, with the hope and/or intention that such disclosures will enable the forging of a relationship (Leung 2002), but there is the danger that too much information released can generate risks in the real world.

The organization, experience, and even structure of the homespace thus become significantly different as a result of the use of ICTs.

In the wired home, geographies of family space are informed by issues such as the sharing of PC time. Does the PC, like the television, which revolutionized living room space in the earlier generation, become a part of the family's lifestyle? Does the PC occupy a designated space such as the office or the study? This depends on how the PC is "domesticated" (to adapt Silverstone and Haddon's 1996 term) by members of the household. Various modes of domestication are possible, from budgeting to hobbies to communication (see Frohlich et al. 2003: 301).

For women, the "intrusion" of the Internet and PC has transformed everyday life in significant ways. "Homeoffice" is the new space for women to occupy where they carry out functions in two realms – the home and workplace – mediated by the PC, complicating their lives when the demand to fulfill both roles occurs (C. Burke 2001; McGerty 2000). Questions of gendered control over technology, time, and access remain unchanged in most cases. This brings us to a crucial ideological point about the dispersion of ICTs. The use of ICTs must be examined for both their online and offline effects. ICT-generated virtual worlds remain firmly embedded in the social and material one. Online pursuits and existences are extensions/augmentations of the "meat" or real one, but never a substitute. Therefore, since the use of the Internet and experience of online life (for men, women, and children) are dependent upon their offline life, to see the virtual worlds of cybertechnology as distinct from and independent of material conditions is to erase contexts of use. All online work is at some point connected to offline experiences, just as online life might inform everyday, material life. In the case of women, for instance, their roles as caregiver, mother, or wife govern the amount of time they spend online, and even the nature of what they do online: children's homework or personal hobby? health matters or artistic pursuits?

(ii)   Home and Diasporic Space

The Internet also reconfigures another kind of "home": that of the homeland for the diasporic individual/community.

Madhavi Mallapragada (2006) suggests that cyberculture studies shares the same set of concerns as diaspora studies: border and border crossings, location, and questions of home. It is therefore crucial to see how individuals and communities reconfigure the private and the home in electronic space. This leads, I suggest, to a series of questions:

- How is community or home imagined in cyberspace? (Ananda Mitra's useful 2000 study is particularly relevant here.)
- What is the link between the private (home/homepage/blog) and the public?
- How are relations (especially gender) within the home or community reproduced or altered in cyberspace homes?
- Is the construction of a cyberspace home in VR environments a relocation of the home or an extension of it?

Images of "home" now cross national boundaries through the medium of the Internet. This means that a deterritorialization of home in terms of actual, physical displacement (from home/land) is concomitant with a simultaneous persistence and reterritorialization of home in cyberspace. How does a displaced community identify "home" space in an environment that is inherently borderless and that lacks a definite "shape"?

Scholars working with diasporic communities on the World Wide Web have demonstrated how ethnic communities assert their identity in cyberspace through a shared sense of community and history (Franklin 2004; Ignacio 2006). These diasporic groups articulate their ethnic identities and sense of "home" and also bring to the discussions new ways of seeing the new world order.

In terms of politics and cyberspace, the new territories opened up to migrants are a site where the marginalized can find spaces of articulation. While these non-elite cultures in the age of digital globalization may be talking to *each other* rather than "talking back" to mainstream, white cultures, it still remains an important means of keeping the culture visible. In many cases, diasporic communities are at the forefront of political dissent and protest online (Franklin 2004: 106–135, Lieberman 2003). Online interaction, as Lieberman (2003: 75) points out, is what constructs their national identity and diasporic experience. The homeland's culture is *revived*, *revisited*, and *reinforced*. In fact, as Vinay Lal (2003), has demonstrated, retrograde religious propaganda has been facilitated by the Internet and new ICTs (see also Varghese 2003 for the gender angle to this). In short, home culture is augmented through its existence as the subject of conversations, where the conversations generate a community linked by common interests in their "home" (Franklin 2004; Law 2003; Mitra 2000). Transnational cyberpublics of the immigrant are constituted through such practices of online communication, and these cyberpublics exist in a symbiotic relationship with real spaces.

Everyday Life

The Internet is "domesticated" in everyday life when people browse it for information, use it for games and leisure, or use it to communicate. Everyday practices, as Michel de Certeau (1988) has shown, are not always what the corporate software supplier intended, even though the software does control the possibilities of what can be done with it. Everyday life is contingent, invented through use and habits of ordinary people. Everyday life is inherently heterogeneous, multiple, and highly local. In terms of everyday communication and socialization, the Internet is increasingly used as a means of social interaction. People stay in touch with their family, relatives, and friends via email (arguably the most used component of ICTs).

Detailed ethnographic studies (e.g., Howard et al. 2002 in the USA) about user patterns have generated a typology of users: *netizens* (who have been online for a few years and go online everyday to manage their finances, email, or work at their social relationships), *utilitarians* (who are less enthusiastic users and who see the Internet only as a tool), *experimenters* (who mostly use the Internet to retrieve information or for fun), and *newcomers* (who are still learning how to navigate the vast spaces of the Internet and "look in" at the various things the new technologies offer).[5] In most cases involving netizens and even newcomers, the study found that the Internet *significantly* altered their social relationships because of the ease (and low-cost) mode of communication opened up. Increased connectivity from home also means other kinds of "problems" and concerns – such as safety and privacy. Internet addiction and gambling, for instance, have risen astronomically. The National Annenberg Risk Survey of Youth (2006) found that Internet gambling among males in the 18–22 age group doubled from 2005 (Annenberg Public Policy Center 2006b). Another survey by the same institute found that at least 40 percent of adolescent users of social networking sites like MySpace had been contacted by strangers (Annenberg Public Policy Center 2006a). Related to these findings is a greater social anxiety. Families now worry about *what* their children are doing online, and information privacy is now a major concern (Turow and Nir 2002).

In terms of everyday life, however, there is more than just sharing of information, education, and familial connectivity. Often people within families (or those without them) require a space for the expression of emotions and might seek support during particularly stressful times. The Internet also offers a space and a medium for the sharing of trauma and advice on its handling. "Cybersolace," a term coined in 1999 by Klem and colleagues (Beder 2005), refers to such online consolation, caring, and emotional support. The Internet offers the potential for interactive support for various kinds of stressful, depressing, and traumatic situations. The rise of various social support groups marks the emergence of a new kind of public sphere.

Emotion mapping projects such as Christian Nold's Greenwich Emotion Map (2005) and the work of Lisa Parks (2001) use ICTs to remap the spaces of the everyday as emotional spaces. Affective geographies of this kind once again reiterate the basic premise of this book: that cyberspace is recursively linked to the material-real. Emotions are central to our negotiations of space, as geographers have demonstrated

(Kwan 2007; Thien 2005; Thrift 2004). Cybercultural technologies enable us to see and record how people and bodies work through the city and to map an alternative geography. Lisa Parks, for instance, noted the GPS tracking of her movements. Later, looking at the map of her travels, she recalled her feelings toward particular spots and thus generated a subjective map of the area. This record of her personal movements is not captured within a conventional cartographic space but in an alternative mapping – what we can call an *affective geography*.

The New Urban Space

ICTs such as geographical information systems, mobile phones, and the wireless Internet have altered the social processes and experiences of urban space, especially in metropolises across the world.

Global communication and financial networks radiate outward from key urban centers, allowing particular cities to have a global reach. *Within* cities, a high concentration of multinational corporations, research centers, and BPO offices, a high volume of capital, and multicultural demography have a decided impact on the *social spaces* of the city. Yet what is important to understand is that such technologies of spacing do not occur in a vacuum. The Internet relies on "hard," material infrastructure (as noted earlier), that is, geographic and spatial infrastructure, in order to generate unbounded space. What we can argue, however, is that a city's physical spaces are increasingly mediated and experienced *through* the mobile phone, the wireless, and electronic networks. "Cybercity" is a term used to describe this type of wired city where social relations, human movement, and technology are meshed together (Boyer 1996).

A cybercity is *not* a parallel universe of cyberspace and immaterial bodies. Rather, a cybercity is a *hybrid* city where electronic technology, the new media, and the infrastructure of virtual environments are linked with and inseparable from the physical, social, economic, and cultural life of that city. While the new media and digital technology mediate the individual's experience of the city (especially of time and space because of perpetual contact and augmented mobility), they in turn are mediated and informed by user bodies and cultural features of the locality or community. Cybercities are *intersections* of the material and the immaterial, the real and the virtual, the social and the technological, in ways that are unprecedented. A listserv or local area network (LAN) within a campus is an example of how the physical place is overlaid by and networked with electronic spaces. The experience of the cybercity is one of a *dialectic* between the real and the virtual.[6]

People use virtual spaces, mobile phones – with their now ubiquitous opening *spatialized* statement or query of "Where are you?" or "I am at" – or GPS in order to navigate real spaces. Satellite navigation systems (SatNav) govern our driving experience where we increasingly lose the ability to record visual cues about locations, relying entirely on the screen to tell us about them. The experience of the real and the virtual can no longer be separated into distinct realms because they are interpenetrating. As W. J. Mitchell (2003: 120) points out, with GPS and tracking, our fundamental modes of reference itself have been altered. We depend more on screens than on our cognitive skills to navigate spaces and buildings, cities, and streets, which are all "geocoded." The navigation of spaces in the networked city is thus a cross-linkage of digital and physical domains where a GPS monitor or a camera is used to locate everything from a soda machine to the freeway exit. This, I believe, makes for *augmented spaces*: augmented not only in terms of more complex (wired, photographed, videoed, coded, digitized), but also in terms of our own experience of the space. Augmented spaces are not substitutes for the real concrete space but are another way of experiencing it: we first "experience" the building or the route through the GPS monitor or interactive map before physically encountering it.

Cybercities constitute a new paradigm in urban space. If the nineteenth-century city was characterized by geographies of *speed*, *light*, and *power*, the twenty-first-century cybercity, as Nigel Thrift (1996) has presciently argued, can add *communication* as a determining element in the new geography.[7] The "machinic complex" that Thrift identifies in the nineteenth-century urban condition now includes "perpetual contact," which alters our experience of space – whether it is communicating with the office from home, or calling home from work.

Networked cities could be either dominant centers or command centers (P. J. Taylor 2004). Dominant centers are cities with a higher service value: London and New York stand out in this aspect. Command centers are cities that house the headquarters of global service firms. Taylor notes that 21 cities house the headquarters of 100 global service firms, with London and New York again heading the list. However, regional command centers of these large businesses are located transnationally. Taylor's analysis shows that globalization via networked cities is still very Western.

The new urban space is also a space of control. Surveillance cameras (CCTVs), electronic tracking of persons and objects (via mobile phone use, tagging), motion sensors, and telecommunication systems are now common features of malls, multiplexes, stadiums, and public places. While in earlier eras the people and spaces to be monitored were often enclosed and observed through the *physical* gaze (which presupposes a human body doing the observing), contemporary surveillance does away with the very idea of enclosure: all spaces, including wide open ones such as roads, traffic intersections, parks, and playgrounds, can be under the *electronic* "eye" of the camera, which transmits the visual data back to a databank. Surveillance masquerading as security is a veiled form of *power* rooted in a complex structure of capital (profits), property and its protection, and social behavior, one that determines the movements (agency) of the user of that space, transforming contemporary urban societies into "societies of control" (Deleuze 2004).

The dialectic between the real and the virtual, where each feeds into and informs the other, results in what Mitra and Schwartz (2001) term "cybernetic space." Cybernetic space is the effect of a feedback mechanism *between* the two spaces, or what I have identified as a *dialectic*. "Cybernetic space" is a "digital formation" constituted by the social as much as by the technological. If cyberspace literally means "navigable space" ("cyber" is from the Greek word for "navigator"), then cybertechnology now enables us to navigate real space.

The question of the nature of "cybernetic space" thus involves asking further questions about the social, financial, and cultural forces that determine the website, the homepage, the network, the broadband speed, and the regulatory regime. From a cultural studies perspective, treating cyberspace as "cybernetic space" foregrounds issues of power, control, and therefore agency. The material, cultural, and technological substrate of cybernetic space is interlinked within structures of power and regulation, which can, however, be subverted by subcultures and forms of agency.

A new model of urban geography has begun to emerge in the work of Christian Nold. Contemporary geographers such as Nigel Thrift (2004), Deborah Thien (2005), and Mei Po Kwan (2007) have begun to theorize about "geographies of affect" (Thien 2005: 451), focusing on people's responses to road conditions, shopping zones, and acts of negotiating public spaces. The result is a new kind of geography that maps the virtual onto the real, and vice versa. Emotion maps return us to the central thesis of this book: that cyberspace must always return to the real because it is rooted in the real. If affect is a form of experience and a set of embodied practices that produce visible conduct, then emotional geographies result in interesting consequences for cyberspace.

Disaster sites devoted to the 2004 tsunami or Hurricane Katrina are also affective geographies of/in cyberspace that build on highly emotional real events. Such sites transform the geography of the globe in cyberspace by mapping territories in terms of high emotional charges – disasters – and produce acts of responsibility. Cyberculture here can work towards active interventions based upon such a response to emotional maps.

The Network Society, Community, Netdemocracy

Cyberspace and virtual worlds are linked in a "recursive interaction" (Graham 1998) with the material world. Digitization is always "sociodigitization." And if virtual worlds are connected to and rooted in the "real," then what are the possible consequences for the public sphere, politics, and the basis of political action (the community)? These consequences can be articulated as specific questions:

- Does the online presence of a support group *augment* the processes of community building, community action, and therefore community *agency*?
- Does it further the democratic cause?
- Does it expand the realm of the political?

Community consciousness and social interaction are based on greater information about the Other. Thus, with greater information about the world and just about anything, do public consciousness and social engagement increase with the Internet and new media?[8]

In his influential study *The Media and Modernity* (1995), John Thompson argued that "the use of communication media involves the creation of new forms of action and interaction in the social world, new kinds of social relationships and new ways of relating to others and oneself" (p. 4). If, as Thompson suggests, greater communication creates greater interaction with the Other, and if *community* is built through *communication*, through shared interests and exchange, then the ICT revolution in the 1980s and 1990s facilitated this. In fact, as Wellman and Gulia have demonstrated (1999), newer forms of communication encourage the feeling of closeness through sharing of interests across (even) widely separated spaces and foster a willingness to communicate with strangers.

Community technology initiatives – for example, Computer Bulletin Board Systems (BBS) in Santa Cruz and Chicago (1978); the Berkeley Community Memory Project (1979); the Public Electronic Network, Santa Monica (1989) – have always focused on the public space, public sphere, and civil society. Each of these examples marks the reconfiguration of the public sphere via enhanced communication systems. Community Technology Centers (CTCs) and Community Computing Networks (CCNs) are extremely popular forms of the new public space in wired societies and cities. They offer literacy and training, collect local data, and seek to widen citizen ("netizen") participation. They might be very local, neighborhood-based initiatives, but they represent a public space where the new technologies can be accessed, especially by populations who do not have access to computers at home or at work (Servon 2002: 68). For this reason, NGOs seek greater access and a greater role for citizens in decision-making where sufficient numbers of citizens might be able to alter public policy (it is, of course, a moot point whether greater access will ensure greater political participation).

A network society generates a new order of the public space and the public sphere. If the public sphere, as theorized by Habermas (1962/1989), is based on communication among all sections of the public (i.e., for all sections of the public to have access to the means of communication) and mediates between people and institutions, greater connectivity and connection as emerging in the network society ought to produce a more vibrant public sphere. Whether ICTs facilitate this emergence, and the degree of "publicness" of the public sphere even with the Internet, has been the subject of much debate.

Enthusiasts of cyberculture (e.g., Rheingold 1994) see virtual communities as an answer to what is perceived as the erosion of the public in the modern age. It might be possible to return to sharing, common values, and conviviality in the spaces of the virtual, and eventually help the (re)construction of a global civil society. It must, however, be admitted that strong suspicions exist as to whether online discussions, arguments, and commitments translate into on-the-ground changes. For example – as cited in Chapter 2 on popular culture – studies of ethnic and community-based social networking sites have revealed that such civic or community engagement rarely goes beyond the discursive. In other words, it does not move from the talking to the doing (see Byrne 2007)!

Studies of network society in the USA such as those by Oliver Boyd-Barrett (2004) and David Silver (2004) suggest that while grassroots-level mobilization is facilitated by the ICTs, it does not alter the exclusivity of cyberspace. As we shall see, protocol controls and corporate monopolies do control the shape, texture, and use of cyberspace and thus communication. Others like Gary Chapman (2004) and Lovink (2002), looking at cultural movements, tactical media, and countermovements, see a local-level resistance to "technoglobalism" as building into transnational networks of resistance through the effective harnessing of ICTs. Douglas Schuler and Peter Day (2004) summarize the prospect as follows: "Information and knowledge [in network societies] are harnessed as key resources of communicative action, through which social goals can be achieved" (p. 354). Networks of advocacy, action, and agency at the community level build on and feed into larger networks at national and global levels, thus creating a civil society across geographical and cultural borders.

Independent media centers (IMCs or indymedia) look toward underrepresented people and give them space on news channels and open publishing, thus widening and democratizing civil society. Closely paralleling movements for global justice, media activism, radical democracy, and free software, indymedia's diversity and democracy are key elements in the reconfiguration of civil society in the digital age (see Morris 2004).

However, the question of civil society and the public sphere being facilitated through ICTs depends on

- access (costs, availability, speed);
- responses (of institutions to public emails and feedback);
- qualities (of communication).

In itself, the availability of a medium of communication does not guarantee a truly *public* "public sphere." Racial, economic, gender, and regional inequalities in access mean that the public sphere in cyberspace is once more constructed by the (techno-)elite, while the marginal (often racial/ethnic minorities or women) remain at the periphery. ICTs have helped the already empowered to acquire greater power, while the disadvantaged remain on the margins.

Iris Marion Young (1990), in a critique of the community, argues that the glorification of the community is a negation of difference. Communities can be formed only when a homogenization takes place, leading to an erasure of difference (1990: 229). Extending Young's concerns, in cyberspace identities are fluid, arbitrary, and even unconnected with "real" ones. This means that cyberspace encourages and facilitates a false sense of unity and community among individuals – even when such unity does not exist in the real world. Yet, difference, disorder, and asymmetry are constant features of the real world we inhabit. To ignore this aspect of the real, flesh-and-blood world we occupy in favor of an illusory homogenized community in cyberspace is to create a public space unconnected with the real.

To see the public sphere as constituted *only* through rational discourse or reasoned debate (as Habermas suggests) is to prepare a set of norms that construct both the nature of the public sphere and access. Why does the public sphere, for example, have to be formed only of rational debate? Since human life includes other dimensions such as emotions, affect, and sentiment, why does debate have to be cast in legal, rational frameworks alone? Does this mean that individuals and communities seeking justice or redress for their grievances, for instance, have to resort to the language of the law or reasoned debate in order to be heard in the "public sphere"? Are expressions of "private" sentiments a disqualifying element in this public sphere?

Thus the quality of the public sphere that is formed through networks is as important as the fact of its formation. This will include addressing crucial questions and concerns, such as the nature of content on the Internet and the "controllers" of this content, how disadvantaged people might be trained to get jobs in the knowledge economy, and how to develop curricula to enable children to acquire the skills needed for the information age. Thus, the nature of the cyberspace public sphere loops back to the nature of the material one.

Wikis are an excellent example of the debates about public cyberspace and content regulation. With their "open" nature (anyone is free to edit, delete, or modify their organization including links), wikis constitute an entirely different order of both knowledge databasing and public space. With little preprogramming, wikis might be the next move in the democratization of knowledge itself. Launched in 2001, Wikipedia is perhaps the largest and fastest-growing open source database ever. The absence of monopolistic control over the material on Wikipedia might trouble scholarly work, but it represents the next step in the freeing of knowledge from the hands of corporate, professional knowledge workers and commercial interests. If we accept Habermas's argument that the public sphere is based on informed communication and rational debate, then the sources of "informed" debate must be kept free for everyone to access. That is, wikis, open source, and knowledge sharing are key features of ensuring proper and complete access to reliable information to make up a quality public sphere. Peer-to-peer networks, wikis, and open source movements within cybercultures are therefore key moments in this creation and expansion of the public sphere.

Since digital culture is finally embedded in the material, the nature of a digital public sphere is more than likely to be informed and even controlled by the very (unequal) forces that shape material realities. To see a cyberspace public sphere or civil society as an end in itself is utopian. However, what is possible is to see such goal-oriented networking as the augmentation of movements for social justice in the material world, a digital public sphere that alters the texture of the material public sphere, and a space of flows of information that impinges upon material realities in order to make for a more just world. Until and unless this networked public sphere influences material realities for a greater number of people – and this might mean freeing the controls under which ICTs now operate – it remains "virtual" (in the sense of potential, but not actual).

Organizations have outlined specific areas in which communities can be strengthened and empowered via ICTs. PolicyLink (2007) suggests:

- neighborhood information systems that help data collection;
- e-advocacy for policy making;

- Internet-based microenterprise support;
- digital inclusion initiatives for training.

These are all civil initiatives that may or may not involve the state, but which enable citizens to use the informational economy for their own, local benefits.

In 1999 an online protest to campaign against the imposition of a new telephone dialing system (11 digits to be dialed for a local call) was launched in the western region of Los Angeles. Termed a "public uprising" by news media, the "Stop the Overlay" Campaign used ICTs and the Internet extensively – an instance, according to William Dutton and Wan-Ying Lin (2002), of cyberdemocracy and cyberadvocacy. In cyberdemocracy, the web complements all other media channels. It bypasses the traditional "gatekeepers" and (as in the case of the anti-WTO protests in Seattle in 1999) brings together geographically dispersed organizers to focus on local issues. The ICTs also play an important role in the pace of organization and mobilization of public support. Most importantly, they reconfigure the networks of communication by influencing who speaks, on what, and to whom. They link (with cheaper access) the intellectual, the homemaker, the student, and the grocer, helping each and all of them to talk with the policymaker or the local official.

In order to see how the civil society and netdemocracy could be more than simply utopian, consider their gendered nature. How does democracy in the age of ICTs empower women? Does it *augment* women's role in decision-making, their participation in the public sphere, and their quality of life in the private one? The World Bank identifies a set of parameters, including access and usage, content, employment, education, policy, and participation in decision-making, among others, to measure the gendered use of ICTs (World Bank n.d.).

Studies of the gendered nature and use of cybertechnologies have focused on specific regions across the world. Women in India use the Internet for personal activity rather than for professional work, and their use of ICTs depends on family responsibilities and domestic arrangements. This suggests, unsurprisingly, that women's use of and work on the Internet are embedded in their context (Internet and Mobile Association of India 2006). In many places NGOs and voluntary organizations have taken to ICTs in a big way. E-businesses owned and operated by women have grown since the late 1990s (Sassen 2002: 114). Women's newsgroups such as Women's eNews (www.womensenews.org) collect and disseminate vast amounts of news everyday.

If the *apparatgeist* of ICTs is perpetual contact and augmentation, then it appears as though, at least since the late 1990s, cybertechnologies have been empowering women in particular segments of society. While access remains the key area where expansion can take place (in terms of infrastructure and costs), there definitely seems to be a greater degree of participation by women. In the case of developing nations, this augmentation is of course more metropolitan than rural, but it marks a decided improvement over the previous generation's access to information.

The Governance of Cyberspace

The most widespread myth about cyberspace is that it is truly free and ungovernable. As such, it represents the most democratic public sphere ever.

Scholars like Mark Poster (2006) believe that the Internet enables the creation of new political cultures and networks (Poster is writing in particular about China and Singapore). On the one hand Poster is right to point to the freedoms that the Internet offers for political participation. However, he ignores broader forms of control over the use of the Internet exerted by the governments of those same countries (see Kalathil 2003 for a study of China and the Internet, and Tran 2007 for the Burmese context). Private communications between people work through common protocols that are part of a network, thus calling into question the very idea of "private correspondence." On a smaller but no less significant scale, employers monitor the Internet use and email communications of their employees – again demonstrating that the Internet is not the free space it is made out to be.

Recent work by Milton Mueller (2002), Shanthi Kalathil and Taylor C. Boas (2003), and Alexander Galloway (2004) has also explored and exposed the myth of the Internet-as-freedom. Mueller focuses on attempts to control the DNS (Domain Name System) root and IP (Internet Protocol) addresses. He terms the Internet Corporation for Assigned Names and Numbers (ICANN) a nascent international regime that frames the rules to handle the governance and regulatory problems of a global resource across national boundaries (Mueller 2002: 212, 217).

The set of rules that defines a technical standard, directs netspace, and regulates flows is termed a "protocol" (Galloway 2004: 74). It is a system of distributed management, is anti-authority, decentralized, and flexible, and can accommodate contingency. It is a type of controlling logic operating outside institutional, governmental, and corporate power (2004: 122). As Galloway points out, even though the Internet is a distributed and decentralized network, protocol, put in place by institutions or corporate bodies, serves as a mechanism of control because it is far too expensive not to enter into the "protocological community" (Galloway 2004: 147).

Hackers, independent and tactical media, and some forms of Internet art (such as cyberfeminist art from the Critical Art Ensemble), however, constitute a subversion of the norms. They work from within the community, seeking to free data (including software) from regulation of any kind. Hackers and tactical media disturb the protocol code through viruses and crashes which work their catastrophic effect by exploiting flaws *within* the computer's own code.

Issues of copyright have exercised legal thinkers in the digital era. When the Digital Millennium Copyright Act (DMCA) was enacted in 1998, it was an attempt to ensure copyright protection for software and digital products.[9] The controversies over NAPSTER and music-copying technologies have been cultural debates: who can own copyright, the freeing of knowledge and technology from monopolistic control, and the government's right to monitor usage, among others.

A useful argument about the question of copyright – and therefore of knowledge sharing – comes from a non-legal perspective in cultural theory. Mark Poster (2006) suggests that digital objects are   not governed by the market because they are copied and distributed at almost no cost. Copyright seeks to control the practices of digital technology, but the practices are firmly tied to the technologies themselves.

It is pertinent, in conclusion, to ask whether the task of ensuring security, safety, privacy, and equality (of access) is now the prerogative of private conglomerates and corporations rather than the state. In the age of globalized technologies, ICANN and other such "bodies" determine Internet use and mobile communications. Often, such bodies are not subject to state control but exist outside the nation-state and its machinery. What is the role of the state in ensuring equality of access in such cases? This question is, I believe, a key one in interpreting ICTs and cybercultures.

This chapter has proceeded from the assumption that cyberspaces represent an augmentation of existing public spaces and extend into another realm the communities and sites of political action and agency that exist in the real public sphere. It has explored the formation of new public spaces and the alteration of urban spaces by cybercultural technologies, treating cyberspace as a realm of social practices and politics. It has mapped the changing nature of the workplace, the city, the home, and homeland. It has also explored the emergence of new forms of civil society participation (netdemocracy) and the role of institutions in freeing/restricting the nature and content of cyberspace. It has argued that virtual spaces always return to the real because their impact (or lack thereof) can only be measured by the ways in which they affect the material lives of people. It has therefore studied the emancipatory, regulatory, community-developing, and commercialization aspects of cybercultures.

NOTES

1   The Internet Advertising Bureau founded in 1994 began issuing guidelines for banner ad sizes in 1996.
2   For studies of the image in Netvertising, see Barbara Stern et al. (2005); for mobile advertising see Perlado and Barwise (2005); for brands and advertising in computer games, see Nichols et al. (2006).
3   Mark Poster has argued that the very notion of "identity theft" marks a shift from an earlier era. Theft was something associated with *material* objects that could be stolen. As Poster puts it, "digital networks thus extend the domain of insecurity to objects that had been relatively safe" (2006: 101). With this, identity is an object that can be stolen.

4 The question of whether such online social networking and virtual socializing are a means of overcoming difference is debatable. In the case of Indians socializing on the World Wide Web, for instance, Yahoo! reported how social networking was also based on caste. Apparently, Orkut groups bond around caste, and Yahoo! writes: "The burst of caste consciousness in the netspace is unprecedented" (Anon 2008).

5 Similar studies have been done for the UK: see Anderson and Tracey (2002).

6 The cybercity is not without its ironies. People gravitate towards windows that enable them to hear better on their mobile phones, seek chargers to recharge their mobile phone batteries, look for electric points for their laptops, or search for spaces where the wireless connection works better. As Mitra and Schwartz (2001) point out, people seek out specific physical structures and spaces *in order to* enter virtual spaces!

7 However, communication itself can be *synchronous* (as in a telephone call) or *asynchronous* (as in email or phone messages). Asynchronous communication minimizes the need for presence (since the message can be transmitted, retrieved, and responded to later), reduces transport costs, and facilitates multiple activities.

8 Some surveys have found that the average American's knowledge of public affairs has not demonstrably improved with the explosion of 24-hour cable TV news and the proliferation of the Internet. One survey found that "today's citizens are about as able to name their leaders, and are about as aware of major news events, as was the public nearly 20 years ago" (Pew Research Center 2007).

9 DMCA made software-cracking codes and attempts to circumvent anti-piracy programs illegal. The Act has attracted the anger of civil rights activists and fair use doctrine supporters (Featherly 2007a).

7 CYBERCULTURES
New Formations

CHAPTER PLAN

Race in/and Cyberspace

Postcolonizing Cyberculture

Rights and Cyberspace

Environmentalism in the Internet Age

If, as Pierre Lévy (2001: xvi) suggests, cyberculture is a "set of technologies ... practices, attitudes, modes of thought and values," then it follows that we need to look at material infrastructure, political ideologies, emotional responses, subversive appropriations, and the exploitative potential of cyberculture. This book has demonstrated the linkages between the three "wares," locating technological "devices" and processes in ideologies, economic policies, and politics, and showing that ICTs are as political as any other technology, if not more, because their globalization means that they directly impinge upon a greater mass and variety of people than other technologies. In this chapter I focus on specific issues that help us rethink the politics of cyberculture. Admittedly, this is an excessive politicization of technology.

Critical cyberculture studies is concerned with a wide variety of issues, most of which have serious political agendas and consequences. Of these, the three most significant would be: race studies, human rights, and environmentalism.

Race in/and Cyberspace

In the mid-1990s numerous European and American companies set up customer support operations and transaction processing services in India, mainly in the cities of Bangalore, Chennai, and Hyderabad. Driven by the logic of cost reduction, outsourcing and call center work have boomed since then. (Companies have reported 20–30 percent savings on costs, according to the NASSCOM Strategic Review 2007.) The ability to speak English on the part of the Indian workforce has also helped.

The work includes late-night hours (including a graveyard shift starting at 1 or 2 a.m. to match European or American real time) and shifts last up to 8 hours. There are often 150 calls to take during this period. The industry is marked by very high worker burnout and attrition due to the stresses of repetitive call taking, late hours, and extended commutes. Poor health has been the first symptom of these working modes. Women, in particular those who also have household and family responsibilities, are worse affected. Most of the recruits are trained to speak American English, with an emphasis on accent training. Very often, the Indian call center employee also works under an alias – the Indian name is almost never used, and instead names such as "Sarah" or "Nick" are employed. There is also high pressure to perform, often leading to stress and anxiety.

Call center work and outsourcing present good examples of the informational economy, space–time compression of the globalization process, and the new "spaces of flows." But they also mark the subordination of vast numbers of Indians to Western economic and industrial needs. The cost differential of labor here might be promising to Western industry, and might even offer higher pay to Indian workers (in comparison with the general salary structures in India), but it also incorporates serious work and organizational issues such as those listed above. Issues of identity – through accent training and the use of pseudonyms – provide a psychological angle to the call center question. Westernized intense and normative pressure works on the stress levels of the employee. As Phil Taylor and Peter Bain (2005) point out, these are neo-imperialist and indeed racist practices. Cyberculture's space–time compression and flows are the consequence, indeed construction, of such racialized labor practices (Shome 2006). What is evident is that cyberculture and technology, which rely extensively on global human actors, is *racially* organized. Nearly a decade ago, at the beginning of the call center culture, Timothy Luke had prophetically pointed to this "structure" of cyberspace:

> The cyberspatial resources of global computer nets permit virtual enterprises to employ thousands of poor women in Jamaica, Mauritius or the Philippines in low-paid, tedious data entry or word-processing jobs for firms in London, Paris, or San Diego. Cyberspace permits dromo-economic entrepreneurs to virtualize segments of a core workplace at these peripheral locations. (1999: 37; see also Downey 2002)

Luke gestures here at the center–periphery divide of cybercultures – a divide that returns to the nineteenth century's colonial structure.

This divide is not to be seen exclusively as an economic condition: it is also cultural. Racial identities determine the languages of cybercultures, the articulations in cyberspace, and the kind of artifacts that cybercultures facilitate and promote. Thus the dominance of the English language and of white, Euro-American cultures on the

World Wide Web is at the expense of other cultural presences, for example Chicano/a, Yoruba, or Dalit (the so-called untouchable, subaltern lower castes of India). What should be evident is, I am suggesting, that we see cyberspace as *materially and culturally raced*.

If race is less a biological category than a social construction, it follows that social structures, including technology, determine, inform, and alter racial identities. Markers of race are derived from culture – including technology – and not from biology. Hence it becomes necessary to see how technocultures encode race.

The Internet is a component of ICTs, and ICTs are central to the process of globalization, which is itself closely aligned with neocolonialism, newer forms of economic and cultural imperialism, and unequal power relations between the so-called First and Third Worlds. ICTs that generate cyberspaces are built in the "real" world, through material artifacts (hardware and buildings) and through the labor of actual people (construction workers, software engineers), many of whom are non-white. Cyberspace may be built through the efforts of non-white workers, but profits and administrative control are rarely in their hands. Global media and the World Wide Web are owned and administered by companies in First World nations. Further, many of these conglomerates and companies are located in countries that have had a long history of racism.

The fundamental question with regard to race in cybercultures is: if online identities can be/are masked and invisible, how does it matter whether one is black, white, or brown? A response to this question is something that has been implicit throughout this book: cyberspace is rooted in, recursively linked to, and informed by the real.

Thus, our real-life identities inform our attitudes, responses, and experiences of cyberspace. Our online presence cannot be "decontaminated" – I use the term deliberately, in order to invoke the taboos of racial contamination from earlier colonial eras – of our real-life racial identities because our "handling" of cyberspace is based on cognitive abilities, experiences, and knowledge drawn from the racialized and gendered material world. More importantly, after being online as a white man, a black woman returns to and continues to live in the real world as a *black woman*, not as her online avatar.

In other words, what cyberculture effects is a spectrality of racial identities: you carry your racial identity as a ghost into *Second Life* or your avatar, and you bring back your experience as a deracinated avatar into your real one. This is the spectrality of race in cyberspace: like a revenant, racial identity in cyberspace is one that begins by coming back from the real.

The real (racial, ethnic, gender) identity enters online spaces through various means.

- The language used in online communication, as researchers have demonstrated, reveals racial identities (Lockard 2000; Warschauer 2000).
- Racial identities are commodified and circulate in cyberspace and popular representations of cyberspace (in films, for instance), just as in other media.

- Dedicated African, Chicano, and minority websites seek to locate race and particular cultures in cyberspace, in many cases seeking an online community formation (diasporic groups, for instance, as studied by Franklin 2004).

Lisa Nakamura (2002: xiii) coined the term "cybertypes" to describe images of racial identity engendered by the new communication technologies. The Internet propagates and reinforces older forms of racial stereotypes. Cybertyping also includes the rhetoric of the "postbody" (Nakamura 2002: 5), where men, women, and minorities are freed of their oppressive racialized, diseased, or gendered bodies. The "type" that circulates most often – the "standard" body for virtual worlds – remains clearly white. The Internet retains the "aura" of the native only as long as the native stays native: that is, raced. Once the native begins to adopt white or fluid identities, he or she is rejected as "inauthentic" (Nakamura 2002: 6). Even future subjectivities, as embodied in digital and virtual artworks such as Kostya Mitenev's UNDINA (digbody.atlant.ru/undina), that help us assemble bodies rely on stereotypes of black or dark aliens and blond heroes (visible also in the highly raced game *Counter-strike*, where the "terrorists" are marked as Muslim by their headgear). These cybertypes also treat the raced body as dissociated from other structures that embed (black) bodies: language, economy, and class. As Jennifer González (2000) points out, all historical markers are erased in order to create the hybrid body, a "*subject* distilled from the assembled components of the *body*" (her emphasis).

What is interesting is that, on the one hand, cybercultures encourage multiple and fluid identities. On the other, it becomes necessary for corporations, projects, and theorists to identify their employees, representations, and subjects by their racial identities. In effect, then, "posthuman" identities are not for the natives, who need to retain their black/brown identities and bodies. The quest for diversity in cybercultures demands a retention of black or brown identities for some subjects.

More important in Nakamura's theorization is her argument that the black race has always been postmodern and virtual. If postmodernism is the decentering and fragmentation of subjectivity, then the black race has always been off-center, marginal, and fragmented. The cyber-turn in culture means that their decentered location is carried over into cyberspace. In Nakamura's words:

> While everyone in cyberspace is disoriented, people of color in cyberspace come to the medium already in this state, already marginalized, fragmented, and imbricated within systems of signification that frame them in multiple and often contradictory ways. (2002: xvi)

Her critique of cyberculture gathers force later:

> The celebration of the "fluid self" that simultaneously lauds postmodernity as a potentially liberatory sort of worldview tends to overlook the more disturbing aspects of the fluid, marginalized selves that already exist offline in the form of actual marginalized peoples, which is not nearly so romantic a formulation. (2002: xvi)

For marginalized people in the real world, the fluid identities of cyberspace hold no charm. To be "free" in cyberspace might provide a temporary thrill, but it does not change their marginal, material realities.

Virtual identities, as Howard Rheingold (1994) and Sherry Turkle (1995) see it, are liberatory: for one can *choose* an identity. In social, economic, and labor practices across the world, virtual identities are imposed on non-white cyber-workers. Thus the call center "executive" in Bangalore (India) who identifies herself as "Sarah" or "Jane" continues to fall prey to an older racialized structure in which the aim of the native was to be as white as possible in order to gain acceptance by the colonial master. The romance of a new identity only reinforces the older actual marginalization of the non-white races where the ambition of the marginal race is to become white(r). In other cases, the romance of cyberspace is not one shared by workers. Materialist critiques of the new informational economy (e.g., Downey 2002; Terranova 2000) have shown how the so-called "virtual" masks real labor, for whom identity remains embodied, grounded, and embedded in concrete conditions.

Increasingly, minorities and other racial "types" have taken to the Internet. Subcultural groups have emerged and diasporic communities formed – all of which tends to complicate the Internet-as-white phenomenon. Rhythm of Life (www.rolo. org) is a non-profit organization that raises money to provide both computer skills and job training to the black working poor and working class in the San Francisco Bay Area. The Afro-Futurist collective (www.afrofuturism.net) provides a clearinghouse for a discussion on how the work of African American and African Diasporic artists and intellectuals can and does intersect with the latest breakthroughs in technology.

Even as such races acquire a degree of computer literacy and power, cybercultures celebrate the end of the body. Just when blacks or Hispanics seek and establish a presence on the World Wide Web – as racialized bodies, foregrounding racial identity and skin color – cybercultures promote a fragmented and non-identitarian politics. This continues the Western/white strategy of marginalizing non-white identities. If once (during colonialism) it rejected the "native" (non-white) as barbaric, it now rejects the native as non-raced. Since the battle for equality and democracy has been on the basis of race, and since exploitation is governed mainly by the color of the skin, to do away now with racial identity is to refuse any chance of agency to the black or the Hispanic.

The hype around the freedoms of cyberspace – including identity changes, surfing, limitlessness – recalls the tropes of the colonial period when mobility was always associated with the white man. Differential speeds of access to the Web, smoother entries into electronic domains, and the very structure of institutional access between races (even in First World metropolises) means that travels through the virtual world are raced.

The colonization of global media networks by predominantly white corporations is an example of the raced nature of the "information revolution." Further, this revolution is based on the labor of multiracial peoples. As Nakamura has argued, the technology industry tries to create a "cosmetic multiculturalism" (2002: 21) where the racial problems within America are quietly elided in favor of a representation of technological democracy. Labor statistics about African Americans at the upper levels of technocapitalist organizations, however, tell a different tale.

Postcolonizing Cyberculture

Recent work on cyberculture's imperial and imperialist imaginary (Ebo 2001) examines the highly uneven impact of cybertechnology on developing nations. However, this anxiety on the part of critics to see cybercultures as a new wave of Westernization, while not being without some justification (the dominance of English as the language of the Internet and the computer game does foster such an anxiety), leaves little room for a nativization and vernacularization – or what I call "postcolonizing" – of cybercultures.

"Postcolonial studies," as I see it, is essentially a critique of Eurocentric thought and practice – in the epistemological, literary-cultural, political, and economic domains. The "postcolonial" is an approach/literature/culture that critically engages with a history of oppression, colonialism, racism, and injustice. The focus of the critique is, therefore, race and its manifestations in hegemonic, dominant, and oppressive forms in culture. Since its "foundational" text, Edward Said's *Orientalism* (1978), postcolonial studies has, besides addressing Eurocentric and racialized cultural formations, incorporated critiques of patriarchy and heterosexual normativism through women's studies and queer studies. In the 1990s it turned to studies of globalization, seeing this as an extension of earlier forms of colonialism and imperialism (for studies of the link between postcolonial studies and globalization theory, see Brennan 2004). It has addressed questions of nationalism and national identities, ethnic and minority rights, hybridity and migrancy, development policies, and global consumer culture as exhibiting disturbing parallels with the colonial age.

For my purposes here, I see postcolonial studies as necessarily having to address that most efficient tool of globalization (Castells 1989, 1996; Giddens 1991): information technology and its practices. Retaining postcolonial studies' emphasis on race and Eurocentrism enables cyberculture studies to address the racialized nature of the age of information, of the unequal (racialized, gendered) social life of information and its technologies where Euro-American "sites" control the lives, labors, and identities of non-white races across the world and where "cybertypes" abound in virtual worlds.

Globalization, as noted earlier, thrives on the exploitation of resources (labor, intellect, natural materials, markets) of the Third World by the First World, a feature of nineteenth-century colonialism. Migrant workers (mainly from India and Asia) built Silicon Valley, which eventually headquartered the research and commercial aspects of the computer revolution. Business process outsourcing (BPO) works that enable global networking depend almost entirely on Asian labor.

"Postcolonizing cyberculture" refers to a process of interpretation and appropriation (of cyberspace) that is alert not only to the racially determined exploitative conditions of globalized ICT labor, but also to the emancipatory potential of cybercultures. It includes "glocalized" digital cultures where global technologies are made to serve the purposes of local archivization and social actions. It involves the development of very local digital practices such as New Delhi's "Cybermohalla," where language registers subvert the dominance of English and digital technology is pressed into the service of geographically localized needs and politics. It involves, as I have proposed (Nayar 2008d), locating and examining the significance and impact of ICTs in everyday life, marginalized cultures, and diaspora studies.

Postcolonial approaches to cyberculture also interrogate the digitization and databasing of information and populations in projects such as the Human Genome Project (HGP). The HGP will store data from the ethnic and racial populations of the world. But no mention is made as to the controlling authority behind this information: who will own it? Will the indigenous populations whose samples have been taken to database the DNA of their community/tribe have access to it? Will they be allowed to determine the dissemination of information?

Population studies has always been driven by the need to know the locations, movements, and behavior of people. Vagabonds and nomadic tribes have always been "tracked" so as to enable the state to know their exact location and anticipate any "trouble" (Beier 1985; Higgs 2004). Genomic projects carry much more than the numbers of people or their locations: they carry within them a particular human body's behavioral patterns and tendency to particular diseases. Originally, African Americans were *not* included in the genomic survey of the human race. After persistent demands, DNA samplings from African Americans were also included. This exclusion is a throwback to the colonial age when Africans did not figure in tracts on humanity, except as primitives and animal-like species. In effect, it would have meant a normative human genetic code, drawn from a narrow section of the population, as "representative" of all humans.

It is crucial as to whose genetic make-up is used as a baseline or standard because medical, health, and other research will use it as a model. In fields like pharmacogenetics (where medicines will be prepared according to genetic make-up), no medicines will be designed for the African American genetic profile. Genomic projects collect genetic materials from minority and Third World communities, but commercial interests might possibly exclude this economically weaker "gene pool" from getting drugs suited to their genetic make-up (see Jackson 1999, 2001; Nayar 2006a). A postcolonial approach to such projects maps the underlying ideologies and exploitative mechanisms at work within contemporary technoscience, and links such projects with older colonial ones such as mapping, population studies, and ethnography.

Central to such a postcolonial approach to cybercultures is the question of knowledge. Knowledge is gathered from peripheries and theorized about in the West (as postcolonial critics from Edward Said onwards have argued), and the modes of interpretation have always been determined by Western epistemologies. Databases such as the HGP constitute another moment in the history of such knowledge gathering. Digitization, as Mike Featherstone and Couze Venn (2006) have argued, runs the risk of perpetuating older divides of First World "theory" and interpretation and "Third World" informants. What alternative modes of knowledge gathering and intellectual networks are available for non-Western academics and theorists that would destabilize knowledge/interpretation in the West? Featherstone and Venn, discussing the New Encyclopedia Project (ongoing since 2001), note that native forms and traditions of knowledge have been neglected in the case of South India even though, ironically, most knowledge experts hail from Bangalore in South India (2006: 4–5). A global archive of knowledge, they argue, demands databasing different traditions of knowledge that would then help destabilize existing Euro-American systems of classification and interpretation. In short, Featherstone and Venn propose a vernacularization that disturbs the Occidental modes of knowledge work, systems of thought, and intellectual regimes – a process commonly associated with nativism within postcolonial studies.

Enabled by digitization, the New Encyclopedia Project "has the potential to be both archive and a device for classifying and de-classifying knowledges and objects of the world" (Featherstone and Venn 2006: 5).[1] The Internet is not a "neutral content delivery system" (p. 10), and this means we need to worry about the nature of the medium, the question of access, the classificatory systems used, the traditions of knowledge that have been incorporated in the global archive of the New Encyclopedia Project, and the commodification of knowledge. What is needed is a deliberate and careful freeing of space between archive and encyclopedia. Featherstone and Venn therefore propose "encyclomedia" as a term: one that frees the project of the pedgagogic ("pedia") component while referring to the circulating, spiraling, and connecting structure of global knowledges (p. 15). Newer forms of storage and transmission (iPods that are used for creating and podcasting in educational institutions) mean that newer, radical connections can be forged, which destabilize the hierarchic structures of traditional encyclopedias. *Encyclomedia* asks us to be conscious of the process of knowledge formation.

Postcolonial approaches to cyberculture would include such digital projects that self-consciously work with local traditions of knowledge and resist Western modes as seen in traditional encyclopedias. The postcolonial tackling of globalization would include such a vernacularization of knowledge itself.

Resistance to globalizing cybercultures began to appear from the 1990s. The postcolonial era has seen the rise of a global civil society. Ethnic, linguistic, and minority identities are now asserted on multiple, global locations without (necessarily) a territory (such as the nation-state). The solidarity forged between ethnic identities in Asia and America (by Americans of Asian origin) reshapes the very contours of "Asia" and "America," and the relation between the two. Such solidarities are increasingly facilitated by the global telecommunications technologies. Non-governmental organizations (NGOs), transgovernmental organizations, and activists link across the globe through these technologies. In a postcolonial world, such networks can be the source of a democratic, interventionary, and resistant civil society. Local communities, building solidarities with other like-minded communities, often become postcolonial in that they resist imperialism from within the metropolis. Thus the anti-World Trade Organization (WTO) protest marches in Seattle in 1999 can be seen as critiques of and resistance to globalization.

Notions of home and cultural nativism can work as modes of resistance and assimilation within globalized cultures. When a portal for non-resident Indians (NRI) was launched in 2000 (under Google groups), the launch was described as "a cyberhome for non-resident Indians" (groups.google.co.in/group/). The description gestures at the reconfiguring of homespace, this time without the regional, linguistic, and even physical variations between, say, Guwahati and Bangalore. It "acts as a link for the global NRI community." It goes on to state that:

> It addresses issues that are relevant to the NRI – from homesickness to raising kids abroad to coping with new cultures. More than anything else, NRI Online provides a platform for NRIs to get together where they can discuss issues that affect them.

It concludes with: "NRI Online also aims to lobby the Indian government for changes as well as raise the image of India abroad." The actual website (www.nriol.com) contains links to a poet's corner, exclusives, news reports, and a "community" link with sub-links to NRI questions, NRI happenings, Indian baby names, a culinary club, and a host of links on visas and insurance. Its popular pages (popular by its own declaration) include: "Indian languages, Indian monuments, Indian temples and Indian tourism." The rhetoric suggests a nativism, a retrieval of national and cultural identity via ICTs. If the postcolonial is marked by an attempt to retrieve native selves/cultures (insofar as this is desirable and possible), then these "homes" in cyberspace constitute a postcolonial appropriation.

Foregrounding race matters and aligned with the postcolonial approaches to hybrid identities, ambivalence, subjectivities, and the sexuality/gender issue, the work of recent scholars has been instrumental in opening up cyberculture studies in fascinating new ways.

Critics of hypertexts, such as Jaishree Odin (1997), have argued that cyberspace with its multivocality and non-linear "arrangement" is ideally postcolonial because, like the postcolonial, cyberspace refuses homogenization. The postcolonial stance in such cases appears to be a rewriting of the languages of cyberspace itself – a phenomenon identified by Ashcroft and colleagues (1989) in relation to the newly independent nations and their literary-linguistic moves *vis-à-vis* their former colonial masters/cultures.

The work of Latin American performance artist Guillermo Gómez-Peña (www.pochanostra.com/) and Cybermohalla (www.sarai.net) is an attempt to postcolonize cyberculture via an appropriation of cyberspace itself.[2] The Critical Art Ensemble's work (www.critical-art.net/) moves a step further in bringing gender and sexuality into their "queering" of technology, even though it does remain predominantly white. Building on what he terms the "cultural fears of the West" in the wake of 9/11, Gómez-Peña constructs the "new barbarians" and ethno-cyborgs. With "geisha-apocaliptica," "piedad postcolonial," and other images of hybrid bodies that utilize images of violence, torture, and war, Gómez-Peña proposes a radically different use of the Internet – what he terms "Aztec high-tech." The deliberate mix of identities in his ludic work with Iranian artist Ali Dadgar – where "viewers" must match the character to the name using their racial/cultural description as clues – points directly at racial profiling in the wake of 9/11. His work "The Fourteen Commandments" critiques Puritanism, homogenization, and essentialisms, and calls for multiplicities across national and racial borders where the subalterns constitute a public. Cybermohalla, as I have argued elsewhere, presents a very localized transformation, and the creation of a postcolonized space, via ICTs (Nayar 2007b, 2008a).

These works are postcolonial because they resist the dominant cybertypes, celebrate hybridity, seek multiplicities rather than homogeneity, and often critique First World strategies of war, imperialism, domination, and stereotyping. They could extend to radically postcolonial acts of resistance – where hacking, page-stealing, online campaigns, and other acts (often termed "cyberterrorism") are racially inflected and target First World, Euro-American policies and politics. More importantly, like postcolonial literature in general, they give space for the expression of local cultures and alternative identities. They "vernacularize" cyberspace even as they construct larger online communities that generate awareness of and resistance to domination. Just as the English language and the English book were appropriated by anticolonial movements in the nineteenth century, the language, architecture, and organization of cyberspace are being appropriated by non-white cultures.

However, even as we recognize the potential of such resistant artistic and cultural work, we must also acknowledge that they remain at the level of representation. True, they reveal the flaws in dominant forms of (racialized and gendered) representation and suggest alternative, more emancipatory forms. The extent of these acts of representation in intervening in the material conditions of labor and ICT work or larger economic shifts remains (unfortunately) debatable. These works have been used to garner support, but their "tactical" interventions are yet to be concretized as a counter to dominant "strategies" (to invoke Certeau's 1988 terms). That is, while it is exciting to see such works as Gómez-Peña's or Critical Art Ensemble's with a powerful "politics of representation" (that 1990s phrase!), their transformative power at the ground level of politics remains to be seen. There is also the risk that such art forms themselves become icons of the "postcolonial exotic" (Huggan 2001), providing images for the consumption of First World audiences.

Postcolonizing cyberculture thus far remains at the level of representations, but (to be more optimistic) opens up – and this is no small achievement – the space of the screen to the Other. Aligning Roger Silverstone's argument alongside Niamh Thornton's (2007) work on Guillermo Gómez-Peña, a postcolonial approach to cyberculture would include:

- an attention to the cybertypes (i.e., cultural representations) circulating in cyberspace;
- the raced material conditions (labor, knowledge workers) that produce cyberspace;

- the complicity of (postcolonial) nation-states with global, Euro-American-driven informationalism and knowledge formation;
- the alternative modes of expression possible for the vernacular and the local;
- an examination of the unequal power relations between races in cyberculture engendered by technologies of software and hardware (in terms of the computer education of minorities, for example, or access in their own languages);
- the opening up of the screen to cultural difference, where the screen is literally the space of the Other that demands a moral response.

It also includes more on-the-ground work through use of the Internet and communication systems. Bharat Mehra persuasively argues that cyberculture research has thus far not addressed questions of "democratic social change" and the creation of "valid social knowledge" (2006: 206). He therefore pleads for Action Research (AR) in cyberpower so as to benefit marginalized groups. This kind of AR research includes more participatory alliances among women, minorities, and other such disenfranchised groups. It seeks to work with the expertise at *local* levels. Such online communities organize ideas and programs of intervention with local knowledge and keeping local interests and needs in mind. This decentralizes not only knowledge but also administration, and is an effective political intervention in the social structures.

Political solidarities in developing nations can be built through ICTs. For example, during the Seattle demonstrations against the WTO, the Independent Media Center registered a million and a half hits, even more than CNN. The international peace marches of 2003 were organized through email. Households and public/civil society linkages are clearly facilitated through the new technologies, and can help generate a newer, more democratic form of the public sphere.

ICTs facilitate an "interculturalism" to refer to the cultural exchanges that are enabled by globalization. Interculturalism refers to exchanges among cultures, performed by individuals or unofficial groups, without obeying national boundaries (Bharucha 2001: 5). The World Wide Web is an important medium of these exchanges, and can enable the building of solidarities between marginalized, subaltern communities (for instance, the linkage between Dalits, Aboriginals, and blacks).

What a postcolonial approach calls for is a reconceptualization of cyberspace itself, as seen above. It alerts us to the metaphors of cyberspace (as frontier and as spaces of travel – "surfing," "information highway" – traditionally associated with European, and later American cultures), even as it proposes new tropes (such as Cybermohalla). The postcolonial approach and appropriation could, as Claire Taylor and Thea Pitman argue, "refus[e] to offer cyberculture or blogs for the imperial gaze" (2007a: 265).

Rights and Cyberspace

New contexts of technoglobalization and technocapitalism mean that there are new contexts in which human rights have to be defined, limited, ensured, and protected.

- How does the discourse of human rights negotiate the new spaces of virtualities and electronic communications?
- Is the right to communicate a human right?
- Are rights to access human rights?

Debates about the new informational order have often focused on the use of ICTs to increase global awareness of human rights violations and state and government attempts to regulate the Internet (Drake and Jørgensen 2006: 5–6). Yet there is a lot more to human rights in the informational age than just these two issues.

The World Summit on Information Society (WSIS) created a Human Rights Caucus (HRC) in 2002. It called on governments to list all the internationally agreed rights but also to ensure that other provisions like spectrum management, national ICT regulation, and labor rights were fully consistent with the world human rights conventions. In 2003, the WSIS's Civil Society Declaration called for shaping information societies for human needs, proposing that nations come together to "build a people-centred, inclusive and development-oriented Information Society, where everyone can create, access, utilize and share information and knowledge" (www.itu.int/wsis). This Declaration set out communication and knowledge rights as central to both human rights and the information society. The ICT Task Force called for bridging the "digital divide" by fostering a "digital opportunity" that would ensure "development for all." This call focused on pragmatic matters like education, capacity-building, and connectivity (www.itu.int/wsis/docs/geneva/official/dop.html). In the 2002 "Millennium Development Goals and Economic, Social and Cultural Rights" of the UN Committee on Economic, Social, and Cultural Rights and the UN Commission on Human Rights, special rapporteurs on economic, social, and cultural rights linked development rights to human rights.

Organizations such as Internet Rights (www.internetrights.org.uk/) are key players here because they furnish fact sheets of rights, legal remedies in case of perceived infringement, and modes of legal control and surveillance. The GreenNet CSIR Toolkit Briefing (available on the Internet Rights website) highlights more specific problems such as "Electronic Rights in the Workplace" (Mobbs 2002).

The lack of access in regions such as rural India or the interior of Africa, as well as within impoverished ghettoes (mostly of minorities) in First World cities, privatization, censorship restricting online content, and regulation of Internet Service Providers (ISPs) prevent access and fuller use of ICTs. Beth Kolko (2006) has examined the policies governing Internet infrastructure and development in Central Asia. Her work is crucial because it links rights to access to larger issues of state control, funding, development policies, and infrastructure and once again grounds cyberspace in the material and the economic.

Rikke Jørgensen (2006) proposes measures to ensure compliance of national regulation with freedom of expression norms, spreading awareness of online communication and information access in school syllabuses, and the establishment of low-cost Internet access and proper mechanisms to ensure continuous development of a public domain of information. These, argues Jørgensen, will create a context for freer expression and communication.

Human rights and their effective "enforceability" in the global information society involves economic, political, social, and cultural issues. These include what Robin Gross (2006) has termed "communication rights," conceptualized as an important constituent of human rights. The principles involving communication rights are:

- national sovereignty over domestic information policies;
- protection for the intellectual "commons";
- intellectual property rights that should promote creativity;
- promotion of open source software;
- intellectual freedom.

Rights such as the right to privacy and intellectual property rights, as many thinkers observe (e.g., Gross 2006; Hosein 2006), are often at odds with such communication rights.

"Communication" is, of course, intrinsically (and etymologically) linked to "community." The right to communicate, especially via mass emailing and Internet listservs, has been used from the 1990s to organize support, campaigns, and resistance. In the aftermath of the 2004 tsunami and Hurricane Katrina (2005), websites and online campaigns mustered political, economic, and social support as aid agencies used the Internet as the speediest mode of mass communication. ICTs have arguably altered the spaces of association for individuals and organizations. This means that human rights campaigns now find new spaces of association.

Heike Jensen (2006) has argued that women's human rights can be strengthened via the use of ICTs. Looking at the women of the South, Jensen notes the potential ICTs have in terms of community building, employment opportunities, and disseminating information. In a related vein, Birgitte Kofod Olsen (2006) looks at the interface of minority rights and the GIS. Olsen proceeds from the conventional structures (usually legal and state-driven) for minority protection and argues a strong case for regulatory mechanisms that ensure

- rights of access;
- transparency in information gathering about ethnic minorities;
- cultural rights of the minorities in cyberspace (a theme addressed above in the discussion of postcolonialism and cyberspace).

The right of association has indeed slipped into the right to communicate here, but it has also attracted massive state surveillance and control (the Iranian government's efforts at monitoring Internet activity, China's surveillance of blogging, and the US Patriot Act are examples).

Political development as envisaged by these documents and thinkers is measured through indicators such as the freedom of expression, access to information, privacy protection, and transparency and participation in decision-making. Groups like Social Watch (www.socialwatch.org) are therefore central to the monitoring of violations in these areas.

However, until such time as these declarations and recommendations become enforceable and justiciable, they might remain mere rhetorical moves. What is important (despite that gloomy prognostication) is that there are quicker ways of finding information and legal remedies than ever before. Transparency and access to accountable bodies (or individuals) are achievements that might yet go a long way in human rights initiatives.

A key development in the direction of globalizing rights discourses is an initiative like the Geospatial Technologies and Human Rights project of the Science and Human Rights program of the American Association for the Advancement of Science (AAAS 2007). GIS, GPS, and other modes are used to prepare databases and geographical distribution of environmental disasters, atrocities, and diseases. First deployed effectively in 2004, high-resolution commercial satellite imagery by the US Agency for International Development (USAID) and the US Department of State confirmed ethnic cleansing in Darfur (www.usaid.gov/locations/sub-saharan_africa/sudan/satelliteimages.html). During hearings in The Hague at the Eritrea-Ethiopia Claims Commission, Eritrea provided evidence of Ethiopian misconduct with high-resolution imagery and photographs that showed extensive damage to homes, public buildings, and fields (see the Permanent Court of Arbitration records at www.pca-cpa.org/showpage.asp?pag_id=1151). Human Rights Watch used high-resolution imagery and other geospatial data to document civilian deaths during Operation Iraqi Freedom (Human Rights Watch 2003). In April 2007 using Google Earth software, the US Holocaust Memorial Museum put up the Crisis in Darfur database to document and publicize the human rights violations from the region (see www.ushmm.org/conscience/).

Environmentalism in the Internet Age

How do the new communications and transportation networks affect society and the natural landscape? It is a truism that new technologies can have a disruptive influence on the environment. However, they can also significantly alter individual and communitarian relationships with the environment.

The obvious use of ICTs would be, as can be imagined from earlier discussions, environmentalist campaigns. Advocacy, propaganda, and information dissemination through the availability of biodiversity databases are greatly facilitated by ICTs. Information about even remote areas can now be accessed and thus generate interest among activists and pressure groups. When the campaign to prevent a salt-processing facility (by Mitsubishi) at San Ignacio Lagoon in Mexico took to the Internet from 1995, it marked a historic moment in Internet-based conservation advocacy (Scherr 2002).

Communications and transport systems deconcentrate settlements and therefore development patterns. Smoother communication and transport mean that far-flung areas adjoining metropolises also develop as "satellites." Growing mobility means that there is a greater degree of flexibility in finding locations for offices or housing. Wired homes and environments mean greater flexibility for workers and employers alike, and deconcentrates workspaces. These are processes of "fragmentation" and "recombination" (W. J. Mitchell 2002: 53).

Mitchell (2002: 58–9) offers a few possibilities for conservation in the new wired era:

- using inexpensive, distributed intelligence to create more efficient electrical supply, vehicle, and building service systems, with better coordination;
- repurposing and revitalizing older urban structures: wiring older buildings of great architectural character does not damage them, and they can be fitted out for new forms of work and economic activity where the architecture itself can become a part of the attraction, leading to architectural preservation and historic neighborhood conservation;
- wiring basic units would mean that more places can have 24-hour populations instead of a commuter population that empties the town for much of the day: local neighborhoods can develop local services blended into the locality while being connected to the wider world.

Wiring neighborhoods might also result in emigration to non-metropolitan areas when people opt for spaces with better *natural* amenities and physically attractive regions. Thus Bend, Oregon, and communities in Deschutes and Crook counties are booming as people migrate, and empirical studies show that Internet penetration in these areas is high among those who identified themselves as members of conservation groups. Amenity-influenced migration by techno-savvy populations changes the culture and land-use patterns of the region (Leavitt and Pitkin 2002: 101–102, 105).

Environmentalists and activists have turned to the Internet in a major way in an effort to create global environmental systems and databases. Biodiversity informatics is a new field working with earth sciences, computational science, and software engineering. In the USA the National Science Foundation has identified bioinformatics as having the highest priority for knowledge creation in the biosciences. Biodiversity data from natural history institutions are being prepared for regions, species, and genomic domains. Data thus stored are now usable by research and teaching institutions through Species Analyst (a software that enables any user to query multiple databases simultaneously), allowing users to model, predict, and analyze species occurrences. Such databases – the "green Internet" – help activists and conservationists to work towards preservation/conservation of biodiversity, map species movements, and through analyses of pest species even redesign agricultural landscapes (Krishtalka et al. 2002).

The electronic linking of disaster sites, environmental accidents, and human rights violations constitutes an *alternative world vision* facilitated by ICTs.

Roger Silverstone argues that the mass media are a "space of appearance" (2007: 25–55). The Other appears to us, is made known to us, only on our screens. The world appears and is constituted in its appearance as difference on the screen. It is appropriate to conclude with an elaborated version of this argument. Initiatives concerning human rights, environmentalism, and race studies online are such "spaces of appearance." Here, in virtual space, there exists the possibility that we can see *and* respond to the suffering of the Other: that when the suffering Other calls to us from Darfur, Rwanda, or the Andamans, we can reach out.

Leela Gandhi's (2006) innovative reading of anticolonial Englishmen and their "politics of friendship" with Indians suggests the formation of such communities. Gandhi proposes that in the case of many dissidents in nineteenth-century Europe, individuals "betrayed" their national interests and ideologies (her examples include C. F. Andrews, E. M. Forster, and the vegetarian movement) because they valued their friendship with Indians and other cultures above all else. This "ethico-political practice of a desiring self inexorably drawn toward difference," Gandhi writes, resulted in an "affective cosmopolitanism" (2006: 17). Linking Gandhi and Silverstone's arguments, I see virtual, cybercultural initiatives such as the AAAS projects as enabling an *affective geography* of the world and of humanity itself.

The screen, the database, and geospatial maps of suffering recast the world not as oceans or *terra firma* but as sites of atrocity, deprivation, and pain. The virtual enables the creation of such "affective communities" where, despite one's "real" geographical, racial, or gendered locations, a whole new politics of affinity is possible. Such a cosmopolitanism of affective communities can surely happen only with ICTs. The ethical imperative is to recognize:

1. difference;
2. suffering;
3. the possibility of affinity.

This imperative is a *political* one, and this imperative must drive the future of cybercultures. What I have termed "postcolonizing cybercultures" with its emphasis on race, human rights, and environmentalism is a move towards a whole new affective geography of the material world that first appears virtually on our screen. By starting online and moving towards the concrete in terms of aid, refuge, understanding, and affect, we have a chance to actualize the "virtual."

NOTES

1 Wikipedia, Featherstone and Venn rightly point out, constitutes a destabilizing project where the cult of the expert is undermined (2006: 10). As we have noted in Chapter 6 on the public sphere, wikis constitute, along with the open source movement and blogging, an important means of ensuring the free access and flow of information, thereby ensuring a truly *public* public sphere.

2 According to Gómez-Peña, *pocha nostra* is a Spanish neologism meaning "our impurities" or even "the cartel of cultural bastards" (cited in N. Thornton 2007: 113). The postcolonial obsession with impurity and hybridity is reflected in the neologism itself.

CONCLUSION

This book has surveyed the various manifestations and dimensions of the informational age by foregrounding the thesis that cybercultures must be treated as recursively linked to, rooted in, and informed by the real, material world. Virtual worlds and online culture, it has argued, at some point "connect" with fleshly bodies, social structures of race and gender, cultural beliefs, and conditions of political economy and politics.

Chapter 1, "'Reading' Cybercultures," introduced the main thesis of the book: that cybercultures and virtual worlds have a *material* dimension. The "hardware" of virtual worlds and digital games is made of bodies, cities, concrete, cables, sentiments, workspaces, and labor that are subject to the dynamics of race, class, gender, economic inequalities, governance, and injustice. The chapter began with a brief account of the "information society" in a globalized world. Globalization and technocapitalism were the first topics discussed in the section "Key Issues in Cyberculture Studies." This section went on to discuss materiality and corporeality (that is, the theme of the fleshly body in digital cultures). It looked at the existence of many forms of the "digital divide" – inequality of access, quality, and expansion of digital technologies and cultures. E-governance, a significant issue in the political aspect and application of cybercultural technologies, was also examined here. This section raised the issues of identity, civil society in the age of digital cultures, class, race, space and geography, risk, the mediapolis, and aesthetics. Each of the discussions here served as introductions to further elaboration later in the book.

The chapter concluded with an examination of three "approaches" to cybercultures. Ethnographies of cyberspace would include a study of software design and their applications at the user end, the creation of online communities and networks, popular cultural forms of such technologies, the cultural identities that emerge in the new technospaces, and the political economy of cyberculture. *Apparatgeist* theory, first articulated in the context of mobile communications, addresses the "spirit" and "logic" of cybercultures. Chapter 1 proposed that the *apparatgeist* of cybercultures is a dual one: "perpetual contact" (as Katz and Aakhus 2002 suggest for mobile phones) and augmentation. A cultural studies approach would address questions of agency, power, and identity. This book's use of a cultural studies approach means that it treats cyberculture as an articulation between three crucial elements or actors: *hardware* (the machines, computers, cable networks), *software* (programs), and *wetware* (humans), where all three are deeply embedded in the social and historical contexts of the technology, and therefore also other "elements" or factors such as gender, race, symbolic and cultural forms, economy, politics, and identity. The book proposes that it is not possible to see cybercultures as simply ICTs without reference to questions of power, identity, ideology, and culture. This means paying attention to questions of politics: if there is a politics (and profit) involved in the production of cybercultures, there is also a politics in its consumption.

Chapter 2, "Popular Cybercultures," opened with a description of four main features of popular cybercultures: *convergence*, *remediation*, *consumption*, and *interactivity*. Convergence, as Henry Jenkins (2006) termed it, is the coming together of various applications across multiple media forms on a common platform or interface. Remediation, as first elaborated by Bolter and Grusin (1999), is the paradox where technology on the one hand tries to make the audience feel as though it is right there at the scene without any mediating technology (*immediacy*), and on the other draws attention to the medium itself (*hypermediacy*). Consumption refers to the consumer culture engendered by the new media technologies – from personalized search engines to products. Interactivity between audience and the producer and artifact marks new media cultures, where the audience/user exercises options and even co-constructs the technology or medium.

Having introduced these key concepts, the chapter examined various "genres" in cybercultures. *Cyberpunk*, the literary genre that represents life in a wired world, introduces a "posthuman" philosophy with the cyborg. *Posthumanism* believes that the human body's limitations – age, disease, appearance, disability – can be overcome and its capabilities – looks, intelligence, strength, disease resistance – augmented through technological intervention. The discussion of cyberpunk focused on the body (which is increasingly rendered into data, or modified as a cyborg), reproduction (generating a cultural anxiety about cloning), time and space, the environment (a post-apocalyptic world in most cyberpunk fiction and film), and information. It also presented the feminist critique of cyberpunk, which sees technology as embedded in patriarchy and capitalism and therefore exploitative and inherently unjust.

Computer games represent the most rapidly proliferating form of cybercultures. This section opened with a discussion of the social nature of games and their interactive element. The "new sociability" that emerges with gaming was also scrutinized, with the conclusion that gaming, especially of the LARP kind, marks the emergence of a new form of both sociability and public culture. The discussion then moved to consider the development of new skills, the narrative "structure" of games, role-playing, and, finally, the *racial* and *gendered* politics of gameworlds, arguing that the character in the game is configured at the interface of the "real" human player and the computer-generated figure on the screen, and is thus not completely autonomous. Gameworlds are framed in particular ways, in terms of both their production and consumption, and are often based on stereotypes of gender, race, and nationality.

Fans online constitute an important popular culture manifestation of cybercultures. Fan associations and texts are important means of bringing individuals into contact with other like-minded individuals and thereby forming a community. Online fan communities are an example of a cultural intimacy that develops despite geographical and temporal distances. Fansites are archives, documenting enormous amounts of detail about their chosen icon, as well as informational spaces, official or vernacular (i.e., unofficial), that are built around a particular celebrity. Online fandom enables many individuals to transcend their political, social, and cultural backgrounds to come together as a community united through a common focus of adoration that may have nothing to do with their "true" community. Online fans often transcend or ignore other "affiliations" of ethnic identity, race, place, and belief systems to constitute a community based on a common taste or preference. Fan politics, this section proposed, is also subject to its own politics of consumerism and questions of agency and identity. It argued that fans and fan associations spill over from the virtual world into the real, and that the contacts and power centered around the virtual fan community are instrumental in altering social-public arrangements in the material world.

New media art includes virtual reality performances, hypertext creations, and interactive art installations. Movies on mobile phones, visuals on desktops, music on the web, web telephony, and literary texts in SMS format are new forms of visuality, aurality, textuality, and tactility. Convergence culture within cybercultures gives an enormous amount of power to the user to design interfaces, aesthetics, and modifications within the computer world. The section on new media art explored "digitextuality" (the convergence of multiple forms of media in the digital age where print, audio, video, and graphics can be simultaneously accessed and processed through one common software application). Convergence, this section argued, also includes the convergence of technology into the human body. New media art that involves the audience (seen in exhibitions like TEXT RAIN) reanimate the audience, and hence could be described as active audience art. Many forms also embody the principle of "remediation," where new media forms emerge out of old ones. New media art, this section argued, refuses to separate the artifact from the audience viewing it, shifting the artifact from being simply a spectacle or a view to being an environment.

Podcasting and iPods have emerged as popular technologies usable for entertainment, information, and education. In this section, I suggested that podcasting has two key features: *customization* and *augmented distribution*. Unlike the Walkman or Discman, which treated the listener simply as a passive consumer, podcasting transforms the consumer into a producer. In terms of its role in education and the university, podcasting becomes a way of creating an alternate mode of knowledge creation and transmission, one that is not dependent upon institutions.

Genomic art is the newest trend on the Euro-American art scene. Using concepts and ideas from genetic engineering and biomedical sciences, these art forms – virtual installations, body modifications using computers and software – from Stelarc, Eduardo

Kac, and others seek to represent the possible evolution of the human. Treating such art as "posthuman art," this section argued that it explores and exhibits the possibilities of the human form. This involves particular aesthetic modes such as the monstrous and the grotesque, and the creation of "informational bodies" where the medium and the body are indistinguishable (what Eugene Thacker 2004a has called "biomedia"). However, such posthuman art forms also encode their own politics because, I argued, they represent the human tendency to take charge of destiny itself.

In the last section of this chapter, I addressed the now ubiquitous phenomenon of social networking. Social networking sites (SNSs) that enable the construction of profiles (private, public, or semi-public) have become the rage, especially among youth across metropolises. Social networking, this section argued, blurs the distinction between private and public. The theme of privacy in social networking – also the subject of major cultural and parental anxieties – was addressed, with the proposal that the exclusivity and monitoring of SNSs replicates conditions of exclusivity, privacy, and patrolling in real life. SNSs also enable the augmenting of social relations. Friendships are increasingly mediated and technologized through online interactions, and the SNS is a key mode of generating "friendships." Social networking also empowers the individual in terms of the acquisition of "social capital." For young people, social networking is a mode of self-representation and display. Hence profile management online, where users project a sense of their good "taste," becomes a central mode of generating and publicizing a *social* identity. Online networking, often leading to offline relations and friendships, has major *material* relations. Thus, online profile management is now an integral component of real-life identities because people increasingly meet both online and offline.

Chapter 3, "Bodies," studied the emergence of new forms of networked, wired, electronically linked, and modified human bodies. In the opening section of this chapter, it was argued that the posthuman is this networked and modified human body that does not fit in any precise fashion the definition of human or machine. The body is first *disembodied* and later *re-embodied* in a process I call *e-mergence*, where the merger of wetware (the organic body) and software (electronic circuitry) causes the emergence of a new form of the human itself. This posthuman e-mergence could occur through aestheticization (which includes high-tech body modification), digitization, and informatization (which includes the databasing of the body and more radical reconfigurations such as cryogenics and transhumanism). However, as this section argued, such a posthuman also becomes another consumer body.

In the next section of this chapter I explored the "connected" body, where the body is mediated by technology and technology itself becomes an extension of the body. I argued that the connected body occupies multiple spaces simultaneously, even as identity itself extends beyond the body and its skin. The posthuman experience is one of disembodiment and re-embodiment (what I called *e-mergence*). The body is "disembodied" when it is converted into a database. Yet it is also re-embodied, with subjectivity moving out of the body and into the cybernetic circuit. E-mergence is a phenomenon where the posthuman exists in a *symbiotic relationship* with technology, and where technology is no longer simply a functional or instrumental device but a *component* of the posthuman's identity itself. I also argued here that with the increasingly technological dependence of the body, all reality becomes mediated – what Mark Hansen (2006) has termed the "mixed reality" paradigm. Re-embodiment and e-mergence return us to the body, but the *body-in-technics*, whose convergence with technology facilitates augmented perception.

In the final section of Chapter 3 I explored the political consequences of this e-mergence of the posthuman. I suggested that we are in an age of "cyborg identity" because we do not experience our mobile phones or PCs as different entities but as our *selves*. The e-mergence of the posthuman suggests that identity is not *localized in* or *restricted to* a body any more. And yet a paradox exists at the heart of cyber-cultures: in an age when everything can be individualized and people can shop, work, play, or govern without stepping out of the home – an extreme example of the privatization and "disappearance" of the body – the individual can be, theoretically speaking, connected to the world 24/7. This dual move of privatization/disappearance and publicization/connection is a characteristic of the digital age. I reject the idea of a wholly virtual citizen body because, as I demonstrated in the chapter, for women and minorities who have sought rights and privileges based on their bodies, the transcendence of the body is a curse rather than a blessing for the simple reason that for them the physical body is *political*. Welfare, employment, medical services, voting rights, and citizenship are made available to the individual based on the color, ability, and ethnic identity of the *physical* body. Without a physical body, no "virtual citizenship" is possible. In this section I also looked at the changing configurations of aging, the family, and the "criminal" body. I returned to the book's thesis to show how virtual worlds are built by raced and gendered laboring bodies, arguing that politics must continue to be based on real bodies. Even with e-mergent bodies, I argued, politics, welfare, and rights require a physical body. In the final section, looking at citizenship, I saw agency as being at the core of citizenship and rights. In an age when agency is at least partly the effect of the non-organic material in/attached to our bodies, I argued that we may not be creating new citizens so much as new forms of citizenship practices through a greater participation in cultural "encounters" – transnational, diasporic, multicultural – facilitated by ICTs. A cautionary note was also sounded when I suggested that cyborg bodies could become the new norms for "bodies."

Chapter 4, "Subcultures," explored the ways in which marginal, alternative, and subversive cultures have emerged in cyberspace. Cyber-subcultures are practices that are not recognized or are deemed to be illegal by mainstream state or corporate culture. If cyberspace is a set of social practices, then those practices that do not find acceptance become subcultural. Blogging began as a tangential practice within cyberculture but has now acquired "mainstream" status. This section argued that blogs represent the endless self-construction and self-representation of the new media age, creating a hyperlinked self for public consumption. Blogging becomes a means of dialoguing with the world. The blogosphere is a realm that is constructed by users through the deployment of ICTs, and could become the basis of community formation.

Technologies of self-representation include webcams. Women's use of webcams, I argued, converts the everyday into a spectacle. It becomes a mode of controlling one's representation, and thus a means of empowerment for women. It enables the ordinary individual to become a performer for the world to see.

From these relatively "safe" forms of cyber-subculture, the chapter moved to a discussion of cybercrime and hacking. ICTs generate new forms of thieving. The section looked at a classification of the various forms of cybercrime, noting that hackers are often individuals who break into mainframes as a challenge rather than to steal. Hackers therefore become figures of *cybercultural resistance* where they symbolize "unauthorized" access. Hacking can be seen as a form of passing or masquerade where false identities in a fluid medium like the Internet enable hackers to bypass controls. Hacking is subcultural because it reconfigures technology and social relations by subverting the rules, laws, and social norms regarding the use of technology.

The chapter then considered hacktivism, tactical media, and cyberterrorism. Hacktivism, or politically motivated hacking, is used most often as a propaganda form. It turns cyberspace into a contested public space, extending into cyberspace the concerns, politics, and activism of the real-life public space. Hacktivism, I proposed, is linked to the new social movements of the twentieth century.

Tactical media emerged as a response to the corporatized or statist media forms that seek to stifle diversity of opinion. Tactical media use all forms of media, are temporary, and are "open source." They spread misinformation, track misinformation, stage virtual sit-ins, and damage the state or corporate information networks.

Finally, I turned to cyberterrorism. Cyberterrorism is the action by a group of people using computer networks to vandalize and destroy a nation/group's electronic, financial, and physical infrastructure for a political purpose. As state and corporate control over cyberspace increases, and more and more financial transactions take the electronic route, cyberterrorists find these technologies useful.

The next genre to be considered within cyber-subculture was online fandom. This constitutes a new form of community formation that helps people of similar tastes and objects of adoration to come together in cyberspace, irrespective of their material or geographical locations. Very often fan work such as slash fiction works in opposition to mainstream celebrity or fan culture.

The very opposite of fan cultures online is perhaps cyberhate. This section looked at the racialized, sexist, and virulent cybercultures that are visible today. Right-wing websites extend their ideologies into cyberspace. Just as hacktivists use ICTs to spread their anti-state campaigns or environmental groups use them to spread awareness, radical right-wing groups can use them to spread hatred.

Cyberfeminism seeks the appropriation of ICTs for women's use and emancipation. Resisting the masculinist and therefore patriarchal ideology of ICTs, cyberfeminists seek to free cyberspace. Feminist cyberpunk is a subcultural movement that believes there is an inherently diabolical link between cyberculture, technology, capitalism, and patriarchy. Writers such as Marge Piercy and Pat Cadigan consider the theme of bodily transcendence to be an escape from the realities of gender- and race-based oppression. They problematize the "alien" theme so common to SF and mainstream cyberpunk. Feminist cyberpunk writers redefine technology in terms of its use, and include magic, spirituality, and emotions as equally important responses to and modes of appropriation of ICTs. Feminist cyberpunk also sees technology as rooted in a specific social and cultural context. Extending the concerns of cyberfeminism, cyberfeminist art from groups such as VNS Matrix turns the patriarchal and sexist rhetoric and tropes about women into modes of self-representation. In-your-face sexuality and control over their bodies mark cyberfeminist art forms. This type of art underscores how technology can be appropriated by women to empower themselves.

Cyber-subcultures, this chapter concluded, extend into another realm, and with a greater degree of connectivity, community, and visibility, already-existing and resistant forms of thought, beliefs, and practices.

Chapter 5, "Gender and Sexualities," opened with an account of how women are affected by and affect technologies through a quick survey of the feminist critiques of technoscience. It then moved on to discuss women and cyberspace. Examining the issue of embodiment and technology, the first section mapped the "home" – traditionally a "feminine" space – as a space of embodied existence where certain routine actions are carried out repetitively. With ICTs, women creating their own homepages experience a different sort of embodiment. The use of webcams and blogs, I argued, helps women to escape their identities and create new ones.

This section also looked at cyberspace's continuing portrayal of women as objects for manipulation, arguing that the "escape" or "transcendence" of the body celebrated by cyberculture enthusiasts is not a desired aim for minority women. Taking up the argument outlined in Chapter 3, this section reiterated that the body cannot be transcended because identity, agency, politics, and justice continue to be predicated upon the physical body.

The chapter then moved on to consider gendered uses of cyberspace. Women's networks, for example, exemplify the gendered appropriation – both material and discursive – of the new media and new environments. While traditional patriarchal discourses about women persist in cyberspace, the realm still remains a possible source of augmented female participation in public spaces. The section proposed that potential uses of cybercultures do not apply to all women. The differential use of and access to ICTs for, say, white, African, and Southeast Asian women workers remain key issues. Hence the paradox that cyberspace as a counter- and feminist cyber-public sphere, with augmented identities, freedoms, mobilities, and agency, is made possible by women workers who will themselves never have (access to) such identities, freedoms, mobilities, or agency.

In some cases, however, cyberspace reconfigures the public space and the public sphere because it allows for new forms of debate, expression, and opinion making that are not restrained by norms of "rationality" and "reason."

In the third section I turned to the "sexual Internet," a survey of the sexualized World Wide Web. Studying the dominance of cybersex as a commercial development of the Internet and ICTs, this section located the freedom of cyberspace as an influential factor in the rise of cyberflirting and various forms of cybersex (a typology from various critics and studies was also provided). This section also examined feminist responses to the sexual Internet. Some feminists see cyberculture as extending and reinforcing stereotypes from real life, while others see it as liberating for women to explore alternative sexualities and preferences. Pornography online, the section argued, runs recursively whereby customers' preferences feed further variations and developments back into the online sex industry.

In the final section, the chapter turned to cyberspace as a site for alternative sexualities. It dealt with appropriations of cyberspace by queers and intersex groups where anonymity and connectivity reduce risk and extend opportunities for solace, romance, advice, and community.

Chapter 6, "Public Spaces," focused on the nature of public space and the public sphere as transformed through the proliferation of ICTs. Its key argument was that while cyber-public space cannot be assumed to be an entirely new space, it marks the augmentation of existing public spaces and an extension into another realm of the communities, sites of political action, and agency that exist in the real public sphere. Public spaces are also, I argued, spaces of surveillance through the use of CCTVs and display monitors.

I first looked at the nature of cyber*space* itself, starting with global cultural spaces. These include online spaces created by diasporic communities, the extensive commercialization of cyberspace through advertisements, and the spread of religion and beliefs through cybertechnologies.

Global restructuring through ICTs has meant that metropolises are now "soft cities" or global cities, networked to each other and operating as nodes in the flows of finance. However, I argued that this restructuring is not always equal because in many cases it involves an exploitative relation between cities and regions.

I then examined the methods of mapping cyberspace – via Internet usage, the space of information, home, and diaspora. Wired homes are now the norm, and they significantly alter the way the private/family space is experienced. Diasporic communities reconfigure geographical displacement by meeting in cyberspace. The technologies also affect everyday lives when home/office distinctions break down, as does the private/public divide. Regular users of the World Wide Web and ICTs also "map" cities differently, through the use of GPS or through information hotspots.

Local communities have begun to address neighborhood problems and initiate discussions online, thus marking a new form of social interaction and local intervention. A *network society* generates a new order of the public space and the public sphere by opening up access to participation in the public debate for even housebound men and women. It expands the reach of the local governing body and enables citizenry to connect. While much of this space and the nature of the public sphere depend on access, quality of communication, and responses (by the authorities), they also open up access to new forms of knowledge (such as wikis) that might be less "controllable."

The chapter proposed that social movements in cyberspace have the ability to affect real lives. Cyber-public space and the public sphere offer the possibility of an augmentation of movements for social justice in the material world, providing a digital public sphere that alters the texture of the material public sphere.

The chapter concluded that despite attempts to keep the World Wide Web "open," forms of control increase. The governance of cyberspace is a contentious issue, and institutions, nation-states, and corporate bodies assert a great deal of power in regulating this "public space."

Chapter 7, "Cybercultures: New Formations," offered a postcolonial approach to cybercultures, even though this approach might be seen as undergirding the entire book. It looked at the raced nature of cyberspace, especially in cybercultures' political economy in the context of business process outsourcing (BPO), labor (Asian and non-white workers), language (the dominance of English), posthuman identities (marked by fluidity and bodily "transcendence"), and racialized representations (in games). It argued for the "postcolonizing" of cyberspace – a process of interpretation and appropriation (of cyberspace) that is alert not only to the racially determined exploitative conditions of globalized ICT labor, but also to the emancipatory potential of cybercultures. This involves mapping the underlying ideologies and exploitative mechanisms at work within contemporary technoscience and a postcolonial tackling of globalization that would include a vernacularization of knowledge itself. The chapter thus looked at attempts by minorities and diasporic peoples to appropriate digital worlds for their own purposes. A postcolonial approach to cybercultures, it proposed, would include:

- an attention to the cybertypes (i.e., cultural representations) circulating in cyberspace;
- the raced material conditions (labor, knowledge workers) that produce cyberspace;
- the complicity of (postcolonial) nation-states with global, Euro-American-driven informationalism and knowledge formation;
- the alternative modes of expression possible for the vernacular and the local;
- an examination of the unequal power relations between races in cyberculture engendered by technologies of software and hardware (in terms of the computer education of minorities, for example, or access in their own languages);
- the opening up of the screen to cultural difference, where the screen is literally the space of the Other that demands a moral response.

The chapter then moved on to consider human rights in the informational age. Does the right of access to communication and cyberspace constitute a human right? Exploring this question, the chapter focused on "communication rights," minority rights in cyberspace, the modes of documenting and protecting rights of assembly, women's rights, and cultural rights in the digital age. In its concluding section, the chapter explored the role of digital technologies within environmentalism. Using a few case studies where digital technologies have enabled the reinforcement of biodiversity initiatives, it concluded that a "green Internet" is a major contribution of ICTs. The conclusion proposed that ICTs can help generate an alternative world vision, where the Other, the stranger, and the suffering can make their appearance and elicit a response. The virtual might be the space where an affective geography of the world is possible when the screen opens us to the Other. The virtual enables the creation of such "affective communities" where, despite one's "real" geographical, racial, or gendered locations, a whole new politics of affinity is possible. The chapter concluded by arguing that "postcolonizing cybercultures," with an emphasis on race, human rights, and environmentalism, is a move towards a whole new affective geography of the material world that first appears virtually on our screen.

GLOSSARY

Agency
Agency is the capacity of individuals to make choices to alter the course of their lives, and to implement those choices. Agency in social theory is the cornerstone of identity and rights, where the demand for rights is the demand for individuals to be able to pursue their goals, ambitions, and aims without hindrance.

Avatar
An avatar is an online identity. It is usually a graphic representation of the user in a virtual environment. It can be modified and made to look like anything the user wishes, and it can also be made to perform actions in the online environment. The term comes, incidentally, from Hindu mythology, where it signifies the reincarnations or earthly manifestations (appearances on earth) of gods. Its first use may have been in Lucasfilms' online game *Habitat*, dating back to the 1980s.

Blogging
Blogging is the construction of online diaries or blogs, which often include personal webpages that are available for public reading and response. Blogging has been defined as "reverse-chronological posting of individually authored entries that include the capacity to provide hypertext links and often allow comment-based responses from readers" (Bruns and Jacob 2006: 2–3).

Convergence
Convergence is the coming together of various applications across multiple media forms on a common platform or interface that allows the user to view webpages, make a telephone call, record music, and broadcast material.

Cyberculture
The electronic environment where various technologies and media forms converge: video games, the Internet and email, personal homepages, online chats, personal communications technologies (PCTs, such as the cell phone), mobile entertainment and information technologies, bioinformatics and biomedical technologies.

Cyberpunk

Cyberpunk is a science fiction genre that emerged in the 1980s which works mainly with cybertechnology, including virtual reality, often positing subcultures in a world of technocorporate capitalism.

Cyberspace

Cyberspace describes the worlds and domains generated by digital information and communications technologies (ICTs). It is seen, in this book, as a set of relations and actions in electronic space.

Cyborg

A portmanteau term coined by Manfred Clynes and Nathan Kline in 1960, cyborg means a *cyber*netic *org*anism. It refers to a man–machine system where the human body, and sometimes the mind, is interfaced with technological (including computer) systems.

Digital Divide

This term is used to describe the uneven nature of access to and quality of Internet access, electronic communication, and cybercultures in general. It gestures primarily at the difference in digital cultures – including production, dissemination, and use – between First World and Third World nations, though the "divide" within the former is also increasingly described under the same rubric.

Digitextuality

Digitextuality refers to the convergence of multiple forms of media in the digital age where print, audio, video, and graphics can be simultaneously accessed and processed through one common software application.

Emoticons

Emoticons are facial icons meant to convey emotional states. Derived from "emotion" and "icons," they represent a new language that has evolved with cybercultures and SMS communications.

Gameworld

Gameworld refers to the virtual worlds created by the software. It functions with its own set of rules and narrative conventions, whether it be strategic planning to build a civilization or take down an enemy unit.

Global Cities

Global cities are cities linked to global flows of finance, data, and ideas, often working as nodal centers for the transmission of these flows and possessing an urban architecture that is delocalized, containing the same chrome/glass/hardware structures as any other city.

Hacking

Hacking is the unauthorized entering of a computer database for any purpose. Now treated as a new form of crime, hacking has also led to the glorification of the hacker as a person who breaks security codes when he – it is invariably a male – penetrates computer systems. The *hacktivist* is a hacker who uses his computer skills for political ends in order to effect social change.

Hacktivism
Hacktivism is electronic activism that takes apart databases, hacks into mainframes, and creates electronic disturbance for political purposes.

Information Society
This term is used to describe the age of massive expansion of information and communications technologies (ICTs) over the last decades of the twentieth century – and the increasing reliance on electronic exchange/linkage of data, money, and markets.

Mixed Reality
The "mixed reality" paradigm as identified by Mark Hansen (the term was coined by artists Monika Fleischmann and Wolfgang Strauss) rejects the theme of bodily transcendence in virtual realities. This paradigm suggests that the body is the interface to the virtual, playing a crucial role in crossings between virtual and physical realms. It thus reinstates the body at the center.

MP3
MP3, a music-sharing technology, enables music to be compressed to about 1/10 of its actual size so that it can be stored and transmitted more easily. This technology was made open source in 1989 by Fraunhofer-Institut für Integrierte Schaltungen (FIIS-A). From the 1990s the technology enabled users to "rip" music, and has as a result become synonymous with music piracy (Featherly 2007b).

Nanotechnology and Nanomedicine
"Nano" is one billionth of a meter, roughly six carbon atoms in width. Nanotechnology seeks to engineer and manipulate matter and processes at the level of the atom. Nanomedicine is the medical application of nanotechnology. It involves the repair of body organs at the level of cells and even molecules such as protein.

Network Society
A term increasingly used to describe the wired nature of cities and societies across the world. Network cities are linked to global flows of commerce, consumer culture, and even politics. These are wired, hyperconnected cities where public debates, essential services, leisure, governance, and commerce are all technologically mediated with software, computers, and the Internet.

The Posthuman
Another term for cyborged bodies, where organic bodies are modified through surgical, chemical, and technological interventions and networked with software and hardware in order to restore, augment, or modify their "natural" abilities and conditions. The posthuman is an *e-mergence*, a congeries of wetware (organic), software (computer codes), and hardware (prostheses, electronic implants, and computer chips) whose interaction with/experience of the world is mediated through technology.

Posthumanism

Posthumanism is a point of view, ideology, and belief that the limitations of the human body – age, disease, appearance, disability – can be overcome and its capabilities – looks, intelligence, strength, disease resistance – can be augmented through technological intervention.

Protocol

The set of rules that determine the allocation of Internet addresses, domain names, and servers.

Remediation

Remediation is the double and contradictory logic whereby media technology seeks to simultaneously erase and highlight the process of mediation. Older forms of media are "remediated" by newer forms – for example, web TV combines cinema, TV, and the World Wide Web. This process involves two logics – that of *immediacy* (by which the process of mediation, the medium itself – say the computer – seems to become invisible) and *hypermediacy* (where the quantum of media available to the subject itself multiplies).

Social Networking Sites

Web-based services where people can host profiles, chat, and communicate, social network sites are a kind of virtual social-public space.

Subculture

Usually a group of practices occurring on the fringes of mainstream culture, and frequently in opposition to it. These could be cultures formed around particular political ideas, fashion, or taste in music. Subcultures are unofficial cultural formations that seek to escape or subvert state and corporate power, often through the use of similar technologies. With the advent of ICTs, subcultures have taken to online lives and communities that work at breaking the corporate stranglehold of information, software, and cultural meanings.

Subvertisements

These are spoofs or humorous reworkings of advertisements, often carrying political messages about corporate strategies, profiteering, or government oppression.

Tactical Media

Tactical media are based on temporary alliances provoked by an immediate issue or event that utilize media forms to protest, campaign, and organize opinions for anti-government or anti-corporate purposes.

Transcoding

Technically, transcoding is simply file conversion – from .GIF images to a video clip to audio files to print. In cultural theory, it is taken to represent the shift between the cultural "layer" and the computer "layer."

BIBLIOGRAPHY

Aarsand, P. A. (2007) "Computer and Video Games in Family Life: The Digital Divide as a Resource in Intergenerational Interactions." *Childhood* 14 (2): 235–256.

Aarseth, E. (2004) "Genre Trouble." *Electronic Book Review*. Accessed December 25, 2007 from www.electronicbookreview.com/thread/firstperson/vigilant.

Aarseth, E. (2006) "How We Became Postdigital: From CyberStudies to Game Studies." In D. Silver and A. Massanari (Eds.), *Critical Cyberculture Studies*. New York: New York University Press, pp. 37–46.

Amani, B. and Coombe, R. J. (2005) "The Human Genome Diversity Project: The Politics of Patents at the Intersection of Race, Religion, and Research Ethics." *Law and Policy* 27 (1): 152–188.

American Association for the Advancement of Science (AAAS) (2007) "Geospatial Technologies and Human Rights." Accessed from shr.aaas.org/geotech/whatcanGISdo. shtml#rc.

Anderson, B. (1991) *Imagined Communities: Reflections on the Origins and Spread of Nationalism*, rev. ed. London: Verso.

Anderson, B. and Tracey, K. (2002) "Digital Living: The Impact (or Otherwise) of the Internet on Everyday British Life." In J. Turow and A. L. Kavanaugh (Eds.), *The Wired Homestead: An MIT Press Sourcebook on the Internet and the Family*. Cambridge, MA: MIT Press, pp. 139–163.

Anker, S. and Nelkin, D. (2004) *The Molecular Gaze: Art in the Genetic Age*. Cold Spring Harbor, NY: Cold Spring Harbor Laboratory Press.

Annenberg Public Policy Center (2006a, September 20) "Online Contact by Strangers Common on Adolescent Social Networking Websites." Accessed December 4, 2007 from www.annenbergpublicpolicycenter.org/NewsFilter.aspx?mySubType=Finding.

Annenberg Public Policy Center (2006b, October 2) "More Than 1 Million Young People Use Internet Gambling Sites Each Month." Accessed December 4, 2007 from www.annen bergpublicpolicycenter.org/NewsFilter.aspx?mySubType=Finding.

Anon (2001) "Yahoo! Drops Porn from Portal." *Contemporary Sexuality* 35 (5): 9.

Anon (2005) "Podcasting in Medicine." *Journal of Visual Communication in Medicine* 28 (4): 176.

Anon (2008) "Social Network Sites Budding on 'Caste Bonding' Now." *Yahoo! India News*, February 11.

Anti-Defamation League (n.d.) "Extremism in America: About the Ku Klux Klan." Accessed October 25, 2007 from www.adl.org/learn/ext_us/kkk/.

Appiah, O. (2004) "Effects of Ethnic Identification on Web Browsers' Attitudes toward and Navigational Patterns on Race-Targeted Sites." *Communication Research* 31 (3): 312–337.

Arizpe, L. (1999) "Freedom to Create: Women's Agenda for Cyberspace." In W. Harcourt (Ed.), *Women@Internet: Creating New Cultures in Cyberspace*. London: Zed, pp. xii–xvi.

Ashcroft, B., Griffiths, G., and Tiffin, H. (1989) *The Empire Writes Back: Theory and Practice in Post-Colonial Literatures*. London and New York: Routledge.

Atkins, B. (2006) "What Are We Really Looking At? The Future-Orientation of Video Game Play." *Games and Culture* 1 (2): 127–140.

Atton, C. (2004) *An Alternative Internet: Radical Media, Politics and Creativity*. Edinburgh: Edinburgh University Press.

Aurigi, A. and Graham, S. (1998) "The 'Crisis' in the Urban Public Realm." In B. Loader (Ed.), *Cyberspace Divide: Equality, Agency and Policy in the Information Society*. London: Routledge, pp. 57–80.

Bach, J. and Stark, D. (2005) "Recombinant Technology and New Geographies of Association." In R. Latham and S. Sassen (Eds.), *Digital Formations: IT and New Architectures in the Global Realm*. Princeton and Oxford: Princeton University Press, pp. 37–53.

Badmington, N. (2004) *Alien Chic: Posthumanism and the Other Within*. London and New York: Routledge.

Balsamo, A. (1996) *Technologies of the Gendered Body: Reading Cyborg Women*. Durham, NC: Duke University Press.

Barbrook, R. (1997) "The Digital Economy: Commodities or Gifts?" Accessed December 26, 2007 from www.imaginaryfutures.net/2007/04/05/the-digital-economy-by-richard-barbrook/.

Bassett, C. (1997) "Virtually Gendered: Life in an On-Line World." In K. Gelder and S. Thornton (Eds.), *The Subcultures Reader*. London: Routledge, pp. 537–550.

Beck, U. (1992) *Risk Society: Towards a New Modernity*. London: Sage.

Beder, J. (2005) "Cybersolace: Technology Built on Emotion." *Social Work* 50 (4): 355–358.

Beer, D. (2008) "Social Network(ing) Sites… Revisiting the Story So Far: A Response to Danah Boyd and Nichole Ellison." *Journal of Computer-Mediated Communication* 13: 516–529.

Beier, A. L. (1985) *Masterless Men: The Vagrancy Problem in England 1560–1640*. London: Methuen.

Bell, D[aniel]. (1973) *The Coming of Post-Industrial Society: An Essay in Social Forecasting*. Harmondsworth: Penguin.

Bell, D[avid]. (2001) *An Introduction to Cybercultures*. London: Routledge.

Bell, D. (2007) "Cybercultures Rewriter." In D. Bell and B. M. Kennedy (Eds.), *The Cybercultures Reader*, 2nd ed. London and New York: Routledge, pp. 1–9.

Bell, D. and Kennedy, B. M. (Eds.) (2002) *The Cybercultures Reader*. London and New York: Routledge.

Bell, D. and Kennedy, B. M. (Eds.) (2007) *The Cybercultures Reader*, 2nd ed. London and New York: Routledge.

Bell, D., Loader, B., Pleace, N., and Schuler, D. (2004) *Cyberculture: The Key Concepts*. London and New York: Routledge.

Benzie, R. (2007) "Facebook Banned for Ontario Staffers." *The Star*, May 3. Accessed from www.thestar.com/News/article/210014.

Berry, R. (2006) "Will the iPod Kill the Radio Star? Profiling Podcasting as Radio." *Convergence* 12 (2): 143–162.

Bharucha, R. (2001) *The Politics of Cultural Practice: Thinking through Theatre in an Age of Globalization*. Delhi: Oxford University Press.

Biber, J. K., Doverspike, D., Baznik, D., Cober, A., and Ritter, B. A. (2002) "Sexual Harassment in Online Communications: Effects of Gender and Discourse Medium." *CyberPsychology and Behavior* 5 (1): 33–42.

Biddlecombe, E. (2004) "Cell Phone Users are Finding God." *Wired.com*, August 19. Accessed from www.wired.com/culture/lifestyle/news/2004/08/64624.

Biever, C. (2006) "The Irresistible Rise of Cybersex." *New Scientist* 190 (2556): 30–32.

Bijker, W. E. (1995) *Of Bicycles, Bakelites, and Bulbs: Toward a Theory of Sociotechnical Change*. Cambridge, MA: MIT Press.

Binnie, J. (1995) "Trading Places: Consumption, Sexuality and the Production of Queer Space." In D. Bell and G. Valentine (Eds.), *Mapping Desire: Geographies of Sexualities*. London: Routledge, pp. 182–199.

Bloch, L.-R. and Lemish, D. (1999) "Disposable Love: The Rise and Fall of a Virtual Pet." *New Media and Society* 3 (1): 283–303.

Boase, J., Horrigan, J. B., Wellman, B., and Rainie, L. (2006) "The Strength of Internet Ties." *Pew Internet and American Life Project*. Accessed November 30, 2008 from www.pewinternet.org/pdfs/PIP_Internet_ties.pdf.

Boies, S. C., Knudson, G., and Young, J. (2004) "The Internet, Sex, and Youths: Implications for Sexual Development." *Sexual Addiction and Compulsivity* 11: 343–363.

Bolding, G., Davis, M., Sherr, L., Hart, G., and Elford, J. (2004) "Use of Gay Internet Sites and Views about Online Health Promotion Among Men Who have Sex with Men." *AIDS Care* 16 (8): 993–1001.

Boler, M. (2007) "Hypes, Hopes and Actualities: New Digital Cartesianism and Bodies in Cyberspace." *New Media and Society* 9 (1): 139–168.

Bolter, D. J. and Gromala, D. (2003) *Windows and Mirrors: Interaction Design, Digital Art, and the Myth of Transparency*. Cambridge, MA: MIT Press.

Bolter, D. J. and Grusin, R. (1999) *Remediation: Understanding New Media*. Cambridge, MA: MIT Press.

Borchgrave, A. de, Cilluffo, F. J., Cardash, S. L., and Ledgerwood, M. M. (2001) *Cyberthreats and Information Security: Meeting the 21st Century Challenge. A Report of the CSIS Homeland Defense Project*. Washington, DC: Center for Strategic and International Studies.

Bowen, L. M. (2005) "Reconfigured Bodies: The Problem of Ownership." *Communication Theory* 15 (1): 23–38.

boyd, D. M. and Ellison, N. B. (2007) "Social Network Sites: Definition, History, and Scholarship." *Journal of Computer-Mediated Communication*, 13 (1). Accessed July 18, 2008 from jcmc.indiana.edu/vol13/issue1/boyd.ellison.html.

Boyd, J. (2003) "The Rhetorical Construction of Trust Online." *Communication Theory* 13 (4): 392–410.

Boyd-Barrett, O. (2004) "US Global Cyberspace." In D. Schuler and P. Day (Eds.), *Shaping the Network Society: The New Role of Civil Society in Cyberspace*. Cambridge, MA: MIT Press, pp. 19–42.

Boyd-Barrett, O. (2006) "Cyberspace, Globalization and Empire." *Global Media and Communication* 2 (1): 21–41.

Boyer, C. (1996) *Cybercities: Visual Perception in the Age of Electronic Communication.* Princeton: Princeton University Press.

Braidotti, R. (1996) "Cyberfeminism with a Difference." Accessed November 18, 2007 from www.let.uu.nl/womens_studies/rosi/cyberfem.htm.

Brennan, T. (2004) "From Development to Globalization: Postcolonial Studies and Globalization Theory." In N. Lazarus (Ed.), *The Cambridge Companion to Postcolonial Literary Studies.* Cambridge: Cambridge University Press, pp. 120–138.

BridgeToTheStars.Net (2008, July 9) "Pullman's Identity Stolen on Facebook." Accessed November 20, 2008 from www.bridgetothestars.net/news/category/philip-pullman/.

Briggs, A. and Burke, P. (2002) *A Social History of the Media: From Gutenberg to the Internet.* Cambridge: Polity.

Bruns, A. and Jacob, J. (2006) *Uses of Blogs.* New York: Peter Lang.

Byrne, D. N. (2007) "Public Discourse, Community Concerns, and Civic Engagement: Exploring Black Social Networking Traditions on BlackPlanet.com." *Journal of Computer-Mediated Communication*, 13 (1). Accessed July 18, 2008 from jcmc.indiana.edu/vol13/issue1/byrne.html.

Burke, C. (2001) "Women, Guilt, and Home Computers." *CyberPscyhology and Behavior* 4 (5): 609–615.

Burke, S. K. (2000) "In Search of Lesbian Community in an Electronic World." *CyberPsychology and Behavior* 3 (4): 591–604.

Burkhalter, B. (1999) "Reading Race Online: Discovering Racial Identity in Usenet Discussions." In M. A. Smith and P. Kollock (Eds.), *Communities in Cyberspace.* London: Routledge, pp. 60–75.

Butler, J. (1990) *Gender Trouble: Feminism and the Subversion of Identity.* London: Routledge.

Butler, J. (1993) *Bodies that Matter: On the Discursive Limits of "Sex."* London: Routledge.

Butler, J. (2002) "Is Kinship Always Heterosexual?" *Differences* 13 (1): 14–44.

Cadora, K. (1995) "Feminist Cyberpunk." *Science Fiction Studies* 22: 357–372.

Calleja, G. (2007) "Digital Game Involvement: A Conceptual Model." *Games and Culture* 2 (3): 236–260.

Castells, M. (1989) *The Informational City: Information Technology, Economic Restructuring and the Urban–Regional Process.* Oxford: Blackwell.

Castells, M. (1996) *The Rise of the Network Society.* Oxford: Blackwell.

Castells, M. (2000) *End of Millennium,* 2nd ed. Malden, MA: Blackwell.

Castells, M. (2001) *The Internet Galaxy: Reflections on the Internet, Business, and Society.* Oxford: Oxford University Press.

Castells, M. and Hall, P. (1994) *Technopoles of the World: The Making of Twenty-First Century Industrial Complexes.* London: Routledge.

Castronova, E. (2001) "Virtual Worlds: A First-Hand Account of Market and Society on the Cyberian Frontier." Center for Economic Studies and Ifo Institute for Economic Research Working Papers Series, Paper No. 618. Accessed December 26, 2007 from papers.ssrn.com/sol3/papers.cfm?abstract_id=294828.

Certeau, M. de (1988) *The Practice of Everyday Life.* Tr. Stephen Randall. Berkeley: University of California Press.

Chan, B. (2005) "Imagining the Homeland: The Internet and Diasporic Discourse of Nationalism." *Journal of Communication Inquiry* 29 (4): 336–368.

Chapman, G. (2004) "Shaping Technology for the 'Good Life': The Technological Imperative versus the Social Imperative." In D. Schuler and P. Day (Eds.), *Shaping the Network Society: The New Role of Civil Society in Cyberspace*. Cambridge, MA: MIT Press, pp. 43–66.

Charnigo, L. and Barnett-Ellis, P. (2007) "Checking Out Facebook.com: The Impact of a Digital Trend on Academic Libraries." *Information Technology and Libraries* 26 (1): 23–24.

Children Now (2001) "Fair Play? Violence, Gender and Race in Video Games." Accessed January 12, 2008 from publications.childrennow.org/publications/media/fairplay_2001b.cfm.

Chow-White, P. A. (2006) "Race, Gender and Sex on the Net: Semantic Networks of Selling and Storytelling Sex Tourism." *Media, Culture and Society* 28 (6): 883–905.

Clerc, S. (2002) "Estrogen Brigades and 'Big Tits' Threads: Media Fandom On-line and Off." In D. Bell and B. M. Kennedy (Eds.), *The Cybercultures Reader*. London and New York: Routledge, pp. 216–229.

Cockburn, C. (1985) *Machinery of Dominance: Women, Men and Technical Know-how*. London: Pluto.

Coleman, S. (2005) "Blogs and the New Politics of Listening." *Political Quarterly* 76 (2): 272–280.

Consumer Affairs (2006) "Connecticut Opens MySpace.com Probe." *Consumer Affairs*, February 5. Accessed November 30, 2008 from www.consumeraffairs.com/news04/2006/02/myspace.html.

Cooper, A. (1999) "Sexuality and the Internet: Surfing into the New Millennium." *CyberPsychology and Behavior* 1: 181–187.

Cooper, A., McLaughlin, I. P., and Campbell, K. M. (2000) "Sexuality in Cyberspace: Update for the 21st Century." *CyberPsychology and Behavior* 3 (4): 521–536.

Coopersmith, J. (2006) "Does Your Mother Really Know What You *Really* Do? The Changing Nature and Image of Computer-Based Pornography." *History and Technology* 22 (1): 1–25.

Cowan, D. E. (2005) "Online U-topia: Cyberspace and the Myth of Placelessness." *Journal for the Scientific Study of Religion* 44 (3): 257–263.

Critical Art Ensemble (2001) *Digital Resistance: Explorations in Tactical Media*. New York: Autonomedia.

Crogan, P. (2006) "The Question of Computer Games." *Games and Culture* 1 (1): 72–77.

Cronin, B. and Davenport, E. (2001) "E-Rogenous Zones: Positioning in the Digital Economy." *Information Society* 17: 33–48.

Cross, K. (2001) "Framing Whiteness: The Human Genome Diversity Project (As Seen On TV)." *Science as Culture* 10 (3): 411–438.

Cubitt, S. (1998) *Digital Aesthetics*. London: Sage.

Cyberspace Policy Research Group (CyPRG) (2001) "Webbing Governance: Global Trends across National Level Public Agencies." Accessed November 5, 2007 from www.cyprg.arizona.edu/publications/acm.rtf.

Daly, M. (1990/1978) *Gyn/Ecology: The Metaethics of Radical Feminism*. Boston: Beacon.

Daneback, K., Månsson, S.-A., and Ross., M. A. (2007) "Using the Internet to Find Offline Sex Partners." *CyberPsychology and Behavior* 10 (1): 100–107.

Davis, K. (1995) *Reshaping the Female Body: The Dilemma of Cosmetic Surgery*. New York and London: Routledge.

Day, P. and Schuler, D. (2004) "Prospects for a New Public Sphere." In D. Schuler and P. Day (Eds.), *Shaping the Network Society: The New Role of Civil Society in Cyberspace.* Cambridge, MA: MIT Press, pp. 43–66.

De Mello, M. (2000) *Bodies of Inscription.* Durham, NC: Duke University Press.

Dear, M. and Flusty, S. (1999) "The Postmodern Urban Condition." In M. Featherstone and S. Lash (Eds.), *Spaces of Culture: City, Nation, World.* London: Sage, pp. 64–85.

Deery, J. (2003) "TV.com: Participatory Viewing on the Web." *Journal of Popular Culture* 37 (2): 161–183.

Deleuze, G. (2004) "Postscript on Societies of Control." In S. Graham (Ed.), *The Cybercities Reader.* London and New York: Routledge, pp. 73–77.

Denning, D. E. (1991) "Hacker Ethics." Research Center on Computing and Society. Accessed October 14, 2007 from www.southernct.edu/organizations/rccs/resources/research/security/denning02/introduction.html.

Denning, D. E. (2000) "Cyberterrorism." Testimony before the Special Oversight Panel on Terrorism Committee on Armed Services, US House of Representatives. Archived at www.cs.georgetown.edu/~denning/infosec/cyberterror.html. Accessed November 18, 2007.

Dhillon, A. (2007) "Blogger Enraptures and Enrages India." *Telegraph,* October 7. Accessed October 17, 2007 from www.telegraph.co.uk/news/worldnews/1565404/Blogger-enraptures-and-enrages-India.html.

Dibbell, J. (1993) "A Rape in Cyberspace or How an Evil Clown, A Haitian Trickster Spirit, Two Wizards, and a Cast of Dozens Turned a Database into a Society." *Village Voice,* December 21, pp. 36–42. Accessed November 18, 2007 from ftp://ftp.lambda.moo.mud.org/pub/MOO/papers/VillageVoice.txt.

Doane, M. A. (1999) "Technophilia: Technology, Representation, and the Feminine." In J. Wolmark (Ed.), *The Cybersexualities Reader.* Edinburgh: Edinburgh University Press, pp. 20–33.

Dodge, M. (2004) "Geographies of E-Commerce: The Case of Amazon.com." In S. Graham (Ed.), *The Cybercities Reader.* London and New York: Routledge, pp. 221–225.

Dodge, M. and Kitchin, R. (2001) *Mapping Cyberspace.* London and New York: Routledge.

Döring, N. (2000) "Feminist Views of Cybersex: Victimization, Liberation and Empowerment." *CyberPsychology and Behavior* 3 (5): 863–884.

Döring, N. and Gundolf, A. (2006) "Your Life in Snapshots: Mobile Weblogs." *Knowledge, Technology, and Policy* 19 (1): 80–90.

Döring, N. and Pöschl, P. (2006) "Images of Men and Women in Mobile Phone Advertisements: A Content Analysis of Advertisements for Mobile Communications Systems in Selected Popular Magazines." *Sex Roles* 55: 173–185.

Dowland, P., Furnell, S., Illingworth, H., and Reynolds, P. (1999) "Computer Crime and Abuse: A Survey of Public Attitudes and Awareness." *Computers and Society* 18 (8): 715–726.

Downey, G. (2002) "Virtual Webs, Physical Technologies, and Hidden Workers: The Spaces of Labor in Information Internetworks." *Technology and Culture* 42 (2): 209–235.

Drake, W. J. and Jørgensen, R. F. (2006) "Introduction." In R. F. Jørgensen (Ed.), *Human Rights in the Global Information Society.* Cambridge, MA: MIT Press, pp. 1–50.

Du Gay, P., Hall, S., Janes, L., Mackay, H., and Negus, K. (1997) *Doing Cultural Studies: The Story of the Sony Walkman.* London: Sage.

Dutton, W. H. and Lin, W.-Y. (2002) "E-Democracy: A Case Study of Web-Orchestrated Cyberdemocracy." In J. Armitage and J. Roberts (Eds.), *Living with Cyberspace: Technology and Society in the 21st Century.* New York: Continuum, pp. 98–119.

Dwyer, C., Hiltz, S. R., and Passerini, K. (2007) "Trust and Privacy Concern Within Social Networking Sites: A Comparison of Facebook and MySpace." *Proceedings of AMCIS 2007.* Accessed from csis.pace.edu/~dwyer/research/DwyerAMCIS2007.pdf.

Ebo, B. (Ed.) (2001) *Cyberimperialism? Global Relations in the New Electronic Frontier.* Westport, CT: Praeger.

Eisenstein, E. (1979) *The Printing Press as an Agent of Change: Communications and Cultural Transformation in Early Modern Europe,* 2 vols. Cambridge: Cambridge University Press.

Elias, N. (2000) *The Civilizing Process: Sociogenetic and Psychogenetic Investigations,* rev. ed. Oxford: Blackwell.

Eliot, T. S. (1993/1917) "The Love Song of J. Alfred Prufrock." In T. S. Eliot, *Collected Poems 1909–1962.* New Delhi: Rupa, pp. 13–17.

Ellen-Case, S. (1995) "Performing Lesbian in the Space of Technology: Part II." *Theatre Journal* 47 (3): 329–343.

Ellison, N. B., Steinfield, C., and Lampe, C. (2007) "The Benefits of Facebook 'Friends': Social Capital and College Students' Use of Online Social Network Sites." *Journal of Computer-Mediated Communication,* 12 (4). Accessed July 18, 2007 from jcmc.indiana.edu/vol12/issue4/ellison.html.

Eriksson-Zetterquist, U. (2007) "Gender and New Technologies." *Gender, Work and Organization* 14 (4): 305–311.

Ervin, K. S. and Gilmore, G. (1999) "Traveling the Superinformation Highway: African Americans' Perceptions and Use of Cyberspace Technology." *Journal of Black Studies* 29 (3): 398–407.

Escobar, A. (1996) "Welcome to Cyberia: Notes on the Anthropology of Cyberculture." In Z. Sardar and J. R. Ravetz (Eds.), *Cyberfutures: Culture and Politics on the Information Superhighway.* New York: New York University Press, pp. 111–137.

Esen, R. (2002) "Cyber Crime: A Growing Problem." *Journal of Criminal Law* 66 (3): 269–283.

Eskelinen, M. (2001) "The Gaming Situation." *Game Studies* 1 (1). Accessed September 1, 2007 from www.gamestudies.org/0101/eskelinen/.

Everett, A. (2003) "Digitextuality and Click Theory: Theses on Convergence in the Digital Age." In A. Everett and J. T. Caldwell (Eds.), *New Media: Theories and Practices of Digitextuality.* London and New York: Routledge, pp. 3–28.

Feather, J. (2000) *The Information Society: A Study of Continuity and Change.* London: Library Association.

Featherly, K. (2007a) "Digital Millennium Copyright Act." *Encyclopedia of New Media,* online. Accessed April 4, 2008 from sage-ereference.com/newmedia/Article_n72.html.

Featherly, K. (2007b) "MP3." *Encyclopedia of New Media,* online. Accessed April 4, 2008 from sage-ereference.com/newmedia/Article_n166.html.

Featherstone, M. and Burrows, R. (Eds.) (1998) *Cyberspace/Cyberbodies/Cyberpunk: Cultures of Technological Embodiment.* London: Sage.

Featherstone, M. and Venn, C. (2006) "Problematizing Global Knowledge and the New Encyclopaedia Project: An Introduction." *Theory, Culture and Society* 23 (2–3): 1–20.

Ferree, M. C. (2003) "Women and the Web: Cybersex Activity and Implications." *Sexual and Relationship Therapy* 18 (2): 385–393.

Finn, J. and Banach, M. (2000) "Victimization Online: The Downside of Seeking Human Services for Women on the Internet." *CyberPsychology and Behavior* 3 (5): 785–796.

Fischer, C. (1988) "The Telephone Industry Discovers Sociability." *Technology and Culture* 29: 32–61.

Fisher, W. A. and Barak, A. (2000) "Online Sex Shops: Phenomenological, Psychological, and Ideological Perspectives on Internet Sexuality." *CyberPsychology and Behavior* 3 (4): 575–589.

Fisher, W. A. and Barak, A. (2001) "Internet Pornography: A Social Psychological Perspective on Internet Sexuality." *Journal of Sex Research* 38 (4): 312–323.

Fishwick, P. (2006) "An Introduction to Aesthetic Computing." In P. Fishwick (Ed.), *Aesthetic Computing*. Cambridge, MA: MIT Press, pp. 3–27.

Fiske, J. (1989) *Understanding Popular Culture*. Boston: Unwin Hyman.

Fiske, J. (1992) "The Cultural Economy of Fandom." In L. A. Lewis (Ed.), *The Adoring Audience*. London: Routledge, pp. 37–42.

Flanagan, M. (2002) "Hyperbodies, Hyperknowledge: Women in Games, Women in Cyberpunk, and Strategies of Resistance." In M. Flanagan and A. Booth (Eds.), *Reload: Rethinking Women + Cyberculture*. Cambridge, MA: MIT Press, pp. 425–454.

Foley, C., Holzman, C., and Wearing, S. (2007) "Moving Beyond Conspicuous Leisure Consumption: Adolescent Women, Mobile Phones and Public Space." *Leisure Studies* 26 (2): 179–192.

Franco, J. (2006) "Langsters Online: K.D. Lang and the Creation of Internet Fan Communities." In S. Holmes and S. Redmond (Eds.), *Framing Celebrity: New Directions in Celebrity Culture*. London and New York: Routledge, pp. 269–283.

Franklin, M. I. (2004) *Postcolonial Politics, the Internet and Everyday Life: Pacific Traversals Online*. London: Routledge.

Fraser, N. (1992) "Rethinking the Public Sphere: A Contribution to the Critique of Actually Existing Democracy." In C. Calhoun (Ed.), *Habermas and the Public Sphere*. Cambridge, MA: MIT Press, pp. 109–142.

Friedman, E. J. (2007) "Lesbians in (Cyber)space: The Politics of the Internet in Latin American On- and Offline Communities." *Media Culture and Society* 29(5): 790–811.

Friedman, T. (1995) "Making Sense of Software: Computer Games and Interactive Textuality." In S. G. Jones (Ed.), *Cybersociety: Computer-Mediated Communication and Community*. London: Sage, pp. 73–89.

Friedman, T. (1999) "Making Sense of Sim City." *First Monday* 4 (4). Accessed January 12, 2008 from www.firstmonday.org/ISSUES/issue4_4/friedman/index.html.

Frohlich, D. M., Dray, S., and Silverman, A. (2003) "Breaking Up Is Hard to Do: Family Perspectives on the Future of the Home PC." In J. Turow and A. L. Kavanaugh (Eds.), *The Wired Homestead: An MIT Press Sourcebook on the Internet and the Family*. Cambridge, MA: MIT Press, pp. 292–324.

Fromme, J. (2003) "Computer Games as a Part of Children's Culture." *Game Studies* 3 (1). Accessed September 2, 2007 from www.gamestudies.org/0301/fromme/.

Frosch, D. (2007) "Pentagon Blocks 13 Web Sites from Military Computers." *New York Times*, May 15. Accessed from www.nytimes.com/2007/05/15/washington/15block.html.

Fuchs, C. (2003) "'Death is Irrelevant': Cyborgs, Reproduction, and the Future of Male Hysteria." *Genders* 18: 114–115.

Fuller, M. (2005) *Media Ecologies: Materialist Energies in Art and Technoculture*. Cambridge, MA: MIT Press.

Furnell, S. (2002) *Cybercrime: Vandalizing the Information Society*. London: Pearson.

Gajjala, R. (2003) "South Asian Digital Diasporas and Cyberfeminist Webs: Negotiating Globalization, Nation, Gender and Information Technology Design." *Contemporary South Asia* 12 (1): 41–56.

Gajjala, R. and Mamidipudi, A. (1999) "Cyberfeminism, Technology and International 'Development.'" *Gender and Development* 7 (2): 8–16.

Gajjala, R. and Mamidipudi, A. (2002) "Gendering Processes within Technological Environments: A Cyberfeminist Issue." *Rhizomes* 4. Accessed November 16, 2007 from www.rhizomes.net/issue4/gajjala.html.

Galloway, A. (2004) *Protocol: How Control Exists after Decentralization*. Cambridge, MA: MIT Press.

Gandhi, L. (2006) *Affective Communities: Anticolonial Thought and the Politics of Friendship*. New Delhi: Permanent Black.

Garrelts, N. (2005a) "Negotiating the Digital Game/Gamer Intersection." In N. Garrelts (Ed.), *Digital Gameplay: Essays on the Nexus of Game and Gamer*. Jefferson: McFarland, pp. 1–19.

Garrelts, N. (Ed.) (2005b) *Digital Gameplay: Essays on the Nexus of Game and Gamer*. Jefferson: McFarland.

Gibson, W. (1984) *Neuromancer*. New York: Ace.

Gibson, W. (1994/1986) *Count Zero*. London: Voyager-HarperCollins.

Giddens, A. (1979) *Central Problems in Social Theory: Action, Structure, and Contradiction in Social Analysis*. Basingstoke: Macmillan.

Giddens, A. (1991) *Consequences of Modernity*. Cambridge: Polity.

Glenn, D. (2003) "Scholars Who Blog." *Chronicle of Higher Education* 49 (39). Accessed November 30, 2008 from chronicle.com/free/v49/i39/39a01401.htm.

Goggin, G. (2006) *Cell Phone Culture: Mobile Technology in Everyday Life*. London and New York: Routledge.

Goggin, G. (2009) "Adapting the Mobile Phone: The iPhone and its Consumption." *Continuum* 23 (2): 231–244.

Gómez-Peña, G. (2001) "The Virtual Barrio." In D. Trend (Ed.), *Reading Digital Culture*. Oxford: Blackwell, pp. 281–286.

González, J. (2000) "The Appended Subject: Race and Identity as Digital Assemblage." In B. Kolko, L. Nakamura, and G. B. Rodman (Eds.), *Race in Cyberspace*. London and New York: Routledge, pp. 27–50.

Goodings, L., Locke, A., and Brown, S. D. (2007) "Social Networking Technology: Place and Identity-Mediated Communities." *Journal of Community and Applied Social Psychology* 17: 463–476.

Gopalan, S. (n.d.) "Role of NCTs in Enhancing Women's Political Awareness." In I. Joshi (Ed.), *Asian Women in the Information Age: New Communication Technology, Democracy and Women*. Singapore: Asian Media Information and Communication Centre, pp. 61–64.

Gossett, J. L. and Byrne, S. (2002) "'Click Here': A Content Analysis of Internet Rape Sites." *Gender and Society* 16 (5): 689–709.

Graham, S. (1998) "The End of Geography or the Explosion of Place? Conceptualizing Space, Place and Information Technology." *Progress in Human Geography* 22 (2): 165–185.

Gray, C. H. (1997) *Postmodern War: The New Politics of Conflict*. London: Routledge.

Gray, C. H. (2001) *Cyborg Citizen: Politics in the Posthuman Age*. London and New York: Routledge.

Green, N. (2002) "On the Move: Technology, Mobility, and the Mediation of Social Time and Space." *The Information Society* 18: 281–292.

Griffiths, M. D. (1999) "All But Connected (Online Relationships)." *Psychology Post* 17: 6–7.

Griffiths, M. D. (2000a) "Excessive Internet Use: Implications for Sexual Behavior." *CyberPsychology and Behavior* 3: 537–552.

Griffiths, M. D. (2000b) "Does Internet and Computer 'Addiction' Exist?" *CyberPsychology and Behavior* 3 (2): 211–218.

Griffiths, M. D. (2001) "Sex on the Internet: Observations and Implications for Internet Sex Addiction." *Journal of Sex Research* 38 (4): 333–342.

Grochowski, T. (2006) "Running in Cyberspace: O. J. Simpson Web Sites and the (De)Construction of Crime Knowledge." *Television and New Media* 7 (4): 361–382.

Gross, R. (2006) "Intellectual Property Rights and the Information Commons." In R. F. Jørgensen (Ed.), *Human Rights in the Global Information Society*. Cambridge, MA: MIT Press, pp. 107–120.

Guertin, C. (2007) "All the Rage: Digital Bodies and Deadly Play in the Age of the Suicide Bomber." *Fast Capitalism* 3 (1).

Guins, R. (2004) "'Intruder Alert! Intruder Alert!' Video Games *in* Space." *Journal of Visual Culture* 3 (2): 195–211.

Gunkel, D. (2000) "We Are Borg: Cyborgs and the Subject of Communication." *Communication Theory* 10 (3): 332–357.

Habermas, J. (1962/1989) *The Structural Transformation of the Public Sphere*. Tr. T. Burger Cambridge/MA: MIT Press.

Hakken, D. (2008) "Cyberspace." In W. A. Darity, Jr. (Ed.), *International Encyclopedia of the Social Sciences*, Vol. 2, 2nd ed. Detroit: Macmillan Reference USA, pp. 216–217.

Hall, S. (2000) "Who Needs Identity?" In P. Du Gay, J. Evans, and P. Redman, P. (Eds.), *Identity: A Reader*. London: Sage.

Hansen, M. B. N. (2006) *Bodies in Code: Interfaces with Digital Media*. London and New York: Routledge.

Haraway, D. (1991a/1985) "A Manifesto for Cyborgs: Science, Technology and Socialist Feminism in the 1980s." In D. Haraway, *Simians, Cyborgs and Women: The Reinvention of Nature*. New York: Routledge, pp. 149–181.

Haraway, D. (1991b) "The Actors are Cyborg, Nature is Coyote, and the Geography is Elsewhere: Postscript to 'Cyborgs at Large.'" In A. Ross and C. Penley (Eds.), *Technoculture*. Minneapolis: University of Minnesota Press, pp. 21–26.

Haraway, D. (2006) "Encounters with Companion Species: Entangling Dogs, Baboons, Philosophers, and Biologists." *Configurations* 14: 97–114.

Harcourt, W. (1999) *Women@Internet: Creating New Cultures in Cyberspace*. London: Zed.

Harcourt, W. (2000) "The Personal and the Political: Women Using the Internet." *CyberPsychology and Behavior* 3 (5): 693–697.

Harper, M. C. (1995) "Incurably Alien Other: A Case for Feminist Cyborg Writers." *Science Fiction Studies* 22: 399–420.

Harpham, G. G. (1982) *On the Grotesque: Strategies of Contradiction in Art and Literature*. Princeton: Princeton University Press.

Harrison, C. (2006) "Cyberspace and Child Abuse Images: A Feminist Perspective." *Affilia* 21 (4): 365–379.

Hayles, N. K. (1999). *How We Became Posthuman: Virtual Bodies in Cybernetics, Literature, and Informatics*. Chicago and London: University of Chicago Press.

Hayles, N. K. (2008) *Electronic Literature: New Horizons for the Literary.* Notre Dame: University of Notre Dame Press.

Hebdige, D. (1979) *Subculture: The Meaning of Style.* London: Methuen.

Heitzman, J. (2004) *Network City: Planning the Information Society in Bangalore.* New Delhi: Oxford University Press.

Herman, A., Coombe, R. J., and Kaye, L. (2006) "Your Second Life? Goodwill and the Performativity of Intellectual Property in Online Digital Gaming." *Cultural Studies* 20 (2–3): 184–210.

Hermes, J. (2006) "Citizenship in the Age of the Internet." *European Journal of Communication* 21 (3): 295–309.

Herring, S. C. and Paolillo, J. C. (2006) "Gender and Genre Variation in Weblogs." *Journal of Sociolinguistics* 10 (4): 439–459.

Hevern, V. W. (2004) "Threaded Identity in Cyberspace: Weblogs and Positioning in the Dialogical Self." *Identity* 4 (4): 321–335.

Higgs, E. (2004) *The Information State in England: The Central Collection of Information on Citizens since 1500.* Basingstoke: Palgrave Macmillan.

Hine, C. (2000) *Virtual Ethnography.* London: Sage.

Hirst, P. and Woolley, P. (1982) *Social Relations and Human Attributes.* London: Tavistock.

Holland, S. (1998) "Descartes Goes to Hollywood: Mind, Body and Gender in Contemporary Cyborg Cinema." In M. Featherstone and R. Burrows (Eds.), *Cyberspace/Cyberbodies/Cyberpunk.* London: Sage, pp. 157–174.

Hosein, G. (2006) "Privacy as Freedom." In R. F. Jørgensen (Ed.), *Human Rights in the Global Information Society.* Cambridge, MA: MIT Press, pp. 121–147.

Howard, P. E. N., Rainie, L., and Jones, S. (2002) "Days and Nights on the Internet." In J. Turow and A. L. Kavanaugh (Eds.), *The Wired Homestead: An MIT Press Sourcebook on the Internet and the Family.* Cambridge, MA: MIT Press, pp. 45–73.

Huggan, G. (2001) *The Postcolonial Exotic: Marketing the Margins.* London: Routledge.

Human Rights Watch (2003, December 11) "Off Target." Accessed from www.hrw.org/en/reports/2003/12/11/target.

Humphries, H. (2003) "A Philosophical Inquiry into the Nature of Computer Art." *Journal of Aesthetic Education* 37 (1): 13–31.

Ignacio, E. N. (2006) "E-scaping Boundaries: Bridging Cyberspace and Diaspora Studies through Nethnography." In D. Silver and A. Massanari (Eds.), *Critical Cyberculture Studies.* New York: New York University Press, pp. 181–193.

IndiaInfo.com (2008, November 19) "Second Life Romance Costs First Life Marriage." Accessed from lifestyle.indiainfo.com/article/0811192142_second_life_romance_costs_life_marriage/244596.html.

Internet and Mobile Association of India (2006, February 7) "Number of Women Online Crosses the 12 Million Mark." Accessed December 6, 2007 from www.iamai.in/PRelease_Detail.aspx?nid=700&NMonth=2&NYear=2006.

Internet World Stats (2007) "Internet Usage Statistics. The Internet Big Picture: World Internet Users and Population Stats." Accessed November 5, 2007 from www.internetworldstats.com/stats.htm.

Introna, L. D. and Nissenbaum, H. (2000) "Shaping the Web: Why the Politics of Search Engines Matters." *The Information Society* 16 (3): 169–185.

Jackson, F. L. (1999) "African-American Responses to the Human Genome Project." *Public Understanding of Science* 8 (3): 181–191.

Jackson, F. L. (2001) "The Human Genome Project and the African American Community: Race, Diversity, and American Science." In R. A. Zilinskas and P. J. Balint (Eds.), *The Human Genome Project and Minority Communities: Ethical, Social, and Political Dilemmas*. Westport, CT: Praeger, pp. 35–52.

Jackson, L. A., Samona, R., Moomaw, J., Ramsey, L., Murray, C., Smith, A., and Murray, L. (2007) "What Children Do on the Internet: Domains Visited and Their Relationship to Socio-Demographic Characteristics and Academic Performance." *CyberPsychology and Behavior* 10 (2): 182–190.

Jacobs, K. (2004) "Pornography in Small Places and Other Spaces." *Cultural Studies* 18 (1): 67–83.

Janack, J. A. (2006) "Mediated Citizenship and Digital Discipline: A Rhetoric of Control in a Campaign Blog." *Social Semiotics* 16 (2): 283–301.

Jansz, J. and Martens, L. (2005) "Gaming at a LAN Event: The Social Context of Playing Video Games." *New Media and Society* 7 (3): 333–355.

Jenkins, H. (1992) *Textual Poachers: Television Fans and Participatory Culture*. New York and London: Routledge.

Jenkins, H. (1998) "'Complete Freedom of Movement': Video Games as Gendered Play Spaces." Accessed January 12, 2008 from web.mit.edu/cms/People/henry3/complete.html.

Jenkins, H. (2006a) "Game On! The Future of Literacy Education in a Participatory Media Culture." Accessed January 12, 2008 from www.projectnml.org/node/306/.

Jenkins, H. (2006b) *Convergence Culture: Where Old and New Media Collide*. New York: New York University Press.

Jenks, C. (2005) *Subculture: The Fragmentation of the Social*. London: Sage.

Jensen, H. (2006) "Women's Rights in the Information Society." In R. F. Jørgensen (Ed.), *Human Rights in the Global Information Society*. Cambridge, MA: MIT Press, pp. 235–262.

Johnson, S. (2006) *Everything Bad is Good for You: How Today's Popular Culture is Actually Making Us Smarter*. New York: Riverhead.

Jones, O., Williams, M., and Fleuroit, C. (2003) "'A New Sense of Place': Mobile 'Wearable' Information and Communications Technology Devices and the Geographies of Urban Childhood." *Children's Geographies* 1 (2): 165–180.

Jones, S. G. (Ed.) (1995) *Cybersociety: Computer-Mediated Communication and Community*. London: Sage.

Jordan, T. (2002) *Activism! Direct Action, Hacktivism and the Future of Society*. London: Reaktion.

Jørgensen, R. F. (2006) "The Right to Express Oneself and to Seek Information." In R. F. Jørgensen (Ed.), *Human Rights in the Global Information Society*. Cambridge, MA: MIT Press, pp. 53–72.

Jørgensen, R. F. (Ed.) (2006) *Human Rights in the Global Information Society*. Cambridge, MA: MIT Press.

Joshi, I. (n.d.) "Towards Women-Friendly Communication Technologies." In I. Joshi (Ed.), *Asian Women in the Information Age: New Communication Technology, Democracy and Women*. Singapore: Asian Media Information and Communication Centre, pp. 31–60.

Joshi, I. (Ed.) (n.d.) *Asian Women in the Information Age: New Communication Technology, Democracy and Women*. Singapore: Asian Media Information and Communication Centre.

Joshi, S. (2008) "Undersea Cable Breakdown Hits Internet-Based Services." *The Hindu*, February 1, p. 1.

Jung, S. (2004) "Queering Popular Culture: Female Spectators and the Appeal of Writing Slash Fan Fiction." *Gender Forum* 8. Accessed February 6, 2008 from www.genderforum. uni-koeln.de/queer/jung.html.

Juul, J. (2001) "Games Telling Stories? A Brief Note on Games and Narratives." *Game Studies* 1 (1). Accessed September 1, 2007 from www.gamestudies.org/0101/juul-gts/.

Kac, E. (2005a) "The Emergence of Biotelematics and Biorobotics: Integrating Biology, Information Processing, Networking, and Robotics." In E. Kac, *Telepresence and Bio Art: Networking Humans, Rabbits, and Robots*. Ann Arbor: University of Michigan Press, pp. 217–235.

Kac, E. (2005b) "GFP Bunny." In E. Kac, *Telepresence and Bio Art: Networking Humans, Rabbits, and Robots*. Ann Arbor: University of Michigan Press, pp. 264–285.

Kahn, R. and Kellner, D. (2007) "Technopolitics and Oppositional Media." In D. Bell and B. M. Kennedy (Eds.), *The Cybercultures Reader*, 2nd ed. London and New York: Routledge, pp. 618–637.

Kalathil, S. (2003) "Dot Com for Dictators." *Foreign Policy Magazine*, March/April. Accessed February 1, 2008 from www.carnegieendowment.org/publications/index.cfm?fa=view& id=1207&prog=zgp.

Kalathil, S. and Boas, T. C. (2003) *Open Networks, Closed Regimes: The Impact of the Internet on Authoritarian Rule*. Washington, DC: Carnegie Endowment for International Peace.

Katz, J. E. (2006a) "Mobile Communication and the Transformation of Everyday Life: The Next Phase of Research on Mobiles." *Knowledge, Technology, and Policy* 19 (1): 62–71.

Katz, J. E. (2006b) *Magic in the Air: Mobile Communication and the Transformation of Social Life*. New Brunswick, NJ: Transaction.

Katz, J. E. and Aakhus, M. A. (2002) "Making Meaning of Mobiles – A Theory of *Apparatgeist*." In J. E. Katz and M. A. Aakhus (Eds.), *Perpetual Contact: Mobile Communication, Private Talk, Public Performance*. Cambridge: Cambridge University Press, pp. 301–318.

Kellner, D. (1999) "New Technologies: Technocities and the Prospects for Democratisation." In J. Downey and J. McGuigan (Eds.), *Technocities*. London: Sage, pp. 186–204.

Kendall, L. (1996) "MUDder? I Hardly Know 'er! Adventures of a Feminist MUDder." In L. Cherney and E. R. Weise (Eds.), *Wired Women: Gender and New Realities in Cyberspace*. Seattle: Seal.

Kendall, L. (2007) "Cyberculture." *Encyclopedia of New Media*, online. Accessed April 4, 2008 from sage-ereference.com/newmedia/Article_n55.html.

Kennedy, H. W. (2002) "Lara Croft: Feminist Icon or Cyberbimbo? On the Limits of Textual Analysis." *Game Studies* 2 (2). Accessed September 1, 2007 from www.gamestudies. org/0202/kennedy/.

Kennedy, H. W. (2005) "Subjective Intersections in the Face of the Machine: Gender, Race, Class and PCs in the Home." *European Journal of Women's Studies* 12 (4): 471–487.

Kennedy, H. W. (2006) "Beyond Anonymity, or Future Directions for Internet Identity Research." *New Media and Society* 8 (6): 859–876.

Kennedy, T. L. M. (2000) "An Exploratory Study of Feminist Experiences in Cyberspace." *CyberPsychology and Behavior* 3 (5): 707–719.

Killoran, J. B. (2003) "The Gnome in the Front Yard and Other Public Figurations: Genres of Self-Presentation on Personal Home Pages." *Biography* 26 (1): 66–83.

Kilman, C. (2005) "Video Games: Playing Against Racism." Accessed January 12, 2008 from www.tolerance.org/news/article_tol.jsp?id=1228.

Kim, H., Kim, G. J., Park, H. W., and Rice, R. E. (2007) "Configurations of Relationships in Different Media: FtF, Email, Instant Messenger, Mobile Phone, and SMS." *Journal of Computer-Mediated Communication* 12 (4).

Kitzmann, A. (2003) "That Different Place: Documenting the Self in Online Environments." *Biography* 26 (1): 48–65.

Kolko, B. (2006) "Cultural Considerations in Internet Policy and Design: A Case Study from Central Asia." In D. Silver and A. Massanari (Eds.), *Critical Cyberculture Studies*. New York: New York University Press, pp. 119–128.

Kopomaa, T. (2004) "Speaking Mobile: Intensified Everyday Life, Condensed City." In S. Graham (Ed.), *The Cybercities Reader*. London and New York: Routledge, pp. 267–272.

Korzi, M. J. (2006) "The Benefits of Blogs." In A. Rolls (Ed.), *New Media. The Reference Shelf* 78 (2): 68–79.

Krishtalka, L., Peterson, A. T., Vieglais, D. A., Beach, J. H., and Wiley, E. O. (2002) "The Green Internet: A Tool for Conservation Science." In J. N. Leavitt (Ed.), *Conservation in the Internet Age: Threats and Opportunities*. Washington: Island Press, pp. 143–164.

Kwan, M.-P. (2007) "Affecting Geospatial Technologies: Toward a Feminist Politics of Emotion." *Professional Geographer* 59 (1): 22–34.

Lal, V. (2003) "North American Hindus, the Sense of History, and the Politics of Internet Diasporism." In R. C. Lee and S.-L. C. Wong (Eds.), *Asian America.Net: Ethnicity, Nationalism, and Cyberspace*. New York and London: Routledge, pp. 98–138.

Lambiase, J. (2003) "Codes of Online Sexuality: Celebrity, Gender and Marketing on the Web." *Sexuality and Culture* 7 (3): 57–78.

Lange, P. G. (2007) Publicly Private and Privately Public: Social Networking on YouTube." *Journal of Computer-Mediated Communication* 13 (1). Accessed July 18, 2008 from jcmc. indiana.edu/vol13/issue1/lange.html.

Latham, R. and Sassen, S. (2005) "Digital Formations: Constructing an Object of Study." In R. Latham and S. Sassen (Eds.), *Digital Formations: IT and New Architectures in the Global Realm*. Princeton and Oxford: Princeton University Press, pp. 1–33.

Lauritzen, P. (2005) "Stem Cells, Biotechnology, and Human Rights: Implications for a Posthuman Future." *Hastings Center Report* 35 (2): 25–33.

Lauwaert, M. (2007) "Challenge Everything? Construction Play in Will Wright's SIMCITY." *Games and Culture* 2 (3): 194–212.

Law, L. (2003) "Transnational Cyberpublics: New Political Spaces for Labour Migrants in Asia." *Ethnic and Racial Studies* 26 (2): 234–252.

Lawson, H. M. and Leck, K. (2006) "Dynamics of Internet Dating." *Social Science Computer Review* 24 (2): 189–208.

Leavitt, J. N. and Pitkin, J. R. (2002) "Internet Use in a High-Growth, Amenity-Rich Region." In J. N. Leavitt (Ed.), *Conservation in the Internet Age: Threats and Opportunities*. Washington: Island Press, pp. 99–122.

Leckenby, J. D. (2005) "The Interaction of Traditional and New Media." In M. R. Stafford and R. J. Faber (Eds.), *Advertising, Promotion, and New Media*. New Delhi: Prentice Hall of India, pp. 3–29.

Lee, M. J. W., McLoughlin, C., and Chan, A. (2007) "Talk the Talk: Learner-Generated Podcasts as Catalysts for Knowledge Creation." *British Journal of Education Technology* (OnlineEarly Articles). Accessed from www.blackwell-synergy.com/doi/abs/10.1111/j.1467–8535.2007.00746.x?cookieSet=1&journalCode=bjet.

Lee, R. C. and Wong, S-L. C. (Eds.) (2003) *Asian America.Net: Ethnicity, Nationalism, and Cyberspace*. New York and London: Routledge.

Lefebvre, H. (2000) *The Production of Space*. Tr. Donald Nicholson-Smith. Oxford: Blackwell.

Leland, J. (2006) "The Gamer as Artist." In A. Rolls (Ed.), *New Media. The Reference Shelf* 78 (2): 100–103.

Leonard, D. J. (2005) "To the White Extreme: Conquering Athletic Space, White Manhood, and Racing Virtual Reality." In N. Garrelts (Ed.), *Digital Gameplay: Essays on the Nexus of Game and Gamer*. Jefferson: McFarland, pp. 110–119.

Leung, L. (2002) "Loneliness, Self-Disclosure, and ICQ ('I Seek You') Use." *CyberPsychology and Behavior* 5 (3): 241–251.

Lévy, P. (2001) *Cyberculture*. Tr. Roberto Bononno. Minneapolis and London: University of Minnesota Press.

Lieberman, K.-A. (2003) "Virtually Vietnamese: Nationalism on the Internet." In R. C. Lee and S.-L. C. Wong (Eds.), *Asian America.Net: Ethnicity, Nationalism, and Cyberspace*. New York and London: Routledge, pp. 71–99.

Light, J. S. (1995) "The Digital Landscape: New Space for Women?" *Gender, Place and Culture* 2 (2): 133–146. Accessed November 30, 2008 from www.ingentaconnect.com/content/routledg/cgpc/1995/00000002/00000002/art00001.

Lillie, J. J. M. (2004) "Cyberporn, Sexuality, and the Net Apparatus." *Convergence* 10 (1): 43–65.

Lister, M., Dovey, J., Giddings, S., Grant, I., and Kelly, K. (2003) *New Media: A Critical Introduction*. London and New York: Routledge.

Liu, A. (2004) *The Laws of Cool: Knowledge Work and the Culture of Information*. Chicago and London: Chicago University Press.

Liu, H. (2007) "Social Network Profiles as Taste Performances." *Journal of Computer-Mediated Communication* 13 (1). Accessed July 18, 2008 from jcmc.indiana.edu/vol13/issue1/liu.html.

Livingstone, S. (2003) *Young People and New Media: Childhood and the Changing Media Environment*. London: Sage.

Livingstone, S. (2008) "Taking Risky Opportunities in Youthful Content Creation: Teenagers' Use of Social Networking Sites for Intimacy, Privacy and Self-Expression." *New Media and Society* 10 (3): 393–411.

Lockard, J. (2000) "Babel Machines and Electronic Universalism." In B. Kolko, L. Nakamura, and G. B. Rodman (Eds.), *Race in Cyberspace*. London and New York: Routledge, pp. 171–190.

Lovink, G. (2002) *Dark Fiber: Tracking Critical Internet Culture*. Cambridge, MA: MIT Press.

Löwgren, J. (2006) "Articulating the Use Qualities of Digital Designs." In P. Fishwick (Ed.), *Aesthetic Computing*. Cambridge, MA: MIT Press, pp. 383–403.

Luke, T. (1999) "Simulated Sovereignty, Telematic Territory: The Political Economy of Cyberspace." In M. Featherstone and S. Lash (Eds.), *Spaces of Culture: City, Nation, World*. London: Sage, pp. 27–48.

Lupton, D. (1998) "The Embodied Computer/User." In M. Featherstone and R. Burrows (Eds.), *Cyberspace/Cyberbodies/Cyberpunk: Cultures of Technological Embodiment*. London: Sage, pp. 97–112.

MacKenzie, D. (1998) *Knowing Machines: Essays on Technical Change*. Cambridge, MA: MIT Press.

MacKinnon, C. A. (1987) *Feminism Unmodified: Discourses on Life and Law*. Cambridge, MA: Harvard University Press.

MacNay, L. (2000) *Gender and Agency: Reconfiguring the Subject in Feminist and Social Theory*. Cambridge: Polity.

Madhavan, N. (2007) "India Gets More Net Cool." *Hindustan Times*, July 6, 2007. Accessed October 17, 2007 from www.hindustantimes.com/StoryPage/StoryPage.aspx?id=f2565bb8–663e-48c1–94ee-d99567577bdd.

Majid, Y. (2006) *Cybercrime and Society*. London: Sage.

Malaby, T. M. (2007) "Beyond Play: A New Approach to Games." *Games and Culture* 2 (2): 95–113.

Mallapragada, M. (2006) "An Interdisciplinary Approach to the Study of Cybercultures." In D. Silver and A. Massanari (Eds.), *Critical Cyberculture Studies*. New York: New York University Press, pp. 194–204.

Manovich, L. (2001) *The Language of New Media*. Cambridge, MA: MIT Press.

Marshall, P. D. (2004) *New Media Cultures*. London: Hodder Headline.

Mayer-Schönberger, V. and Crowley, J. (2006) "Napster's Second Life? The Regulatory Challenges of Virtual Worlds." *Northwestern University Law Review* 100 (4): 1775–1826.

McGerty, L.-J. (2000) "'Nobody Lives Only in Cyberspace': Gendered Subjectivities and Domestic Use of the Internet." *CyberPsychology and Behavior* 3 (5): 895–899.

McKenna, K. Y. A., Green, A. S., and Smith, P. K. (2001) "Demarginalizing the Sexual Self." *Journal of Sex Research* 38: 302–311.

Meek, A. (2000) "Exile and the Electronic Frontier: Critical Intellectuals and Cyberspace." *New Media and Society* 2 (1): 85–104.

Mehra, B. (2006) "An Action Research (AR) Manifesto for Cyberculture Power to 'Marginalized' Cultures of Difference." In D. Silver and A. Massanari (Eds.), *Critical Cyberculture Studies*. New York: New York University Press, pp. 205–215.

Miah, A. (2005) "Genetics, Cyberspace and Bioethics: Why Not a Public Engagement with Ethics?" *Public Understanding of Science* 14: 409–421.

Miah, A. and Rich, E. (2008) *The Medicalization of Cyberspace*. London and New York: Routledge.

Mignonneau, L. and Sommerer, C. (2001) "Creating Artificial Life for Interactive Art and Entertainment." *Leonardo* 34 (4): 303–307.

Miles, S. (2000) *Youth Lifestyles in a Changing World*. Buckingham: Open University Press.

Miller, D. (1987) *Material Culture and Mass Consumption*. Oxford: Blackwell.

Miller, T. (1993) *The Well-Tempered Self*. Baltimore, MD: Johns Hopkins University Press.

Miller, V. (2008) "New Media, Networking and Phatic Culture." *Convergence* 14 (4): 387–400.

Mitchell, W. J. (2002) "The Internet, New Urban Patterns, and Conservation." In J. N. Leavitt (Ed.), *Conservation in the Internet Age: Threats and Opportunities*. Washington: Island Press, pp. 50–60.

Mitchell, W. J. (2003) *Me++: The Cyborg Self and the Networked City*. Cambridge, MA: MIT Press.

Mitra, A. (2000) "Virtual Commonality: Looking for India on the Internet." In D. Bell and B. M. Kennedy (Eds.), *The Cybercultures Reader*. London and New York: Routledge, pp. 676–694.

Mitra, A. and Schwartz, R. L. (2001) "From Cyberspace to Cybernetic Space: Rethinking the Relationship between Real and Virtual Spaces." *Journal of Computer-Mediated Communication* 7 (1). Accessed November 9, 2007 from jcmc.indiana.edu/vol7/issue1/mitra.html.

Mitra, A. and Watts, E. (2002) "Theorizing Cyberspace: The Idea of Voice Applied to the Internet Discourse." *New Media and Society* 4 (4): 479–198.

Mobbs, P. (2002) "Electronic Rights in the Workplace: Changes to Workers' Rights and Employers' Responsibilities in the New Information Economy." Accessed March 22, 2008 from www.internetrights.org.uk/index.shtml?AA_SL_Session=8fa795873994ed10dd54938b98227a99&x=607.

Moorey-Denham, S. and Green, A. (2007) "The Effectiveness of Online Video Advertising." *AdMap* 481 (March): 45–47.

Morahan-Martin, J. (2000) "Women and the Internet: Promise and Perils." *CyberPsychology and Behavior* 3 (5): 683–691.

Moravec, H. (1988) *Mind Children: The Future of Robot and Human Intelligence.* Cambridge, MA: Harvard University Press.

Morgan, K. P. (1991) "Women and the Knife: Cosmetic Surgery and the Colonisation of Women's Bodies." *Hypatia* 6 (3): 25–53.

Morris, D. (2004) "Globalization and Media Democracy: The Case of Indymedia." In D. Schuler and P. Day (Eds.), *Shaping the Network Society: The New Role of Civil Society in Cyberspace.* Cambridge, MA: MIT Press, pp. 325–352.

Mortensen, T. E. (2006) "WoW is the New MUD: Social Gaming from Text to Video." *Games and Culture* 1 (4): 397–413.

Mossberger, K., Tolbert, C. J., and Gilbert, M. (2006) "Race, Place, and Information Technology." *Urban Affairs Review* 41 (5): 583–620.

Mueller, M. L. (2002) *Ruling the Root: Internet Governance and the Taming of Cyberspace.* Cambridge, MA: MIT Press.

Mulvey, L. (1975) "Visual Pleasure and Narrative Cinema." *Screen* 16 (3): 6–18.

Munt, S. (2001) "Introduction." In S. Munt (Ed.), *Technoscapes.* New York: Continuum.

Muthyala, J. (2008) "Whose World is Flat? Mapping the Globalization of Information Technology." *New Global Studies* 2 (1): 1–23.

Nakamura, L. (2002) *Cybertypes: Race, Ethnicity, and Identity on the Internet.* London and New York: Routledge.

Nakamura, L. (2005) "Talking Race and Cyberspace." Interview (Geert Lovink). *Frontiers* 26 (1): 60–65.

Nakamura, L. (2006) "Cultural Difference, Theory, and Cyberculture Studies: A Case of Mutual Repulsion." In D. Silver and A. Massanari (Eds.), *Critical Cyberculture Studies.* New York: New York University Press, pp. 29–36.

Nake, F. and Grabowski, S. (2006) "The Interface as Sign and as Aesthetic Event." In P. Fishwick (Ed.), *Aesthetic Computing.* Cambridge, MA: MIT Press, pp. 53–70.

NASSCOM Strategic Review (2007) "Executive Summary." Accessed December 14, 2007 from www.nasscom.in/upload/51054/Executive%20Summary.pdf.

National Alliance (2007) "General Principles." Accessed October 25, 2007 from www.natall.com/what-is-na/na1.html#natural.

National Alliance (n.d.) "Amnesty." Accessed October 25, 2007 from www.natall.com/leaflets/amnesty.pdf.

Nayar, P. K. (2004) *Virtual Worlds: Culture and Politics in the Age of Cybertechnology.* New Delhi: Sage.

Nayar, P. K. (2006a) "The Rhetoric of Biocolonialism: Genomic Projects, Culture and the New Racisms." *Journal of Contemporary Thought* 24: 131–148.

Nayar, P. K. (2006b) "Bodies and Spaces: Reading Women In/And Cyberspace." *In-Between* 15 (1): 3–21.

Nayar, P. K. (2007a) "The New Monstrous: Digital Arts, Genomic Arts and Aesthetics." *Nebula* 4 (2). Accessed from www.nobleworld.biz.

Nayar, P. K. (2007b) "The Digital Glocalized." *Writing Technologies.* 1 (1). Accessed from www.ntu.ac.uk/writing_technologies/Currentjournal/Nayar/index.html.

Nayar, P. K. (2008a) "New Media, Digitextuality and Public Space: Reading 'Cybermohalla.'" *Postcolonial Text* 4 (1).

Nayar, P. K. (2008b) "Wetware Fiction: Cyberpunk and the Ideologies of Posthuman Bodies." *ICFAI Journal of English Studies* 3 (2): 30–40.

Nayar, P. K. (2008c) "The Sexual Internet." *eSocialSciences Working Papers.* Accessed February 21, 2008 from www.esocialsciences.com/Articles/displayArticles.asp?Article_ID=1391.

Nayar, P. K. (2008d) "Postcolonializing Cyberculture: Race, Ethnicity and Critical Internet Studies." *LittCrit* 34 (1): 3–15.

Nayar, P. K. (2008e) "The Narrative Tradition of Posthuman Rights." In A. Miah (Ed.), *Human Futures: Art in an Age of Uncertainty.* Liverpool: Liverpool University Press, pp. 196–206.

Negroponte, N. (1995) *Being Digital.* New York: Vintage.

Nelson, C., Treichler, P. A., and Grossberg, L. (1992) "Cultural Studies: An Introduction." In L. Grossberg, C. Nelson, and P. A. Treichler (Eds.), *Cultural Studies.* London and New York: Routledge, pp. 1–16.

Neuborne, E. (2007) "Attract a Crowd." *The Advertiser,* October, pp. 86–90.

Newman, J. (2002) "The Myth of the Ergodic Videogame: Some Thoughts on Player–Character Relations in Videogames." *Game Studies* 2 (1). Accessed September 1, 2007 from www.gamestudies.org/0102/newman/.

Nichols, D., Farrand, T., Rowley, T., and Avery, M. (2006) *Brands and Gaming: The Computer Gaming Phenomenon and Its Impact in Brands and Businesses.* London: Palgrave Macmillan.

Nissenbaum, H. (2004) "Hackers and the Contested Ontology of Cyberspace." *New Media and Society* 6 (2): 195–217.

Nold, C. (2005) Greenwich Emotion Map. Accessed January 12, 2008 from www.emotion map.net.

Norris, P. (2001) *Digital Divide: Civic Engagement, Information Poverty, and the Internet Worldwide.* Cambridge: Cambridge University Press.

O'Leary, S. D. (1996) "Cyberspace as Sacred Space: Communicating Religion on Computer Networks." *Journal of the American Academy of Religion* 64 (4): 781–808.

Odih, P. (2007) *Advertising in Modern and Postmodern Times.* London: Sage.

Odin, J. (1997) "The Performative and Processual: A Study of Hypertext/Postcolonial Aesthetic." Accessed November 29, 2008 from www.usp.nus.edu.sg/post/poldiscourse/odin/odin1.html.

Oehlert, M. (2000) "From Captain America to Wolverine: Cyborgs in Comic Books: Alternative Images of Cybernetic Heroes and Villains." In D. Bell and B. M. Kennedy (Eds.), *The Cybercultures Reader.* London and New York: Routledge, pp. 112–123.

Olsen, B. K. (2006) "Ensuring Minority Rights in a Pluralistic and 'Liquid' Information Society." In R. F. Jørgensen (Ed.), *Human Rights in the Global Information Society*. Cambridge, MA: MIT Press, pp. 263–280.

Ong, A. (1999) *Flexible Citizenship: The Cultural Logics of Transnationality*. Durham, NC: Duke University Press.

Ong, A. (2006) "Mutations of Citizenship." *Theory, Culture and Society* 23 (2–3): 499–531.

Ow, J. A. (2000) "The Revenge of the Yellowfaced Cyborg Terminator: The Rape of Digital Geishas and the Colonization of Cyber-Coolies in 3D Realms' Shadow Warrior." In B. A. Kolko, L. Nakamura, and G. B. Rodman (Eds.), *Race in Cyberspace*. London and New York: Routledge, pp. 51–68.

Palackal, A., Anderson, M., Miller, B. P., and Shrum, W. (2007) "Internet Equaliser? Gender Stratification and Normative Circumvention in Science." *Indian Journal of Gender Studies* 14 (2): 231–257.

Palen, L. and Hughes, A. (2007) "When Home Base is Not a Place: Parents' Use of Mobile Telephones." *Personal and Ubiquitous Computing* 11 (5): 339–348.

Papacharissi, Z. (2002) "The Virtual Sphere: The Internet as a Public Sphere." *New Media and Society* 4 (1): 9–27.

Parker, T. S. and Wampler, K. S. (2003) "How Bad Is It? Perceptions of the Relationship Impact of Different Types of Internet Sexual Activities." *Contemporary Family Therapy* 25 (4): 415–429.

Parks, L. (2001) "Plotting the Personal: Global Positioning Satellites and Interactive Media." *Ecumene* 8 (2): 209–222.

Paul, C. (2003) *Digital Art*. London: Thames and Hudson.

Pearce, C., Fullerton, T., Fron, J., and Morie, J. F. (2007) "Sustainable Play: Toward a New Games Movement for the Digital Age." *Games and Culture* 2 (3): 261–278.

Pedersen, S. and Macafee, C. (2007) "Gender Differences in British Blogging." *Journal of Computer-Mediated Communication* 12: 1472–1492.

Peluchette, J. and Karl, K. (2008) "Social Networking Profiles: An Examination of Student Attitudes Regarding Use and Appropriateness of Content." *CyberPsychology and Behavior* 11 (1): 95–97.

Perlado, V. R. and Barwise, P. (2005) "Mobile Advertising: A Research Agenda." In M. R. Stafford and R. J. Faber (Eds.), *Advertising, Promotion, and New Media*. New Delhi: Prentice Hall of India, pp. 3–29.

Peter, J. and Valkenburg, P. M. (2006) "Adolescents' Exposure to Sexually Explicit Material on the Internet." *Communication Research* 33 (2): 178–204.

Petersen, S. M. (2007) "Mundane Cyborg Practice: Material Aspects of Broadband Internet Use." *Convergence* 13 (1): 79–91.

Pew Research Center (2007, April 15) "Public Knowledge of Current Affairs Little Changed by News and Information Revolutions: What Americans Know: 1989–2007." Accessed December 4, 2007 from people-press.org/reports/display.php3?ReportID=319.

Pink, D. H. (2004) "The New Face of the Silicon Age: How India Became the Capital of the Computing Revolution." *Wired* 12 (2). Accessed November 11, 2007 from www.wired.com/wired/archive/12.02/india.html.

Pitts, V. (2003) *In the Flesh: The Cultural Politics of Body Modification*. New York: Palgrave Macmillan.

Plant, S. (1995) "The Future Looms: Weaving Women and Cybernetics." In M. Featherstone and R. Burrows (Eds.), *Cyberspace/Cyberbodies/Cyberpunk: Cultures of Technological Embodiment*. London: Sage, pp. 45–64.

Plant, S. (1996) "Feminisations: Reflections on Women and Virtual Reality." In L. H. Leeson (Ed.), *Clicking In: Hot Links to a Digital Culture*. San Francisco: Bay Press, pp. 37–38.

PolicyLink (2007) "Bridging the Innovation Divide: An Agenda for Disseminating Technology Innovations within the Nonprofit Sector." Accessed December 5, 2007 from www.policylink.org/pdfs/Innovation_Divide.pdf.

Poon, M. K.-L., Ho, P. T.-T., Wong, J. P.-H., Wong, G., and Lee, R. (2005) "Psychosocial Experiences of East and Southeast Asian Men Who Use Gay Internet Chatrooms in Toronto: An Implication for HIV/AIDS Prevention." *Ethnicity and Health* 10 (2): 145–167.

Poster, M. (2006) *Information Please: Culture and Politics in the Age of Digital Machines*. Durham, NC: Duke University Press.

Power, E. (2006) "The Blog Revolution and How it Changed the World." In A. Rolls (Ed.), *New Media. The Reference Shelf* 78 (2): 9–15.

Private Media Group (2007, November 12) "Private Reports Net Sales 7.5 Million Euro and Net Income 0.5 Million Euro for Q3/07." Accessed November 16, 2007 from www.prvt.com/newsroom/press/view.php?pressid=184.

PR Newswire (2005, April 7) "Industry's First Benchmark Study From Nielsen Entertainment Provides Directional Findings on Emerging Markets, Spending, and Cross-Media Ownership for Interactive Entertainment." Accessed January 12, 2008 from www.prnewswire.com/cgi-bin/stories.pl?ACCT=104&STORY=/www/story/04-07-2005/0003338769.

Pullen, K. (2000) "I-love-Xena.com: Creating Online Fan Communities." In D. Gauntlett (Ed.), *Web.Studies: Rewiring Media Studies for the Digital Age*. London: Arnold, pp. 52–61.

Qian, H. and Scott, C. R. (2007) "Anonymity and Self-Disclosure on Weblogs." *Journal of Computer-Mediated Communication* 12: 1428–1451.

Rak, J. (2005) "The Digital Queer: Weblogs and Internet Identity." *Biography* 28 (1): 166–182.

Rakow, L. and Navarro, V. (1993) "Remote Mothering and the Parallel Shift: Women Meet the Cellular Phone." *Critical Studies in Mass Communication* 20 (3): 144–157.

Rapacki, S. (2007) "Social Networking Sites: Why Teens Need Places Like MySpace." *Young Adult Library Services* 5 (2): 28–30.

Rasmussen, T. (2002) "Internet as World Medium." In G. Stald and T. Tufte (Eds.), *Global Encounters: Media and Cultural Transformation*. Luton: University of Luton Press, pp. 85–105.

Ray, T. S. (2001) "Aesthetically Evolved Virtual Pets." *Leonardo* 34 (4): 313–316.

Rheingold, H. (1994) *The Virtual Community: Finding Connection in a Computerised World*. London: Secker and Warburg.

Rheingold, H. (2002) *Smart Mobs: The Next Social Revolution*. New York: Basic Books.

Robinson, H., Wysocka, A., and Hand, C. (2007) "Internet Advertising Effectiveness: The Effect of Design on Click-Through Rates for Banner Ads." *International Journal of Advertising* 26 (4): 527–541.

Rogerat, C. (1992) "The Case of Elletel." *Media, Culture and Society* 14: 73–88.

Rogers, M. (2000) "A New Hacker Taxonomy." Accessed October 14, 2007 from homes.cerias.purdue.edu/~mkr/hacker.doc.

Röhle, T. (2007) "Desperately Seeking the Consumer: Personalized Search Engines and the Commercial Exploitation of User Data." *First Monday*, 12 (9). Accessed October 16, 2007 from firstmonday.org/issues/issue12_9/rohle/index.html.

Rommes, E. (2002) "Creating Places for Women on the Internet: The Design of a 'Women's Square' in a Digital City." *European Journal of Women's Studies* 9 (4): 400–429.

Ross, M. W. (2005) "Typing, Doing, and Being: Sexuality and the Internet." *Journal of Sex Research* 42 (4): 342–352.

Rothenberg, T. (1995) "'And She Told Two Friends': Lesbians Creating Urban Social Space." In D. Bell and G. Valentine (Eds.), *Mapping Desire: Geographies of Sexualities*. London: Routledge, pp. 165–181.

Rowbottom, J. (2006) "Media Freedom and Political Debate in the Digital Era." *Modern Law Review* 69 (4): 489–513.

Roy, S. (2005) *Globalisation, ICT and Developing Nations: Challenges in the Information Age*. New Delhi: Sage.

Royse, P., Lee, J., Undrahbuyan, B., Hopson, M., and Consalvo, M. (2007) "Women and Games: Technologies of the Gendered Self." *New Media and Society* 9 (4): 555–576.

Rutsky, R. L. (1999) *High Technē: Art and Aesthetics from the Machine Age to the Posthuman*. Minneapolis: Minnesota University Press.

Ryan, M.-L. (1999) "Introduction." In *Cyberspace Textuality: Computer Technology and Literary Theory*. Indiana: Indiana University Press, pp. 1–29.

Ryan, M.-L. (2005) "Peeling the Onion: Layers of Interactivity in Digital Narrative Texts." Accessed December 26, 2007 from lamar.colostate.edu/~pwryan/onion.htm.

Sack, W. (2005) "Discourse Architecture and Very Large-Scale Conversation." In R. Latham and S. Sassen (Eds.), *Digital Formations: IT and New Architectures in the Global Realm*. Princeton and Oxford: Princeton University Press, pp. 242–282.

Said, E. (1978) *Orientalism*. Harmondsworth: Penguin.

Sardar, Z. (2002) "Alt.Civilizations.Faq: Cyberspace as the Darker Side of the West." In D. Bell and B. M. Kennedy (Eds.), *The Cybercultures Reader*. London and New York: Routledge, pp. 732–752.

Sassen, S. (1999) "Digital Networks and Power." In M. Featherstone and S. Lash (Eds.), *Spaces of Culture: City, Nation, World*. London: Sage, pp. 49–63.

Sassen, S. (2002) "Mediating Practices: Women With/In Cyberspace." In J. Armitage and J. Roberts (Eds.), *Living with Cyberspace: Technology and Society in the 21st Century*. New York: Continuum, pp. 109–119.

Sassen, S. (2005) "Electronic Markets and Activist Networks: The Weight of Social Logics in Digital Formations." In R. Latham and S. Sassen (Eds.), *Digital Formations: IT and New Architectures in the Global Realm*. Princeton and Oxford: Princeton University Press, pp. 54–88.

Scherr, S. J. (2002) "Conservation Advocacy and the Internet: The Campaign to Save Laguna San Ignacio." In J. N. Leavitt (Ed.), *Conservation in the Internet Age: Threats and Opportunities*. Washington: Island Press, pp. 186–217.

Schleiner, A.-M. (2001) "Does Lara Croft Wear Fake Polygons? Gender and Gender-Role Subversion in Computer Adventure Games." *Leonardo* 34 (3): 221–226.

Schmidt, J. (2007) "Blogging Practices: An Analytical Framework." *Journal of Computer-Mediated Communication* 12: 1409–1427.

Schuler, D. and Day, P. (Eds.) (2004) *Shaping the Network Society: The New Role of Civil Society in Cyberspace*. Cambridge, MA: MIT Press.

Schut, K. (2007) "Strategic Simulations and Our Past: The Bias of Computer Games in the Presentation of History." *Games and Culture* 2 (3): 213–235.

Schwartz, M. F. and Southern, S. (2000) "Compulsive Cybersex: The New Tea Room." *Sexual Addiction and Compulsivity* 7: 127–144.

Second Life (2007) "What is *Second Life*?" Accessed December 26, 2007 from secondlife.com/whatis/.

Selfe, C. and Selfe, R. (1994) "The Politics of Interface: Power and Its Exercise in Electronic Contact Zones." *College Composition and Communication* 45 (4): 480–504.

Seltzer, M. (1992) *Bodies and Machines*. New York: Routledge.

Servon, L. J. (2002) *Bridging the Digital Divide: Technology, Community, and Public Policy*. Malden, MA: Blackwell.

Sharpe, C. E. (1999) "Racialized Fantasies on the Internet." *Signs* 24 (4): 1089–1096.

Shave, R. (2004) "Slash Fandom on the Internet, Or Is the Carnival Over?" *Refractory* 6. Accessed February 6, 2008 from www.refractory.unimelb.edu.au/journalissues/vol6/RShave.html.

Shields, R. (Ed.) (1996) *Cultures of Internet: Virtual Spaces, Real Histories, Living Bodies*. London: Sage.

Shilling, C. (2005) *The Body in Culture, Technology and Society*. London: Sage.

Shome, R. (2006) "Thinking Through the Diaspora: Call Centers, India, and a New Politics of Hybridity." *International Journal of Cultural Studies* 9 (1): 105–124.

Shome, R. and Hegde, R. S. (2002) "Postcolonial Approaches to Communication: Charting the Terrains, Engaging the Intersections." *Communication Theory* 12 (3): 249–270.

Siapera, E. (2006) "Multiculturalism Online: The Internet and the Dilemmas of Multicultural Politics." *European Journal of Cultural Studies* 9 (1): 5–24.

Silva, V. T. (2005) "In the Beginning Was the Gene: The Hegemony of Genetic Thinking in Contemporary Culture." *Communication Theory* 15 (1): 100–123.

Silver, D. (2004) "The Soil of Cyberspace: Historical Archaeologies of the Blacksburg Electronic Village and the Seattle Community Network." In D. Schuler and P. Day (Eds.), *Shaping the Network Society: The New Role of Civil Society in Cyberspace*. Cambridge, MA: MIT Press, pp. 301–324.

Silverstone, R. (2007) *Media and Morality: On the Rise of the Mediapolis*. Cambridge: Polity.

Silverstone, R. and Haddon, L. (1996) "Design and the Domestication of Information and Communication Technologies: Technical Change and Everyday Life." In R. Mansell and R. Silverstone (Eds.), *Communication by Design: The Politics of Information and Communication Technologies*. Oxford: Oxford University Press, pp. 44–74.

Simon, B. (2007) "Geek Chic: Machine Aesthetics, Digital Gaming, and the Cultural Politics of the Case Mod." *Games and Culture* 2 (3): 175–193.

Slack, J. D. and Wise, J. M. (2006) "Cultural Studies and Communication Technology." In L. A. Lievrouw and S. Livingstone (Eds.), *The Handbook of New Media*. London: Sage, pp. 141–162.

Slocombe, M. (2005) "Men Spend More Money on Video Games Than Music: Nielsen Report." Accessed January 12, 2008 from digital-lifestyles.info/2005/04/11/men-spend-more-money-on-video-games-than-music-nielsen-report/.

Sofia, Z. (1999) "Virtual Corporeality: A Feminist View." In J. Wolmark (Ed.), *The Cybersexualities Reader*. Edinburgh: Edinburgh University Press, pp. 55–68.

Soja, E. (1993) *Postmodern Geographies: The Reassertion of Space in Contemporary Social Theory*. London: Verso.

Sorapure, M. (2003) "Screening Moments, Scrolling Lives: Diary Writing on the Web." *Biography* 26 (1): 1–23.

Soysal, Y. (1994) *The Limits of Citizenship: Migrants and Postnational Membership in Europe*. Chicago: University of Chicago Press.

Spertus, E. (1991) "Why Are There So Few Female Computer Scientists?" MIT Artificial Intelligence Laboratory Technical Report. Accessed November 26, 2007 from ftp:// publications.ai.mit.edu/ai-publications/pdf/AITR-1315.pdf.

Spink, A. and Zimmer, M. (2008) *Web Search: Multidisciplinary Perspectives*. Berlin: Springer-Verlag.

Springer, C. (1999) "The Pleasure of the Interface." In J. Wolmark (Ed.), *The Cybersexualities Reader*. Edinburgh: Edinburgh University Press, pp. 34–54.

Squire, K. (2002) "Cultural Framing of Computer/Video Games." *Game Studies* 2 (1). Accessed September 1, 2007 from www.gamestudies.org/0102/squire/.

Srivastava, L. (2006) "Mobile Mania, Mobile Manners." *Knowledge, Technology, and Policy* 19 (2): 7–16.

Stelarc (1991) "Prosthetics, Robotics and Remote Existence: Postevolutionary Strategies." *Leonardo* 24 (5): 591–594.

Stelarc (2002) "Probings." Interview with Joanna Zylinska and Gary Hall. In J. Zylinska (Ed.), *The Cyborg Experiments: The Extensions of the Body in the Media Age*. New York: Continuum, pp. 114–130.

Sterling, B. (1988a) "Preface." In Sterling (Ed.), *Mirrorshades: The Cyberpunk Anthology*. New York: Ace-Arbor House, pp. ix–xvi.

Sterling, B. (Ed.) (1988b) *Mirrorshades: The Cyberpunk Anthology*. New York: Ace-Arbor House.

Stern, B. B., Zinkhan, G. M., and Holbrook, M. B. (2005) "The Netvertising Image: Netvertising Image Communication Model (NICM) and Construct Definition." In M. R. Stafford and R. J. Faber (Eds.), *Advertising, Promotion, and New Media*. New Delhi: Prentice Hall of India, pp. 30–50.

Stohl, C. and Stohl, M. (2007) "Networks of Terror: Theoretical Assumptions and Pragmatic Consequences." *Communication Theory* 17: 93–124.

Stone, A. R. (2002) "Will the Real Body Please Stand Up? Boundary Stories About Virtual Cultures." In D. Bell and B. M. Kennedy (Eds.), *The Cybercultures Reader*. London and New York: Routledge, pp. 504–528.

Strasser, S. (1982) *Never Done*. New York: Random House.

Stratton, J. (1997) "Cyberspace and the Globalization of Culture." In D. Porter (Ed.), *Internet Culture*. New York: Routledge, pp. 253–275.

Taylor, C. and Pitman, T. (2007a) "Conclusion: Latin American Identity and Cyberspace." In C. Taylor and T. Pitman (Eds.), *Latin American Cyberculture and Cyberliterature*. Liverpool: Liverpool University Press, pp. 263–267.

Taylor, C. and Pitman, T. (Eds.) (2007b) *Latin American Cyberculture and Cyberliterature*. Liverpool: Liverpool University Press.

Taylor, P. and Bain, P. (2005) "'India Calling to the Far Away Towns': The Call Centre Labour Process and Globalization." *Work, Employment and Society* 19 (2): 261–282.

Taylor, P. J. (2004) *World City Network: A Global Urban Analysis*. London and New York: Routledge.

Terranova, T. (2000) "Free Labor: Producing Culture for the Digital Economy." *Social Text* 18 (2): 34–58.

Thacker, E. (2004a) *Biomedia*. Minneapolis: University of Minnesota Press.

Thacker, E. (2004b) "Protocol Is As Protocol Does." Foreword. In A. Galloway, *Protocol: How Control Exists After Decentralization*. Cambridge, MA: MIT Press, pp. xi–xxii.

Thacker, E. (2005) *The Global Genome: Biotechnology, Politics, and Culture*. Cambridge, MA: MIT Press.

Thien, D. (2005) "After or Beyond Feeling: A Consideration of Affect and Emotion in Geography." *Area* 37 (4): 450–456.

Thomas, A. (2006) "Fan Fiction Online: Engagement, Critical Response and Affective Play through Writing." *Australian Journal of Language and Literacy* 29 (3): 216–239.

Thomas, D. (2000) "Criminality on the Electronic Frontier: Corporality and the Judicial Construction of the Hacker." In D. Thomas and B. D. Loader (Eds.), *Cybercrime: Law Enforcement, Security and Surveillance in the Information Age*. London and New York: Routledge, pp. 17–35.

Thomas, D. (2002) *Hacker Culture*. Minneapolis and London: Minnesota University Press.

Thomas, D. and Loader B. D. (2000) "Cybercrime: Law Enforcement, Security and Surveillance in the Information Age." In D. Thomas and B. D. Loader (Eds.), *Cybercrime: Law Enforcement, Security and Surveillance in the Information Age*. London and New York: Routledge, pp. 1–13.

Thompson, J. B. (1995) *The Media and Modernity: A Social Theory of the Media*. Stanford: Stanford University Press.

Thornton, N. (2007) "Body, Nation, and Identity: Guillermo Gómez-Peña's Performances on the Web." In C. Taylor and T. Pitman (Eds.), *Latin American Cyberculture and Cyberliterature*. Liverpool: Liverpool University Press, pp. 111–122.

Thornton, S. (1997) "General Introduction." In K. Gelder and S. Thornton (Eds.), *The Subcultures Reader*. London: Routledge.

Thrift, N. (1996) *Spatial Formations*. London: Sage.

Thrift, N. (2004) "Intensities of Feeling: Towards a Spatial Politics of Affect." *Geografiska Annaler Series B* 86: 57–78.

Thrift, N. (2005) *Knowing Capitalism*. London: Sage.

Thrupkaew, N. (2003) "Fan/tastic Voyage: A Journey into the Wide, Wild World of Slash Fiction." *Bitch: Feminist Response to Pop Culture* 20. Accessed February 6, 2008 from www.bitchmagazine.com/archives/04_03slash/slash.shtml.

Tomasula, S. (2002) "Genetic Art and the Aesthetics of Biology." *Leonardo* 35 (2): 137–144.

Tran, M. (2007) "Internet Access Cut Off in Burma." *The Guardian*, September 28. Accessed February 1, 2008 from www.guardian.co.uk/burma/story/0,,2179427,00.html.

Travers, A. (2003) "Parallel Subaltern Feminist Counterpublics in Cyberspace." *Sociological Perspectives* 46 (2): 223–237.

Turkle, S. (1995) *Life on Screen: Identity in the Age of the Internet*. New York: Simon and Schuster.

Turner, S. S. (1999) "Intersex Identities: Locating New Intersections of Sex and Gender." *Gender and Society* 13 (4): 457–479.

Turow, J. and Nir, L. (2002) "The Internet and the Family: The Views of Parents and Youngsters." In J. Turow and A. L. Kavanaugh (Eds.), *The Wired Homestead: An MIT Press Sourcebook on the Internet and the Family*. Cambridge, MA: MIT Press, pp. 161–206.

Tychsen, A., Hitchens, M., Brolund, T., and Kavakli, M. (2006) "Live Action Role-Playing Games: Control, Communication, Storytelling and MMORPG Similarities." *Games and Culture* 1 (3): 252–275.

United Nations Economic and Social Council (2000, July 25–August 1) "Development and International Cooperation in the 21st Century: The Role of Information Technology in the Context of a Knowledge-Based Global Economy." Accessed March 22, 2008 from www.un.org/documents.

Unsworth, L. (2006) *E-literature for Children: Enhancing Digital Literacy Learning*. London and New York: Routledge.

Van Loon, J. (2002) *Risk and Technological Culture: Towards a Sociology of Virulence*. London and New York: Routledge.

Vargas, J. A. (2005) "Taking the Controllers." *Washington Post*, August 6. Accessed January 12, 2008 from www.washingtonpost.com/wp-dyn/content/article/2005/08/05/AR2005 080501938.html.

Varghese, L. (2003) "Will the Real Indian Woman Log-On? Diaspora, Gender, and Comportment." In R. C. Lee and S.-L. C. Wong (Eds.), *Asian America.Net: Ethnicity, Nationalism, and Cyberspace*. New York and London: Routledge, pp. 235–248.

Veciana-Suarez, A. (2006) "Growing Up Online." In A. Rolls (Ed.), *New Media. The Reference Shelf* 78 (2): 37–40.

Vegh, S. (2002) "Hacktivists or Cyberterrorists? The Changing Media Discourse on Hacking." *First Monday*. Accessed October 16, 2007 from www.firstmonday.org/issues/issue7_10/vegh/index.html.

VNS Matrix (1991) "The Cyberfeminist Manifesto for the 21st Century." Archived at www.sysx.org/gashgirl/VNS/TEXT/PINKMANI.HTM. Accessed October 25, 2007.

Vogelstein, F. (2007) "As Google Challenges Viacom and Microsoft, Its CEO Feels Lucky." *Wired*, April 9. Accessed November 5, 2007 from www.wired.com/techbiz/people/news/2007/04/mag_schmidt_qa?currentPage=all.

Vogt, C. and Knapman, S. (2008) "The Anatomy of Social Networks." *Market Leader* 40. [Knowledge Exchange and Information Center, Mudra Institute of Communication, Ahmedabad, India.]

Wajcman, J. (1993) *Feminism Confronts Technology*. Polity: Cambridge.

Wakeford, N. (2002) "Cyberqueer." In D. Bell and B. M. Kennedy (Eds.), *The Cybercultures Reader*. London and New York: Routledge, pp. 403–415.

Waldby, C. (1997) "Revenants: The Visible Human Project and the Digital Uncanny." *Body and Society* 3 (1): 1–16.

Wall, D. (2001) "Cybercrimes and the Internet." In D. Wall (Ed.), *Crime and the Internet*. London: Routledge.

Wallace, M. (2005) "The Gaming is Virtual. The Profit is Real." *New York Times*, May 29. Accessed December 26, 2007 from www.nytimes.com/2005/05/29/business/yourmoney/29game.html?_r=1&oref=slogin.

Walsh, L. and Barbara, J. (2006) "Speed, International Security, and 'New War' Coverage in Cyberspace." *Journal of Computer-Mediated Communication* 12: 189–208.

Walton, H. (2004) "The Gender of the Cyborg." *Theology and Sexuality* 10 (2): 33–44.

Warf, B. and Vincent, P. (2007) "Multiple Geographies of the Arab Internet." *Area* 39 (1): 83–96.

Warschauer, M. (2000) "Language, Identity, and the Internet." In B. Kolko, L. Nakamura, and G. B. Rodman (Eds.), *Race in Cyberspace*. London and New York: Routledge, pp. 151–170.

Watson, L. (2007) "Pornography and Public Reason." *Social Theory and Practice* 33 (3): 467–488.

Weber, T. (2006) "Why Bill Gates' World is Flat." *BBC News*, January 29. Accessed November 9, 2007 from news.bbc.co.uk/1/hi/business/4660244.stm.

Webster, F. (2003) *Theories of the Information Society*, 2nd ed. London: Routledge.

Wellman, B. and Gulia, M. (1999) "Netsurfers Don't Ride Alone: Virtual Communities as Communities." In B. Wellman (Ed.), *Networks in the Global Village*. Westview, Boulder,

CO. Accessed April 13, 2008 from www.chass.utoronto.ca/~wellman/publications/netsurfers/netsurfers.pdf.

Wellman, B. and Haythornthwaite, C. (Eds.) (2000) *The Internet in Everyday Life*. Malden, MA: Blackwell.

Wheeler, J., Aoyama, Y., and Warf, B. (Eds.) (2000) *Cities in the Telecommunications Age: The Fracturing of Geographies*. London: Routledge.

White, M. (2003) "Too Close to See: Men, Women, and Webcams." *New Media and Society* 5 (1): 7–28.

White, M. (2006) "Television and Internet Differences by Design: Rendering Liveness, Presence, and Lived Space." *Convergence* 12 (3): 341–355.

Whiteside, S. (2008) "Social Networking in the UK: A Summary of an OfCom Report into Attitudes, Behaviours and Use." World Advertising Research Center. [Knowledge Exchange and Information Center, Mudra Institute of Communication, Ahmedabad, India.]

Whitty, M. T. and Carr, A. N. (2003) "Cyberspace as Potential Space: Considering the Web as a Playground to Cyberflirt." *Human Relations* 56 (7): 869–891.

Wilding, F. (1998) "Where's the Feminism in Cyberfeminism?" *N.Paradoxa* 1 (2): 6–13.

Wilkie, T. (1993) *Perilous Knowledge: The Human Genome Project and its Implications*. Berkeley: University of California Press.

Wilkinson, C., Allan, S., Anderson, A., and Petersen, A. (2007) "From Uncertainty to Risk: Scientific and News Media Portrayals of Nanoparticle Safety." *Health, Risk and Society* 9 (2): 145–157.

Williams, J. P. (2006) "Authentic Identities: Straightedge Subculture, Music, and the Internet." *Journal of Contemporary Ethnography* 35 (2): 173–200.

Wilska, T.-A. and Pedrozo, S. (2007) "New Technology and Young People's Consumer Identities: A Comparative Study between Finland and Brazil." *Young* 15 (4): 343–368.

Wilson, S. (2002) *Information Arts: Intersections of Art, Science, and Technology*. Cambridge, MA: MIT Press.

Wilson, S. B., McIntosh, W. D., and Insana II, S. P. (2007) "Dating Across Race: An Examination of African American Internet Personal Advertisements." *Journal of Black Studies* 37 (6): 964–982.

Woledge, E. (2005) "Decoding Desire: From Kirk and Spock to K/S." *Social Semiotics* 15: 235–250.

Wolfe, C. (2007) "Bioethics and the Posthumanist Imperative." In E. Kac (Ed.), *Signs of Life: Bio Art and Beyond*. Cambridge, MA: MIT Press, pp. 95–114.

Wolfe, C. (2008) "Thinking Other-Wise: Cognitive Science, Deconstruction and the (Non) Speaking (Non)Human Subject." Accessed from www.carywolfe.com/txt/Animal_Subjects_06_wolfe.pdf.

Woodland, R. (2002) "Queer Spaces, Modem Boys and Pagan Statues: Gay/Lesbian Identity and the Construction of Cyberspace." In D. Bell and B. M. Kennedy (Eds.), *The Cybercultures Reader*. London and New York: Routledge, pp. 416–431.

World Bank (n.d.) "Indicators for Monitoring Gender and ICT." Accessed December 6, 2007 from go.worldbank.org/VDY0ST50Y0.

World Transhumanist Association (2002) "The Transhumanist Declaration." Accessed from www.transhumanism.org/index.php/WTA/declaration/.

Yar, M. (2006) *Cybercrime and Society*. London: Sage.

Yee, N. (2006) "The Labor of Fun: How Video Games Blur the Boundaries of Work and Play." *Games and Culture* 1 (1): 68–71.

Young, I. M. (1990) *Justice and the Politics of Difference*. Princeton: Princeton University Press.

Zdenek, S. (1999) "Rising up from the MUD: Inscribing Gender in Software Design." *Discourse and Society* 10 (3): 379–409.

Zickmund, S. (2002) "Approaching the Radical Other: The Discursive Culture of Cyberhate." In D. Bell and B. M. Kennedy (Eds.), *The Cybercultures Reader*. London and New York: Routledge, pp. 237–253.

Zimmer, M. (2008) "The Gaze of the Perfect Search Engine: Google as an Infrastructure of Dataveillance." In A. Spink and M. Zimmer (Eds.), *Web Search: Multidisciplinary Perspectives*. Berlin: Springer-Verlag, pp. 77–99.

INDEX